Exploring Federalism

Exploring Federalism

DANIEL J. ELAZAR

THE UNIVERSITY OF ALABAMA PRESS

Library of Congress Cataloging-in-Publication Data

Elazar, Daniel Judah.
  Exploring federalism.

  Bibliography: p.
  Includes index.
  1. Federal government. I. Title.
JC355.E383   1987   321.02   85-20868
ISBN 0-8173-0240-9
ISBN 0-8173-0241-7 (pbk.)

For my son, Jonathan Avraham,
who will write beautiful books
someday.

Contents

Figures and Tables

Figures

Tables

x

Preface

During the past fifteen years, I have moved from a concern with one federal system, that of the United States of America, to a consideration of the comparative dimensions of federal systems. My own curiosity led me into this exploration to discern the extent to which the American system was special, unique, and different, as "everybody" always says it is, and the extent to which it is like other federal systems. My goal was to develop more sophisticated questions of comparison than the simple one that is perhaps the foundation of curiosity about all things political.

To my great pleasure, I discovered that there was a place in my own scheme of things for pursuing these lines of inquiry. I also discovered after reading through the field that, although one could learn a great deal from what had been written already, questions still remained unanswered. This book is a summation and reflection of what I have learned to date. In addition, it is designed to suggest an agenda of questions that have occurred to me as being of particular importance for investigation or, perhaps more accurately, for further investigation.

If this book has any purpose beyond the conveyance of the joy of the exploration, it is to demonstrate that federalism offers a way to approach political phenomena in its own right and is not to be subsumed within other models of political inquiry. If the federalist way has a particular intellectual virtue, it is because, for students of federalism, every good theoretical question must have a practical dimension and vice versa. That is, federal theory, to be good theory, must prove itself empirically, and the practical application of federal arrangements must always rest on some set of theoretical principles. Thus the study of federalism is central to political science because of its linking of theoretical and practical wisdom, which is what all political science should do.

There have been three critical federal experiments in the history of humanity to date. The Israelite tribal federation described in the Bible was the first. More than three thousand years ago, it formulated the founding principle of federalism by transforming the vassel treaty among unequals into a covenant among equal partners (equal at least for the purposes of the covenant) that led to the establishment of a polity of tribes maintaining their liberties within the framework of a common constitution and law. Although external pressures ultimately brought about the demise of the tribal federation as a regime, the Jewish people lived on as the first federal people, and they have continued to use federal principles in their internal organization to the present day. The second was the Swiss Confederation. Seven hundred years ago it preserved liberty in medieval Europe. Later it fostered the principal liberating stream of the Protestant Reformation and survived to create a garden spot in the world, self-governed by free people. The third was the United States of America. Two hundred years ago it became the first modern federation and, more recently, the first federal superpower, which showed the way to combine freedom and federalism in a continental-sized polity. It has been my privilege to have been closely associated with the current manifestations of all three in one way or another and to have divided the writing of this book on location in all three, particularly the first and the last.

Since beginning my comparative studies, I have become directly and intimately involved with efforts to find a federal solution for the conflict between Jews and Arabs over Eretz Israel/Palestine and directly if far less intimately involved in the search for or implementation of federal and quasi-federal solutions to current problems of political organization in Cyprus, Italy, South Africa, and Spain. I have followed closely the recent adjustments of the Brazilian, Canadian, and Swiss federal systems through frequent sojourns in those countries and have come to know firsthand the federal systems of Austria, Australia, India, Nigeria, and Yugoslavia. I was also witness to the failed attempt at devolution in the United Kingdom.

These experiences have been invaluable in furthering my education, not only from the comparative perspective one acquires through active study of different polities and regimes but through the special perspective one gains by trying to apply the fruits of one's knowledge to concrete situations, some of which lend themselves to relatively easy resolutions of problems of constitution and reconstitution through the application of federal principles and others of which are highly intractable and well-nigh insoluble with any set of political principles. I owe a great debt of gratitude to all those actively involved in the public affairs of those peoples and polities with whom I have come in contact in the course of my experiences.

The principal personal benefit that I gained from this effort was contact with many interesting people from whom I have been learning regularly for the past number of years. The greatest measure of my gratitude goes to my colleagues at the Center for the Study of Federalism; Stephen L. Schechter, who coordinated the center's initial effort to enter the international arena and who in the process became my close colleague and fast friend; Ellis Katz and Benjamin Schuster, good friends, who held the fort at the Center for the Study of Federalism while I was involved in my overseas adventures; John Kincaid, first my student and now good friend and collaborator, whose work on the relationship between culture, ideas, and history and whose current role as associate editor of *Publius* both represent major contributions to the overall effort. The staff of the center, headed for the last decade by Mary Duffy, has provided us all and me personally with the support needed to carry out our extensive activities.

In the course of my forays, I have been privileged to participate in the founding of three other federalism-related institutions: the Joint Center for Federal and Regional Studies in Basel, Switzerland; the Jerusalem Center for Public Affairs in Jerusalem, Israel; and the International Association of Centers for Federal Studies (ACFS), the body that links all the various centers for federal studies around the world. The founding of these bodies led me to colleagues and friends to whom I am in debt for advancing my education: Hans Briner and Max Frenkel in Switzerland; Ilan Greilsammer, Moshe Hazani, Jacob Landau, Shmuel Sandler, and Efraim Torgovnik in Israel; and my other colleagues in the ACFS: Ferdinand Kinsky of the Centre International de Formation Européenne (CIFE) in France, Diogo Lordello de Mello of the Instituto Brasileiro de Administracão Municipal (IBAM) in Brazil, Russell Mathews of the Australian Center for Intergovernmental Fiscal Relations, Richard Simeon of the Canadian Institute for Intergovernmental Relations, Robert M. Hawkins of the Sequoia Institute in California, and the late Denis de Rougemont of the Institute for Higher European Studies in Geneva.

I owe a special intellectual debt to two close colleagues and dear friends, Alexandre Marc and Vincent Ostrom. The former, the leading spokesman for the idea of integral federalism, introduced me to that system of thought, which has had a strong impact on federalist thinking in Europe. The work of the latter in developing the concept of constitutional choice has had a profound influence on my own understanding of federalism as a system of government based on choice and design rather than accident or force, which gives federal arrangements their special character. These few words cannot begin to acknowledge my debt to them and the personal sentiments and ties of affection that make the debt so pleasant to bear.

Among the other colleagues from whom I have learned in the course of this adventure are Fried Esterbauer of Austria, Antonio la Pergola of Italy, Jovan Djorjevic of Yugoslavia, Donald Lutz, Elinor Ostrom, Vukan Kuic, Rozann Rothman, Ivo Duchacek, and Deil Wright of the United States, and Filippo Sabetti of Italy and Canada, each of whom has been among my teachers as they have broken new ground in their inquiries.

Special thanks are due my research assistant, Joseph Marbach, for handling the final technical chores of preparing this book for publication and preparing the index.

Support for my research came from several sources, including Bar Ilan University, the Earhart Foundation, the Jerusalem Center for Public Affairs, the John Simon Guggenheim Memorial Foundation, the National Endowment for the Humanities, and Temple University through the Center for the Study of Federalism. All have my deep gratitude. My special gratitude to Richard Ware and Anthony Sullivan of the Earhart Foundation and Joseph Duffy and Phillip Marcus of the NEH for their support of my ideas and efforts.

The catalyst for this book was the invitation extended to me by The University of Alabama Department of Political Science to lecture in comparative federalism in their annual series in 1983. The first draft of this book was prepared for and delivered through that distinguished series. My thanks to Coleman G. Ransome, director of the series, and William Stewart of the department, for the many kindnesses shown me during my stay at the University.

My greatest joy in all of this activity was that associated with the founding and development of the Jerusalem Institute for Federal Studies, now enlarged as the Jerusalem Center for Public Affairs, of which the former remains a principal pillar. The federal idea has its origins in the segment of western Asia which became known more than three thousand years ago as Eretz Israel (the Land of Israel). It has been my privilege to bring back to that land the organized and systematic expression of that idea in its political context through the Jerusalem Center and, via the center, into the Israeli body politic and the larger maelstrom of Middle Eastern politics. That task continues to engage the greater part of my energies in that curious combination of frustration and reward which is so characteristic of the region of which the center is a part.

Daniel J. Elazar
Jerusalem

1

Why Federalism?

Human, and hence scholarly, concern with politics focuses on three general themes: the pursuit of political justice to achieve political order; the search for understanding of the empirical reality of political power and its exercise; and the creation of an appropriate civic environment through civil society and civil community capable of integrating the first two themes to produce the good political life. Political science as a discipline was founded and has developed in pursuit of those three concerns. In that pursuit, political scientists have uncovered or identified certain architectonic principles, seminal ideas, and plain political truths that capture the reality of political life or some significant segment of it and relate that reality to larger principles of justice and political order and to practical yet normative civic purposes.

One of the major recurring principles of political import which informs and encompasses all three themes is federalism—an idea that defines political justice, shapes political behavior, and directs humans toward an appropriately civic synthesis of the two. Through its covenantal foundations, federalism is an idea whose importance is akin to natural law in defining justice and to natural right in delineating the origins and proper constitution of political society. Although those foundations have been somewhat eclipsed since the shift to organic and then positivistic theories of politics, which began in the mid-nineteenth century, federalism as a form of political organization has grown as a factor shaping political behavior. Now, in the crisis of tran-

sition from the modern to the postmodern epochs, the
federal idea is resurfacing as a significant political force just
as it did in the transition from the late medieval to the modern epoch, which took place from the sixteenth to the eighteenth centuries.[1]

Federalism is resurfacing as a political force because it
serves well the principle that there are no simple majorities
or minorities but that all majorities are compounded of
congeries of groups, and the corollary principle of minority
rights, which not only protects the possibility for minorities to preserve themselves but forces majorities to be
compound rather than artificially simple. It serves those
principles by emphasizing the consensual basis of the polity
and the importance of liberty in the constitution and maintenance of democratic republics. Both principles are especially
important in an increasingly complex and interdependent
world, where people and peoples must live together
whether they like it or not and even aspire to do so democratically. Hence it is not surprising that peoples and states
throughout the world are looking for federal solutions to
the problems of political integration within a democratic
framework.

Federalism and the Origins
of the Polity

Since its beginnings, political science has identified three
basic ways in which polities come into existence: conquest
(force, in the words of *Federalist* No. 1), organic development (for the *Federalist,* accident), and covenant (choice).
These questions of origins are not abstract; the mode of
founding of a polity does much to determine the framework
for its subsequent political life.

Conquest can be understood to include not only its most

direct manifestation—a conqueror gaining control of a land or a people—but also such subsidiary ways as a revolutionary conquest of an existing state, a coup d'etat, or even an entrepreneur conquering a market and organizing his control through corporate means. Conquest tends to produce hierarchically organized regimes ruled in an authoritarian manner: power pyramids with the conqueror on top, his agents in the middle, and the people underneath the governing structure. The original expression of this form of polity was the Pharaonic state of ancient Egypt.[2] It was hardly an accident that those rulers who brought the Pharaonic state to its fullest development had the pyramids built as their tombs. Although the Pharaonic model has been judged illegitimate in Western society, modern totalitarian theories, particularly fascism and nazism, have attempted to give it a certain theoretical legitimacy.

Organic evolution involves the development of political life from its beginnings in families, tribes, and villages to larger polities in such a way that institutions, constitutional relationships, and power alignments emerge in response to the interaction between past precedent and changing circumstances, with a minimum of deliberate constitutional choice. The end result tends to be a polity with a single center of power organized in one of several ways. Classic Greek political thought emphasized the organic evolution of the polity and rejected any other means of polity-building as deficient or improper. The organic model is closely related to the concept of natural law in the political order.[3]

The organic model has proved most attractive to political philosophers precisely because at its best it seems to reflect the natural order of things. Thus it has received the most intellectual and academic attention. Just as conquest tends to produce hierarchically organized regimes ruled in an authoritarian manner, however, organic evolution tends to produce oligarchic regimes, which at their best have an aristocratic flavor and at their worst are simply the rule of the many by the few. In the first, the goal is to control the top of the pyramid; in the second, the goal is to control the center of power.

Covenantal foundings emphasize the deliberate coming together of humans as equals to establish bodies politic in such a way that all reaffirm their fundamental equality and retain their basic rights.[4] Even the Hobbesian covenant—and he specifically uses that term—which establishes a polity in which power is vested in a single sovereign maintains this fundamental equality although, in practice, it could not coexist with the system of rule that Hobbes requires.[5] Polities whose origins are covenantal reflect the exercise of constitutional choice and broad-based participation in constitutional design. Polities founded by covenant are essentially federal in character, in the original meaning of the term, whether or not they are federal in structure. That is, each polity is a matrix compounded of equal confederates who come together freely and retain their respective integrities even as they are bound in a common whole. Such polities are republican by definition, and power within them must be diffused among many centers or the various cells within the matrix.

Recurring expressions of the covenant or federal model are found in ancient Israel, whose people started out as rebels against the Pharaonic model; among the medieval rebels against the Holy Roman Empire; in the Reformation era among rebels against the Catholic hierarchy; among the early modern republicans who rebelled against either hierarchical or oligarchic regimes; and in authentic modern federal systems. Frontiersmen generally—people who have gone out to settle new areas where there were no established patterns of governance in which to fit and who, therefore, have had to compact with one another to create governing institutions—are to be found among the most active covenanters and builders of federal institutions beyond that original covenant.

The Federal Idea

As many philosophers, theologians, and political theorists in the Western world have noted, the federal idea has its roots in the Bible.[6] Indeed, the first usage of the term was for theological purposes, to define the partnership between man and God described in the Bible, which, in turn, gave form to the idea of a covenantal (or federal) relationship between individuals and families leading to the formation of a body politic and between bodies politic leading to the creation of compound polities. The political applications of the theological usage gave rise to the transformation of the term "federal" into an explicitly political concept.[7]

The term "federal" is derived from the Latin *foedus,* which, like the Hebrew term *brit,* means covenant. In essence, a federal arrangement is one of partnership, established and regulated by a covenant, whose internal relationships reflect the special kind of sharing that must prevail among the partners, based on a mutual recognition of the integrity of each partner and the attempt to foster a special unity among them. Significantly, *shalom,* the Hebrew term for peace, is a cognate of *brit,* having to do with the creation of the covenantal wholeness that is true peace.[8]

Federal principles are concerned with the combination of self-rule and shared rule. In the broadest sense, federalism involves the linking of individuals, groups, and polities in lasting but limited union in such a way as to provide for the energetic pursuit of common ends while maintaining the respective integrities of all parties. As a political principle, federalism has to do with the constitutional diffusion of power so that the constituting elements in a federal arrange-

cultural, ethnic, or ideological groupings are constituted as federations of "camps," "sectors," or "pillars" and jointly governed by coalitions of the leaders of each. Unions are polities compounded in such a way that their constituent entities preserve their respective integrities primarily or exclusively through the common organs of the general government rather than through dual government structures. Leagues, on the other hand, are linkages of politically independent polities for specific purposes, which function through a common secretariat rather than a government and from which members may unilaterally withdraw. Although neither is a species of federalism, properly speaking, both use federal principles in their constitution and governance. New regional arrangements, which are essentially leagues that emphasize regional development, represent more limited applications of federal mechanisms. There is every reason to expect that in the postmodern world new applications of the federal principle will be developed in addition to the arrangements we already know, including *functional authorities* for the joint implementation of particular tasks and *condominiums* involving joint rule by two powers over a shared territory in such a way that the inhabitants of the latter have substantial self-rule. Thus reality is coming to reflect the various faces of federalism.

A major reason for this evolution lies in the reassertion of ethnic and regional identities, now worldwide in scope, which promises to be one of the major political issues of this generation and the next century. There are some 3,000 ethnic or tribal groups in the world conscious of their respective identities. Of the more than 160 politically "sovereign" states now in existence, more than 140 are multiethnic in composition. More than one-third of those states, 58 to be exact, are involved in formal arrangements using federal principles in some way to accommodate demands for self-rule or shared rule within their boundaries or in partnership with other polities. In sum, although the ideology of the nation-state—a single state embracing a single nation—remains strong, the nation-state itself is rare.[10]

The federalist revolution in Western Europe is taking on two forms. On one hand, Western Europe is moving toward a new-style confederation of old states through the European Community and, on the other, there is a revival of even older ethnic and regional identities in the political arena. As a result, Belgium, Italy, and Spain have constitutionally regionalized themselves or are in the process of doing so, and even France is being forced to move in that direction, at least in the case of Corsica. Portugal has devolved power to its island provinces—as the Netherlands and Denmark have long since done. Switzerland, Germany, and Austria, already federal systems, are undergoing an intensification of their federalist dimensions in one way or another. The issue remains alive, if unresolved, in Britain. The idea of a Europe of ethnic regions is a potent force on that continent.[11]

Most of the new states of Asia and Africa must come to grips with the multiethnic issue. It is an issue that can be accommodated peacefully only through the application of federal principles that will combine kinship (the basis of ethnicity) and consent (the basis of democratic government) into politically viable, constitutionally protected arrangements involving territorial and nonterritorial polities. Although only a few of those states have formally federal systems, as in India, Malaysia, Nigeria, and Pakistan, a number of others have adopted other federal arrangements internally and are combining in multinational arrangements on a regional basis.[12]

Western Asia and the eastern Mediterranean region, known collectively as the Middle East, are no exceptions to this problem of ethnic diversity. Indeed, many of that region's current problems can be traced to the breakdown of

the Ottoman Empire, which had succeeded in accommodating communal diversity within a universal state for
several centuries. The intercommunal wars in Cyprus, Iraq,
Lebanon, and Sudan, not to speak of the minority problems
in Egypt, Iran, and Syria and the Israel-Arab conflict, offer
headline testimony to this reality. Federal solutions are no
less relevant in the Middle East than elsewhere, but especially in the Middle East is the need great for a postmodern federalism that is not simply based upon territorial
boundaries but recognizes the existence of long-enduring
peoples as well.[13]

On the other hand, in the older, more established federal
systems of North America, the reemphasis of ethnic and
cultural differences has challenged accepted federal arrangements. In Canada, this challenge has taken the form of a
provincial secessionist movement and in the United States,
an emphasis on nonterritorial as against territorial-based
subnational loyalties on one hand and a revival of Native
American (Indian) tribal aspirations on the other.[14] Latin
America, the first cultural area outside of the United States
to adopt federal solutions to encourage political liberty,
continues to struggle with the problems of reconciling the
republican dimensions of federalism with its penchant for
autocratic leadership.[15]

In sum, federal forms have been applied to a widening
variety of relationships ranging from federalism in support
of group pluralism and individual liberties in the United
States, to federalism in support of local liberties in
Switzerland and federalism on a linguistic basis in India, to
federalism as a means of gaining mild decentralization in
Venezuela. Federal arrangements to accommodate ethnic
differences are becoming more widespread than ever in
Canada, Belgium, Spain, and the United Kingdom (under
other names), Malaysia, and Nigeria. In every case, these
developments have emerged as practical responses to real
situations.

In most if not all of these cases, whether they know it or not, the various parties have arrived at the point which the late Martin Diamond described as the classic position of federalism—the position expressed by the song that Jimmy Durante, the American comedian, belted out in the film, *The Man Who Came to Dinner:* "Did you ever have the feeling that you want to go, and the feeling that you want to stay?" That is the classic problem for which federalism, as a technology, was invented.

Federalism, Conflict Resolution, and Political Integration

In its quest for a stable and peaceful world, humanity today finds itself confronted with a number of political problems, many of which are seemingly intransigent, whose sources lie in conflicting national, ethnic, linguistic, and racial claims arising out of historical experiences. Some of these problems are headline material almost daily, others are less visible but consistently aggravating, and still others have been temporarily submerged but only await the appropriate moment to reappear further to disturb the worldwide quest for peace. The just resolution of these problems is essential if local and world peace is to be attained on the basis of some approximation of justice, yet in none of these cases is justice a simple matter; hence the conflicting claims of the parties involved have not proved amenable to the usual forms of political compromise. New forms for resolving those problems are desperately needed, for the sake of the parties involved at least as much as for the sake of the world as a whole.

The federal principle offers one possible resource for resolving these problems. As suggested above, using the federal principle does not necessarily mean establishing a federal system in the conventional sense of a modern federal state. The essence of federalism is not to be found in a particular set of institutions but in the institutionalization of particular relationships among the participants in political life. Consequently, federalism is a phenomenon that provides many options for the organization of political authority and power; as long as the proper relations are created, a wide variety of political structures can be developed that are consistent with federal principles.

It is useful to reiterate what is meant by federalism in this context. The simplest possible definition is *self-rule plus shared rule*. Federalism thus defined involves some kind of contractual linkage of a presumably permanent character that (1) provides for power sharing, (2) cuts around the issue of sovereignty, and (3) supplements but does not seek to replace or diminish prior organic ties where they exist.

One cautionary note is necessary: despite all these opportunities for using federalism to resolve problems of political organization and integration, the record of attempting federal solutions has been mixed at best. In some cases, the attempts have been so successful that the polities established have become models of their kind—Switzerland and the United States, for example. In others, federal structures have been introduced but are recognized by objective observers to be essentially window dressing—the USSR and Czechoslovakia, for example. In still others, efforts to introduce federal solutions have simply failed—Ethiopia and Ghana, for example. We will have occasion to examine the cultural, social, economic, and political conditions that influence the success or failure of federal experiments.

There also is the serious problem of "thinking federal," that is, of approaching the problem of organizing political relationships from a federalist rather than a monist or centralist perspective. I would suggest that we can see in the formation of any federal polity some conception of the federal *idea,* some persuasion or ideology that endorsed federal solutions, some particular application of the federal *principle,* and some particular federal *framework.* That leads us to the question of federalism and political integration as presently conceptualized.

The study of political integration has been high on the agenda of contemporary political science. Curiously, however, the relationship between the federal principle and political integration has been almost totally ignored, not only in theory but even in studies of political integration in federal polities. On one level, this curious neglect may reflect the current tendency in political science circles to treat terms like federalism as either too legalistic and hence unsuitable for the behavioral science of politics or too vague for proper scientific definition. On another, the neglect may reflect the currently widespread political science doctrine that every political system has a center and a periphery, "by nature," as it were; that only what happens in the center is politically significant; and that federalism is merely a form of decentralization, perhaps less efficient than other forms because of the various constitutional barriers characteristic of federal systems. Under such terms, political integration becomes a matter of building a strong center and tying the periphery closer to it, hence federal arrangements are either unimportant or represent a way station toward full integration.

Federalism, understood on its own terms, offers an alternative to the center-periphery model, for political integration as for other things political. The matrix model of federalism is polycentric by design. The essence of the federal matrix is conveyed both in the original meaning of the term—a womb that frames and embraces in contrast with a single focal point, or center, that concentrates—and in its contemporary meaning—a communications network that establishes the linkages that create the whole.

Political integration on the matrix model is very different

from integration around a common center. In the first place, the measure of political integration is not the strength of the center as opposed to the peripheries; rather, it is the strength of the framework. Thus both the whole and the parts can gain in strength simultaneously and, indeed, must do so on an interdependent basis. Furthermore, political integration on a federal basis offers possibilities for linkages beyond the limits of the conventional nation-state.

Federalism and Intergovernmental Relations

Since the 1920s, and most particularly during the past twenty years, students of federal systems have engaged in discussions regarding the appropriate framework through which to approach the study of the federal dimensions of those systems. For the most part, this discussion has focused on the terminological grounding of the inquiry—properly, since language is the program for human intellectual effort and the choice of terminology strongly influences the direction and even the outcome of inquiry and research.

The essence of the discussion is between those who prefer to use the terminology of federalism and those who have advocated the abandonment of that terminology for the terminology of intergovernmental relations. Deil Wright, a principal proponent of the latter terminology, has traced the emergence and evolution of the phrase "intergovernmental relations" in the public administration literature since the 1930s.[16] He has used William Anderson's definition of intergovernmental relations as "an important body of activities or interactions occurring between governmental units of all types and levels within the [U.S.] federal system."[17]

Two elements are involved in the emergence of the new terminology. In the first place, there was the beginning of the serious study of the administration of federal systems as separate from the legal and constitutional dimensions of federalism. The former tended to focus on intergovernmental relations, which became a useful term for defining the subject matter of that inquiry and also distinguishing it from what had rightly come to be considered an increasingly arid inquiry into constitutional and legal doctrines which ignored most of the realities of politics and administration that were growing ever more important in a situation of expanding government.[18] The term received an additional impetus in the 1950s and 1960s as a result of the behavioralist revolution in political science, which sought, among other things, to jettison "traditional" terminology, of which the terminology of federalism was considered a prime example, for more "scientific" terminology suitable to a science of politics in which concepts could be defined with greater precision.

The terminology of federalism is part of the classic terminology of political science.[19] As such, it suffers from the plight of all classic terminologies, namely, historically changing usages over a long period of time, which have weakened the possibilities for clear-cut definition, thereby rendering such terminologies less satisfactory for those for whom such definitions are of the essence. On the other hand, the classic nature of the terminology adds to its richness. In that respect, federalism is like democracy or republicanism, classic terms that evoke many nuances and provoke many arguments among undergraduates because they are difficult to define but whose core meaning can be fairly well established within appropriate contexts despite many variations, barring simply incorrect usage. As such, federalism is more like what Max Kadushin has termed a value concept—a term that carries with it an essence, which is interpreted in a variety of ways under different circumstances as long as they adhere to the essentials of the concept so that they serve to allow people to "hone in" on a particular set of deep structural meanings.[20] As a value concept, it does not have a once-and-for-all-time precise definition in the usual scientific sense, although it can be and is defined operationally in well-accepted ways.

Federalism is the generic term for what may be referred to as self-rule/shared-rule relationships; "intergovernmental relations" has to do with particular ways and means of operationalizing a system of government—in the American context, a federal system—ways and means that involve extensive and continuing relations among the federal, state, and local governments or any combination thereof.[21] As we shall see, the American usage and the confusions surrounding it are a result, in no small measure, of the restriction of the term "federalism" to its narrowest possible compass. This restriction is a result of American historical experience with the use of the term since the revolutionary era and the American reluctance to theorize about governmental matters.

On one level, intergovernmental relations can be seen as a universal phenomenon, to be found wherever two or more governments interact in the development and execution of public policies and programs. That definition is implicit in its American usage, but the usage is culture-bound in an unanticipated way. It is a product of the American experience, which, because of its grounding in federalism, understands every governmental unit—federal, state, and local—that meets certain objective criteria to be a government. This interpretation is entirely proper because American federal theory holds that political authority and power reside in the people, who delegate powers through constitutional devices to different governments serving different arenas for different purposes.[22]

This view, however, is not widely shared outside the United States, except insofar as the American usage may have gained currency in other federal systems. The accepted theories of the state in Europe and the Old World hold sovereignty to be indivisible and the state to be the source of all political authority and power. Hence there can be no more than one government per state. According to this theory, every state has a central government, and all other bodies exercising governmental powers are merely "authorities," that is, instrumentalities possessing powers delegated to them by the state or the central government. This theory creates certain problems for European federal systems and is "fudged" in various ways but remains the basic theory of the polity nonetheless. Thus, strictly speaking, there cannot be intergovernmental relations within those systems. At the same time, the phenomenon which the American terms seek to describe clearly does exist, even in the relations between central governments and local authorities in unitary states. If one is willing to accept the American understanding of the polity, the term "intergovernmental relations" becomes useful in focusing on those phenomena regardless of the formal character of the regime.

The statist theory of statehood leads to another complication. "Intergovernmental relations" is an accepted term in international relations (which follows classic European theory) for relations among the central governments of sovereign states.[23] Indeed, the international relations usage antedates the American public administration usage. Thus the international diplomatic arena is full of discussions of intergovernmental relations, with an entirely different meaning from the American usage.

This complication is particularly useful to us in our quest because it points out the different conceptions of sovereignty that underlie the usage. Those different conceptions lead us back to an understanding of why federalism is a prior and more comprehensive concept to which intergovernmental relations is subsidiary, a technical term of great use in exploring the processes within particular political systems, particularly but not exclusively, federal ones, and most effectively, although not exclusively, those that begin with a federalist rather than a statist view of sovereignty.

The question must still be raised as to what extent "intergovernmental relations" can be used as an independent term in other than federal systems. Here we are faced with the irony noted earlier that a term invented in the United States to be scientifically neutral, to get away from the normative connotations of federalism, when used outside of the American context becomes highly normative because it, in fact, defines or redefines the nature of political authority within the political system. For those who are willing to take that normative step or at least to recognize the normative implications of the term, it may also be empirically useful in describing what is, after all, a universal phenomenon of particular significance in our age of highly complex governmental structures, relationships, and processes. In such cases, the subsidiary use of the term "intergovernmental relations" can reinforce the use of the root term "federalism" in the conceptualization of the political order as well as for description and analysis of polities.

Federalism and Consociationalism

In the mid-1950s there was a revival of interest in what Arend Lijphart has referred to as nonmajoritarian democracy, most particularly federalism and consociationalism, as distinctive forms of political organization with their own rules, which are to be understood on their own terms and not as incomplete or deficient expressions of majoritarian democracy.[24] The exploration of both federalism and consociationalism proceeded along parallel tracks for the next two decades. Then in the latter half of the 1970s, students of both began to explore the other's theories in an attempt to determine points of convergence and difference.[25] The exploration grew out of the concrete scientific reality that the two theories seemed to overlap—one might say bumped into each other—in the analysis of particular regimes. Students of federalism, in encountering consociational arrangements, began to talk about "nonterritorial federalism," which seemed to be very close to consociationalism, whereas students of consociationalism began to discover consociational dimensions in federal polities.[26]

Lijphart describes both federalism and consociationalism as forms of nonmajoritarian, as distinct from majoritarian, democracy, which he defines exclusively as the Westminster system. Although his basic distinction points in the right direction, it must be redefined as a distinction between simple and compound majoritarianism. The Westminster system is no doubt the primary example of simple majoritarian democracy, though presumably there are Jacobin systems of simple majoritarianism which are democratic—in France, for example. (Contrasts similar to those between federal and consociational democracy may be drawn between Westminster and Jacobin democracy, but that is not my task here.)

The term "compound majoritarianism" is derived from Publius's argument in *The Federalist* No. 51, in which James Madison presents the compound republic as the best republican remedy for republican diseases, in contrast with the simple republic. The idea of compound versus simple majoritarianism is a subsidiary concept. The term has the advantage of breadth and accuracy because majority rule is not rejected, but majorities are compounded either from distinct territories (territorial democracy) or concurrent groups (consociationalism), not counted through simple addition.

Therein lies the basic similarity between federal and consociational polities. The differences are in the way the majorities are compounded. Federal systems are dependent upon dispersed majorities, generally territorially based, whereas consociational systems are dependent upon concurrent majorities, generally aterritorial in character. Both involve the systemic building of more substantial consensus than in simple majoritarian systems. The prominent examples of dispersed majorities in federal systems are well known: presidential elections in the United States, constitutional referenda in Switzerland, the states as single constituencies in the congressional elections in Brazil, to mention only three examples. Equally well known are the concurrent majority systems in consociational polities: the three "pillars" in the Netherlands, the Austrian grand coalition, the camps and parties in Israel. In both cases it is not that the majority does not rule but that the character of the majority coalition and the effort needed to build it are more substantial and designed to generate broader consensus within the polity as a whole than would be the case with simple majorities.

In discussions of federalism and consociationalism the former is usually presented as quite rigid and the latter as extraordinarily flexible. From one perspective, federal systems are more rigid in the sense that federal arrangements are anchored in constitutions establishing relatively clear-cut frameworks of governmental organization that cannot easily be ignored. Consociational arrangements are far more informal, at most acquiring concrete expression through individual legislative acts directed at specific issues such as language rights or the distribution of support for public institutions, without being anchored in a comprehensive constitutional framework. Seen from the consociational perspective, federalism must appear to be more rigid.

This is not the entire story, however. Federalism is most commonly perceived to be a matter of governmental structure.[27] If a political system is established by compact and has at least two "arenas," "planes," "spheres," "tiers," or "levels" of government, each endowed with independent legitimacy and a constitutionally guaranteed place in the overall system and possessing its own set of institutions, powers, and responsibilities, it is deemed to be federal. Proponents of federalism properly argue that this structural dimension is a key to the operationalization of the federal principle because it creates a firm institutional framework for the achievement of the goals for which federalism was instituted in the first place. This perception is accurate as far as it goes. Students of federalism have come to understand the limits of, as well as the necessities for, a structural approach to federalism. This recognition was born out of experience; many polities with federal structures are not federal in practice—the structures mask a centralized concentration of power that stands in direct contradiction to the federal principle. The structure of federalism is meaningful only in polities whose processes of government reflect federal principles.

Whereas federalism involves both structures and processes of government, consociationalism involves processes only. These processes may be embodied in law at some point, as indicated above, but the closest they come to being embodied in formal structures is through the party system, which is rarely constitutionalized as such. It is the particular process—admittedly institutionalized—of concurrent power sharing that is the principal feature of consociationalism. These processes are subject to change with relative ease when the conditions that generated them change.

Both federalism and consociationalism are political and social phenomena, with consociationalism perhaps even more of a social phenomenon than federalism. Federalism as a political phenomenon, understood according to the modern meaning of political, is essentially limited to relations among governments or polities. Consociationalism emphasizes the existence of essentially permanent religious, ethnic, cultural, or social groups, "camps," or "pillars" around which a particular polity is organized. It is to these that consociationalism is addressed.

A major conclusion that can be drawn from all of this is that federalism is a matter of the form of a polity whereas consociationalism refers to a polity's regime. The term "form" is used here in its classic sense of a permanent arrangement that permeates and shapes every aspect of the polity and is constitutionally anchored. Indeed, consociational regimes tend to be longer-lived when they function within federal polities. Thus Switzerland is perhaps the best-rooted consociational regime. Belgium has preserved consociationalism as it has become more federal, but the Netherlands has lost it for lack of a federal base.[28]

The work of Lijphart and others has emphasized the regime character of consociationalism. He has presented this evidence in connection with his argument that federalism is primarily territorial and consociationalism primarily non-territorial. The list of attributes of each which he presents emphasizes this point. For federalism he identifies five principal attributes:

1. A written constitution which specifies the division of power and guarantees to both the central and regional governments that their allotted powers cannot be taken away;
2. A bicameral legislature in which one chamber represents the people at large and the other the component units of the federation;
3. Over-representation of the smaller component units in the federal chamber of the bicameral legislature;
4. The right of the component units to be involved in the

process of amending the federal constitution but to change their own constitutions unilaterally;

5. Decentralized government, that is, the regional government's share of power in a federation is relatively large compared to that of regional governments in unitary states.[29]

All of the foregoing are constitutionally guaranteed as part of the form of the polity.

On the other hand,

consociational democracy can be defined in terms of two primary attributes—grand coalitions and segmental autonomy—and two secondary characteristics—proportionality and minority veto. Grand coalition, also called powersharing, means that the political leaders of all the significant segments of a plural, deeply divided society, jointly govern the country. Segmental autonomy means that the decision-making is delegated to the separate segments as much as possible. Proportionality is the basic consociational standard of political representation, civil service appointments, and the allocation of public funds, etc. The veto is a guarantee for minorities that they will not be outvoted by majorities when their vital interest is at stake.[30]

None of the foregoing need be constitutionalized, and it is rare that any are.

This point is further strengthened by the recent history of consociational regimes. The Netherlands, presented by Lijphart as the classical model of consociationalism, has, by his account, been declining as a consociational regime since the late 1960s and may no longer be one.[31] Consociationalism in Israel is rapidly giving way to something else as Israel transforms itself from an ideological to a territorial democracy.[32] Lebanon's consociational regime broke down in civil war in the mid-1970s and seems un-

likely to be restored unless a territorial base is provided for
the various minorities (an almost impossible task given the
patterns of settlement in the country that originally led to a
consociational solution).[33] Consociationalism lasted barely
a decade in Cyprus and has now been replaced by a de facto
partition of the island into two territorial states.[34] Surinam
has undergone a revolutionary coup founded on the rejection of consociationalism in favor of an authoritarian regime.[35] Belgium has had more success in retaining its
consociational arrangements primarily because it has
moved in the direction of formal federation on territorial
lines.[36]

In sum, consociationalism appears to be a relatively transient arrangement. Indeed, the classic consociations seem to
last for about two generations before giving way to some
other form of regime. Coincidentally or not, this is about
the length of time that a majority party maintains its majority coalition intact in two-party systems—the United
States, for example, over the entire course of its history as an
independent nation.[37] It seems to be true for other democratic polities as well, hence it may teach us something
about the lifetime of coalitions and their survival capacities.

Students of consociationalism have made the point that
consociational regimes are by nature democratic as distinct
from federal systems, which may or may not be. This issue
is problematic for two reasons, one of which is internal to
consociational regimes and the other of which has to do
with the usage of consociational and federal arrangements
in nondemocratic systems. With regard to the first, it is
generally agreed that consociational regimes are based on
the agreement of elites, each of which must be capable of
maintaining control over its own segment in the grand
coalition. Thus the segments have to be organized internally on hierarchical lines but governed by the people selected to be at the top. So although the regimewide coalition

may be democratic, that is no guarantee that democracy will prevail within the segments. Certainly, there cannot be decentralization with the segments if the segmental leadership is to be able to commit its segment to the terms of the grand coalition agreement. Intrasegmental centralization has, indeed, been a trademark of all consociational systems except for Switzerland, where the deeply rooted federal system has functioned as a countervailing force.[38]

There are regimes that claim to be consociational and are acknowledged as such but that cannot be called democratic. Lebanon is a clear example of one such system. Even before the civil war, when its consociational regime was working, the segments were at best governed by oligarchies of traditional notables drawn from a handful of ruling families.[39] The Lebanese state maintained the trappings of democracy in the form of elections, but it was clear that rule was in the hands of this very small group, who conducted the negotiations within and between the various segments.

The Republic of South Africa, which always considered itself to have consociational leanings, amended its constitution in 1984 to provide for a presidential system of government with three chambers in the national parliament, one representing whites, the second coloureds, and the third Asians, with the relationships among them, the president, and the President's Council explicitly defined as consociational and indeed resembling consociational regimes elsewhere. Undoubtedly there will be considerable dispute as to whether this arrangement is democratic.[40]

Nevertheless the overwhelming majority of consociational regimes are democratic in character and consociationalism was developed as a form of democracy, even if it can be used for other purposes. So, too, federalism was invented as a means to foster democratic republicanism or popular government in the terminology of the eighteenth-century United States. There are two kinds of federal systems—those in which the purpose of federalism is to share power broadly, pure and simple, and those in which the purpose is to give individual national communities a constitutionalized share in the regime. The former is more simply devoted to advancing the cause of popular government; the latter may rely upon other mechanisms for securing popular government and merely add federalism as an extra device. In either case, federal systems have always been introduced in the name of popular government even where they have been a sham. There are only a few exceptions to this rule, such as the United Arab Emirates, where the federation is one of absolutist states and power is shared among their rulers. But even in the Soviet bloc, federalism is presumably designed further to democratize the people's democracies.

What we have before us are two useful means of conceptualizing and describing political systems based on compound rather than simple majoritarianism. Each not only reflects a different means of organizing such polities, but the two are not symmetrical because federalism relates to the form of the polity and consociationalism relates to the character of the regime. To the extent that federalism goes beyond form to function as the character of the regime as well, the two relate to each other on a more symmetrical basis. It is one of the ambiguities of federalism that it is often both form and regime. Consociationalism, on the other hand, relates only to regime. Nevertheless, both reflect the political wisdom that popular government is not only not enhanced by simple majoritarianism but is often defeated by it because civil society in a democracy is both complex and pluralistic and both its complexities and its pluralism must be properly accommodated.

Federalism in Light of Contemporary Political and Social Science

This chapter began with the conflict between different theories of the origins and nature of civil or political society, suggesting that political science has always rested upon three classic models of political organization: the pyramid model, which ultimately derives from a conquest or hierarchical theory of the polity; the center-periphery model, which ultimately derives from the organic theory; and the matrix model, which ultimately derives from the covenant or federal theory. Each of these models is associated with particular political theories and cultures. Their existence in the face of the aforementioned tendencies of human nature is additional testimony to the strength of culture in shaping all human activity and the importance of historical experience in shaping culture. Hence we need to look more closely at the historical and theoretical roots of the conflict between federalist and centralist models and their respective theoretic conceptualizations.

By and large, democratic centralists argue that civil society is organic in nature, representing the organic development of a particular people in a particular place. Federalists, on the other hand, argue that civil society has its origins in a covenant or compact and must be based on consent. This is a classic debate in political science, especially in modern political science, and one that has a great deal of bearing on the study of federal themes and systems. It is closely related to the struggle between Jacobin and federalist democracy, the two competing expressions of modern democratic thought since the American and French Revolutions.

The center-periphery model has become the most widely accepted in contemporary political science and has skewed the way we examine regimes, federal and otherwise. This model has received further impetus from Marxian thought, which is highly compatible with and sympathetic to it. Because so many contemporary social and political scientists, whether or not they are Marxists, are much influenced by Marxian categories, it is no wonder that attempts to conceptualize the polity as a matrix have gone into eclipse, even in the United States, where they were used until the twentieth century. The latter conceptualization is only now being revived in the works of such scholars as Martin Diamond, Vincent Ostrom, Denis de Rougement, and Alexandre Marc, among others. Their writings are part and parcel of the new federalist revolution of the postmodern era.

In his recent book on the federal principle, Rufus Davis, in the classic manner of English scholarship, throws up his hands at the effort to find a common definition of federalism and ultimately rejects the quest as one that interferes with the pragmatic understanding of political systems organized on a federal basis.[41] In this he follows the grand English conceit of rejecting political theory. As a result, he does not do much to advance our knowledge of the subject. William Stewart, on the other hand, focusing on the same problem, has collected several hundred federalist metaphors that have been used to describe American federalism in recent decades and, in the process, has helped us to understand how federalism is useful even though it breeds so wide a variety of modifiers.[42]

It has already been suggested that federalism has to be understood as a classic value concept, like democracy, rather than as a term subject to narrow definition. Examining the larger question of the language of politics, it soon becomes apparent that political science rests on a network of value concepts that set its tone and point its direction, around which definitional arguments rage over the centuries—and properly so. The lack of ability to agree on a single definition for all time for any value concept is not a sign of its weakness but of its strength, not of the futility in seeking political understanding.

The appropriate conclusion to this discussion is that federalism is a root term of massive scope. It embodies a world-view and an approach to the study of political phenomena that come close to being comprehensive. Federalism has its ambiguities, but careful attention can sort them out, so in any particular instance rigorous usage of the term can be maintained.

Partisans of federalism as a vehicle of human organization are prepared to argue that it is particularly helpful in dealing with reality politically, cybernetically, psychologically, and anthropologically. Only the outlines of their argument can be suggested here.

Partisans of federalism would argue that federalism is politically sound because of its compound features, that is, because it establishes polities that are compounded from entities, which maintain their respective integrities and thus work to preserve the liberties of their citizens. Moreover, by providing for a constitutional diffusion of power, federalism enables "ambition to counteract ambition" for the good of the body politic and prevents the consolidation of ambition to the latter's detriment. In short, federalism is designed to prevent tyranny without preventing governance. In this sense it seeks to provide a political remedy for political diseases. One's stance regarding the value of this remedy depends upon one's stance regarding the importance of liberty.

Federalism can be said to be cybernetically sound because it provides for redundancy in the carrying out of governmental functions. The tendency of federalism toward redundancy has been much noted, but the virtues of that tendency have been little noted until the development of cybernetics brought us to a better understanding of how complex systems work and how they can be made to work

well. Cybernetic understanding of how systems work argues that it is precisely the overlapping of institutions and
functions that characterizes federal arrangements that gives
federal systems strength and stability above and beyond
many others. This argument reverses the conventional
wisdom still abroad in the world and provides a theoretical
basis to confirm and explain certain practical observations
made by students of federalism.

Until recently, redundancy was considered to be one of
the unattractive aspects of federalism, something to be tolerated because of federalism's political virtues but minimized whenever possible. This view became especially
prevalent after the rise of the modern science of public administration, which is built on hierarchical principles and
the notion that the larger the institution or organization, the
more efficient it will be. Cybernetics has challenged both
aspects of modern administrative theory and has suggested
that size must be appropriate to the task at hand and that
redundancy is extremely important as a means of providing
"fail-safe" mechanisms to enable operations to continue despite the inevitable errors and failures associated with any
activity. Indeed, as Vincent Ostrom and Martin Landau
have argued, theorists of federalism anticipated cybernetic
theories by two centuries or more.[43]

Federalism can be seen as consistent with human psychology in the way it encompasses and reflects the dynamics
of personality and interpersonal relations. By creating dialectical interaction, federalism encompasses not only differences among humans but differences within humans as
well. If dynamic theories of psychology are correct, the
human personality is forged out of the interaction of several
components that may pull in contradictory directions. Patterns of personal behavior are forged out of the resolution of
these contradictions. Similarly, within federal systems, that
various elements interact and even pull in contradictory

directions generates a creative dialectical tension that can produce better results than if efforts are made to stifle the expression of these different and even contradictory impulses.

Finally, federalism can be said to be consistent with human anthropology because of the fundamental correctness of the covenant theory of the origin of human relationships. There is considerable evidence that human beings, by virtue of their very humanity, grant to or withhold their consent from the institutions and authorities that govern them or the polities within which they are located, even when they are forced to obey. One observes this behavior in children, who, when being told to do something by their parents, frequently comply but refuse to assent to the request (or command), implicitly acknowledging the power and perhaps the authority of the parents to coerce them into acting but withholding their consent to that action. Studies of work groups in factories and other institutions emphasize the distinction between formal authority and informal leadership, which the workers themselves have designated by an implicitly consensual process, showing the latter to be more effective in obtaining results. They offer further demonstration of the essential correctness of the notion that humans compact with one another with regard to the distribution of authority and power whenever they are in the least bit free to do so, even creating contractual relationships when they are formally not free to do so. Thus a theory of political authority that rests upon this understanding of human relationships is more nearly correct than any other.

In the last analysis, the study of federalism directs the attention of political science away from a principal concern with the nature of regimes to a principal concern with the character of political relationships—between political units, between governors and governed, between members of the body politic. In doing so, it forces those concerned with political phenomena to consider questions of political behavior—institutional, group, and individual—first and foremost.

2

What Is Federalism?

Federalism has to do with the need of people and polities to unite for common purposes yet remain separate to preserve their respective integrities.[1] It is rather like wanting to have one's cake and eat it too. Since that is the natural human condition, at least half the work of politics, if not 90 percent of it, is directed to somehow accommodating that logically insoluble problem. Under certain circumstances, federalism is a highly useful device for doing just that. Consequently, federal ideas and arrangements have emerged repeatedly in the course of human history as major devices to try to accommodate that condition.[2] Ours is one of those times.

Federal principles grow out of the idea that free people can freely enter into lasting yet limited political associations to achieve common ends and protect certain rights while preserving their respective integrities. As the very ambiguity of the term "federal" reveals, federalism is concerned simultaneously with the diffusion of political power in the name of liberty and its concentration on behalf of unity or energetic government. The federal idea itself rests on the principle that political and social institutions and relationships are best established through covenants, compacts, or other contractual arrangements, rather than, or in addition to, simply growing organically; in other words, that humans are able to make constitutional choices.

ক

The Federal Matrix and Contrasting Models

Federalism is based on a particular kind of constitutional framework. That framework is most immediately and easily visible in the division of power among a general, or federal, government on one hand and the constituent governments on the other, whether states (as in Argentina, Australia, Brazil, India, Malaysia, Mexico, Nigeria, Venezuela, and the United States), provinces (Canada), *lander* (Austria and West Germany), cantons (Switzerland), or republics (Yugoslavia and the USSR). The constitutional framework goes beyond this division of powers, however, involving as it does the organization of the entire governmental structure of federal polities on a noncentralized basis.[3] Federal polities are characteristically noncentralized; that is, the powers of government within them are diffused among many centers, whose existence and authority are guaranteed by the general constitution, rather than being concentrated in a single center.

Contractual noncentralization, the structured dispersion of powers among many centers whose legitimate authority is constitutionally guaranteed, is the key to the widespread and entrenched diffusion of power that remains the principal characteristic of, and argument for, federal democracy. Noncentralization is not the same as decentralization, though the latter term is frequently—and erroneously— used in its place to describe federal systems. Decentralization implies the existence of a central authority, a central government that can decentralize or recentralize as it desires. In decentralized systems, the diffusion of power is actually a matter of grace, not right; in the long run, it is usually treated as such.

In a noncentralized political system, power is so diffused that it cannot be legitimately centralized or concentrated without breaking the structure and spirit of the constitution. The classic federal systems—the United States, Switzerland, and Canada—have such noncentralized systems. Each has a general, or national, government that functions powerfully in many areas for many purposes, but not a central government controlling all the lines of political communication and decision making. In each, the states, cantons, or provinces are not creatures of the federal government but, like the latter, derive their authority directly from the people. Structurally, they are substantially immune to federal interference. Functionally, they share many activities with the federal government but without forfeiting their policy-making roles and decision-making powers.

Figure 2.1. *The Power Pyramid*

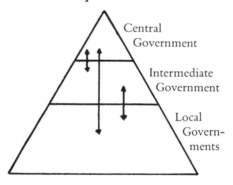

To use other imagery, decentralization implies either a hierarchy—a pyramid of governments with gradations of power flowing down from the top (Figure 2.1) or a center with a periphery (Figure 2.2). The imagery of hierarchy has become the dominant one in most discussions of governmental systems today, adopted in undiluted form from the world of business and the military; the center-periphery imagery has become the favorite of political sociologists. Following Max Weber and Woodrow Wilson, hierarchical or center-periphery arrangements are assumed by most

Figure 2.2. *The Center-Periphery Model*

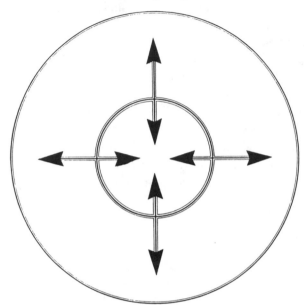

contemporary students of government to be "natural," differing only with respect to whether the locus of control is
bureaucratic (Weber) or parliamentary (Wilson). Not only is
this a misleading imagery for conceptualizing federal systems, but it is not an appropriate basis for organizing democratic polities.[4]

Noncentralization is best conceptualized as a matrix of
governments, with powers so distributed that the rank
order of the several governments is not fixed (Figure 2.3). In
the United States, for example, if the federal government is
primary in the fields of foreign affairs and national defense,
the states are primary in the fields of highways, higher education, and public welfare, and the localities are primary in
matters of elementary and secondary education, housing,
and zoning. The sources of funding may affect the ordering
of governments relative to particular functions but rarely
alter the order significantly.

Figure 2.3. *The Matrix Model*

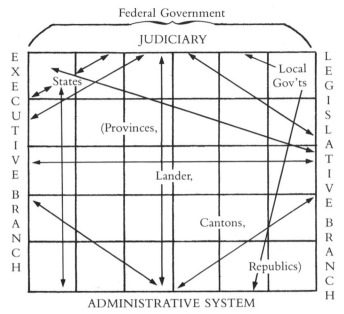

In a matrix, there are no higher or lower power centers, only larger or smaller arenas of political decision making and action. This is a more accurate description of a federal system than that provided by Weber or Wilson. The pyramid model leads to one set of notions as to what represents a national distribution of powers, derived from the imagery of levels and based on the notions of "higher" and "lower." Using the matrix model, the distribution of powers can be seen as involving differential loadings in different arenas for different purposes. As a matter of course, such differential loadings do not indicate a system out of kilter—the way they would were the pyramid model to be used.

The matrix of decision-making centers is linked through formal lines of authority with both formal and informal lines of communication crisscrossing it. The constitution provides the frame or bare bones of the structure, which is fleshed out by formal and informal institutional arrangements, often overlapping. In this sense, the lines of communication serve as the "nerves" of the overall system.

The implications of this kind of constitutional and legal framework are many and varied. The great strength of federalism (including the federal idea and the structures and processes that flow from it) lies in its flexibility (or adaptability), but that very strength makes federalism difficult to discuss satisfactorily on a theoretical level. Even the argument that federalism is particularly flexible goes against much of the conventional discussion of the subject, which, to the extent that it focuses on a juridical understanding of federalism, often emphasizes rigid divisions of power. Although particular federal systems may be inflexible, the federal principle has been successfully applied in a great many different ways, under a wide variety of circumstances, easily justifying the claim of flexibility even as it may seem to complicate theory-building. Flexibility leads to ambiguity, which has great operational advantages even as it creates severe theoretical problems.

Six basic ambiguities can be identified in connection with federalism as a theoretical and operational concept: there are several varieties of political arrangements to which the term federal has properly been applied; federalism is directed to the achievement and maintenance of both unity and diversity; federalism involves both the structure and the processes of government; federalism is both a political and a social-cultural phenomenon; federalism concerns both means and ends; and federalism is pursued for both limited and comprehensive purposes.

The Variety of Federal Arrangements

Federations. People today tend to think of federalism exclusively in its modern form, that is, as some variation of the federal system invented in the United States in the late eighteenth century and embodied in the American federal Constitution, written in 1787. This American application of federal principles was born out of the necessity to come to grips with the problem of the modern nation-state, which, because of the principles of exclusive sovereignty and centralized power upon which it is based, stood in principled opposition to the diffusion of political power and the accommodation of diversity through overlapping jurisdictions. The terms "nation" and "nation-state" are used here in their conventionally accepted sense although that usage is somewhat problematic.

Modern nation-states are of two kinds—those that give political identity to previously existing nations and those that have developed a sense of national identity as concomitant of acquiring a political identity, which requires all residents within the state's territory to acquire a common citizenship as individuals. Germany is a good example of the former. Germans felt themselves to be a nation before they had a single German state (and do now even though they are no longer united within one state); they sought political unity within a state so they could better express their national ties. Britain, on the other hand, achieved political unification as a state before its people developed a common British identity; its rulers used the common political tie to foster that sense.

In some ways, every nation-state had to use political mechanisms to transform some segments of its population into nationals. The device used was the principle of the common citizenship of all individuals within the body politic, eliminating the sole reliance on mediating groups. Thus the nation-state is, at one and the same time, the citizen-state. This understanding becomes very important in considering the development of modern federalism, which is generally used as a device to make possible the fostering of a sense of common citizenship within a polity.

The modern nation-state in its Jacobin manifestations offered new promise for popular and representative government, but it also undermined some of the basic prerequisites for the successful implementation of both. In the words of *The Federalist,* by concentrating power in a single center, it failed to provide "republican remedies for republican diseases." It may have been helpful against entrenched aristocratic privilege, but it also led to a new centralization that deprived many newly freed peoples of their freedom.

The modern nation-state claimed that its combination of territory, government, and people was comprehensive—at least from a political perspective—and hence should be considered exclusive, embracing a single united people and possessing a common center. Modern federalism reflects this claim in its efforts to deal with the problem of creating and maintaining unity in polities where diversity has to be accommodated and, at the same time, is an expression of the interest and effort to try to prevent the simple concentration of power in a single center or, in some cases, the amalgamation of preexisting peoples into one. To link the federal principle with that of the modern state, the framers and proponents of the American Constitution of 1787 had to perform a sleight of hand, to transform the term "federal" as it was known up to that time—what we today term "confederation," or the relatively loose linkage of polities that retain their sovereignty within a permanent league—into something else, an entity whose overarching government could be considered national and would have as much or more original authority as the constituent entities. This sleight of hand was performed through *The Federalist,* which appropriates the term "federal" to describe the latter condition.[5]

The full implications of this change in definition have escaped most commentators on federalism. Modern federalism is based on the linkage of federated or constituent states, which come together to form a larger state in which the question of sovereignty remains, at least in the initial stages, a principal or primary one in public discourse. Precisely because states in the modern sense are supposed to be exclusive in their sovereign powers, the question remains: how can one have two exclusive "sovereigns" sharing the same territory?

In fact, the real meaning of the American federal solution was to provide a way to circumvent the problem of exclusive state sovereignty—in other words, to provide a modern alternative for organizing the polity on an even more democratic basis than that of the Jacobin state. Rather than accepting the sixteenth-century European view of the sovereign state, Americans understood sovereignty to be vested in the people. The various units of government— federal, state, or local—could exercise only delegated powers.[6] Thus it was possible for the sovereign people to delegate powers to the general and constituent governments without normally running into the problem of which possesses sovereignty except in matters of international relations or the like. In matters of internal or domestic governance it was possible to avoid the issue except when political capital could be made out of it. Different governments are purposely designed to serve arenas of different sizes, but since size is not an a priori determinant of importance, they relate to one another as equals with regard to the powers delegated to each, respectively.[7]

Here, then, was a real difference in understanding that made possible the definitional shift. By creating a strong overarching government, it was possible to aspire to the same goals of political unification and integration as the Jacobin state, but by removing sovereignty from the state as such and lodging it with the people, it was possible to arrange for power sharing and to set limits on governmental authority. Out of these two shifts there developed what we have come to know as modern federalism.

Most other modern federal systems have borrowed heavily from the American model. Some have borrowed the federal structure and then not lived up to the intent; others have adopted elements of both and then developed in their own direction. There are three principal models of modern federalism; the American system, the Swiss system, and the Canadian system. The Swiss system is the first modern federation built on indigenous ethnic and linguistic differences that were considered permanent and worth accommodating. The Canadian system is based not only on a multicultural society but on the idea that a federal system can be combined with a parliamentary regime along the Westminister model.

Today federalism has become much more widespread than that. Nineteen of the world's independent states are, by their constitutions, federal, and they contain some 40 percent of the world's population. Table 2.1 lists them and numbers their 304 constituent or associated states plus other autonomous entities in all their diversity.

I have chosen to include all polities that possess formally federal constitutions in Table 2.1 on the grounds that the first test of the existence of federalism is the desire or will to be federal on the part of the polity involved. Adopting and maintaining a federal constitution is perhaps the first and foremost means of expressing that will. At the same time, the will to be federal is frequently paralleled by the will to be other things (for example, a Marxian socialist society) or do other things (for example, conquer an imperial domain) as well, in ways that stand in contradiction to federalism. In such cases, a certain ambivalence is created, to say the least. Often the scales of this ambivalence are, in practice, tipped away from federalism even though the will to be federal remains, at least sentimentally, and continues to be reflected constitutionally. In other cases, the commitment to federalism in practice tips the scales in that direction, leading to a dilution of the striving for those contradictory goals.

Beyond that, in some situations the will to be federal is aborted or restricted by the existence of other "objective" factors—cultural, economic, military, political, or social—that interfere with the implementation of federal principles.

Table 2.1. *Federal Systems*

Name (Constituent Units)	Population (thousands)[a]	Area (sq. mi.)
Argentine Republic (22 provinces + 3 national territories + 1 federal district)	27,863	1,068,302
Commonwealth of Australia (6 states + 4 administered territories + 3 territories + 1 capital territory)	14,616	2,966,150
Federal Republic of Austria (9 *lander*)	7,507	32,376
Brazil (22 states + 4 federal territories +1 federal capital district)	123,032	3,286,488
Canada (10 provinces + 2 territories)	23,941	3,851,809
The Federal and Islamic Republic of the Comoros (3 islands)	298[b]	863
Czechoslovak Socialist Republic (2 republics)	15,312	49,378
Federal Republic of Germany (10 *lander* + 1 associated state)	61,561	96,011
Republic of India (21 states + 9 union territories + 1 federacy[c] + 1 associated state)	683,810	1,269,420
Malaysia (13 states)	13,436	127,581
United Mexican States (31 states + 1 federal district)	67,396	756,066
Federal Republic of Nigeria (19 states + 1 federal capital territory)	77,082	356,669
Islamic Republic of Pakistan (4 provinces + 3 states + 2 tribal areas)	76,770[d]	310,403

Swiss Confederation (26 cantons)	6,329	15,943
Union of Soviet Socialist Republics (15 union republics + 20 autonomous socialist republics + 10 national districts + 8 autonomous regions)	265,542	8,649,540
United Arab Emirates (7 sheikdoms)	1,040	30,000
United States of America (50 states + 2 federacies + 3 associated states + 3 local home-rule territories + 3 unincorporated territories + Indian tribes)	227,640	3,618,467
Republic of Venezuela (20 states + 2 territories + 1 federal district + 2 federal dependencies—72 islands)	13,913	352,144
Socialist Federal Republic of Yugoslavia (6 republics + 2 autonomous provinces)	22,344	98,766

[a]1980 or 1981 figures.
[b]1976 estimate.
[c]Jammu and Kashmir is a federacy.
[d]1978 figure.

Federal Arrangements. Twenty-one additional states are not formally federal but have, in some way, introduced federal arrangements, principles, or practices into their political systems to accommodate the heterogeneity that has given rise to the introduction of federalism in many countries in the first place (Table 2.2). They can be grouped into three basic categories: legislative unions, constitutionally decentralized unitary systems, and consociational unions on a nonterritorial basis. In each of them, the use of federal principles can have important consequences, but the distinction between them and true federations is made real because such principles do not permeate them.

Table 2.2. *Political Systems with Federal Arrangements*

Name (Number of constituent units)	Population (thousands)[a]	Area (sq. mi.)
Antigua and Barbuda (3 independent islands)	75	171
Kingdom of Belgium (2 linguistic + 1 capital region + 3 cultural communities)	9,859	11,783
Union of Burma (4 states + 8 divisions + 1 special division)	32,913	261,218
People's Republic of China (5 autonomous regions + 3 tribal federations + 22 provinces)		
Republic of Colombia (23 departments + 4 intendencies + 3 commissaries)	27,090	440,831
Fiji Islands (consociation of 2 ethnic communities)	663.5	7,095
Republic of Ghana (9 administrative regions)	11,450	92,100
Israel[b]	3,871	7,848
Italian Republic (15 ordinary and 5 special autonomous regions)	57,042	116,318
Japan (47 to-do-fu-ken/prefectures)	116,782	145,834
Republic of Lebanon[c]	2,658	3,950
Kingdom of Netherlands (11 provinces + 1 associated state)	14,144	13,104
Independent State of Papua–New Guinea (2 autonomous island groups)	3,079	178,704
Portuguese Republic (state with 2 autonomous overseas regions)	9,933	35,549

Solomon Islands (4 districts)	228	10,639
Republic of South Africa (4 provinces + 6 homelands)	26,129	437,872
South West Africa/Namibia	1,009	318,261
Spain (17 autonomous regions)	37,746	194,884
Democratic Republic of Sudan (1 constitutionally autonomous + 7 statutorily autonomous regions)	16,126d	967,500
United Republic of Tanzania (2 constituent units)	17,982	364,900
United Kingdom of Great Britain and Northern Ireland (4 countries + 5 self-governing islands)	55,883	94,249
Republic of Vanuatu/New Hebrides (constitutionally regionalized islands)	112	5,700

a1979 or 1980 figures.
bIsrael has limited power sharing in personal status, religious, educational, and language matters for its ethnic and religious communities.
cBefore 1975 Lebanon used the principles of consociational federalism to divide political power among its several ethnoreligious communities. There is currently an attempt to restore these principles.
d1976 figure.

The suggestion that there are technically unitary states that use federal principles worthy of analysis from that perspective should not be treated as a claim that federalism is omnipresent or coterminous with any exercise of power away from the center, de facto as well as de jure. It is not a claim that ineffective centralization is the equivalent of federalism. A technically unitary state is considered to be using federal arrangements when there is a formal agreement between the entities involved that takes on constitutional force (and is often embodied in a constitutional document) as a result of the striking of a bargain that guarantees their respective integrities as specified.

As a result, the goals of such a polity are radically different from those of an undiluted unitary system. In the latter, the trends are historically toward centralization, diluted only by the existence of extrapolitical factors (local, social, ethnic, religious, or other cultural differences). In a sense, the definition of what is governmentally "good" in the system is heavily weighted toward the principle that the more centralized, the better. France is the paradigm of this condition, but England (not the United Kingdom) is another example in which the commitment to strong local government, such as it is, depends almost exclusively on extraconstitutional factors and has meager formal support in the country's political institutions. One could argue that the federal principles built into the United Kingdom to accommodate the peripheral countries within that union are the major bulwark against even greater centralization in England proper. Englishmen with an interest in local control can argue, "If the Scots have it, why can't we?" with some success. Where federal principles are used, on the other hand, the definition of what is governmentally good is related to the commitment to the agreed-upon division of powers; consequently, "good" and "centralization" are not likely to be equated so closely.

Unions. In the case of these polities, there also exists some will toward federation, but it is clearly subordinated to those other considerations. Almost without exception, they are polities that were consciously and deliberately united or compounded out of what were formerly separate countries or peoples by common consent (sometimes precipitated by military action) in such a way as to provide constitutionally for the preservation of some measure of the integrity of the compounding units. Belgium is one such example, although in recent years Belgium has drawn so heavily on federal principles in its efforts to create a viable constitutional framework for the maintenance of unity among

Flemings and Walloons that the distinction exists almost without the difference.[8]

Despite its often imprecise usage, a legislative union can be defined as a compound polity in which the constituent units find their primary constitutional expression through common institutions rather than through their own separateness.[9] The United Kingdom, as its name suggests, is a long-standing legislative union that is assiduous in its rejection of federalist terminology. It is a compound of four countries and several offshore islands. Its polity is based on constitutional arrangements that guarantee Scotland its own local administration, law, established church, and central bank; Wales, a measure of cultural home rule and administrative autonomy; Ulster, home rule with its own legislature; and the islands of Guernsey, Jersey, Man, and Sark off the British coast, substantial constitutional autonomy in their internal government.[10]

Legislative union bears very close resemblance to federal union at several crucial points. Though designed to direct public allegiance to a single national authority, the terms of the union encourage the political system to retain certain noncentralizing elements. The government of the union is established by a perpetual compact that guarantees the constituent parties their boundaries, representation in the national legislature, and certain local autonomies such as their own systems of municipal law. Legislative unions usually unite unequal polities, The centralizing tendencies thereby induced are somewhat counterbalanced by the residual desire for local self-government in the constituent units, which acquires institutional expression.

The constitutional decentralization of unitary states is an ancient device that has appeared in different forms over the centuries. It has already been noted that the Netherlands replaced its protofederal constitution with a union of the original provinces, providing for considerable devolution to them and their municipalities. The Dutch provinces have significant political functions of a character that makes them more important than if one uses strictly administrative and fiscal measures.[11] When the southern provinces seceded in 1831 to form Belgium, the new state adopted a similar constitution and implemented it in an even more devoted way until after World War II. For years, the Belgians glorified in the fact that Belgium was hardly more than a loose league of communes. Internal ethnic pressures have since brought Belgium closer to a federal union of its three regions.[12]

Decentralized unitary states constitutionally guarantee their local governments considerable autonomy in some areas, but local powers are invariably restricted to matters determined by the central authorities to be local and are subject to national supervision, restriction, and even withdrawal, though tradition may militate against precipitous action by the central government in areas where local privileges are well established. Still, as the English experience has shown, even powerful traditions supporting local autonomy have not stood in the way of great reconcentration of power by democratically elected parliaments when such reconcentration has been deemed necessary by parliamentary majority.

Consociations. Some apparently centralized states are actually quasi-federal unions of ethnic (including tribal), religious, or ideological groups that, though not organized territorially, have acquired corporate characteristics of their own and have been able to secure constitutional arrangements designed to preserve their respective integrities within a common polity. Arend Lijphart, Gerhard Lembruch, and others have termed such polities consociational, borrowing the term from Johannes Althusius. The Netherlands with its religioideological "pillars," Belgium with its linguistic communities, Lebanon with its religious communities, and Israel with its ideological parties exemplify this arrangement. In most of these cases, domestic services and responsibilities are shared by the subcommunities that are responsible for serving their adherents under the general aegis of the state.[13]

An additional way in which consociational arrangements are distinguished from federal ones is that the former represent linkages of elites who control centralized and often hierarchical subcommunities, which must remain centralized if the elites are to continue to govern. That is, if the leaders of a particular subcommunity do not have sufficient power to negotiate with their counterparts and to make the results of those negotiations stick within their respective camps, the system breaks down. Thus even territorial decentralization, much less noncentralization, becomes problematic in pure consociational systems.

There has been some discussion between students of consociationalism and students of federalism with regard to the relationship between the two concepts. The former often argue that federalism is merely a matter of structure and that the key to power sharing lies in such phenomena as consociational arrangements. The latter argue in turn that consociationalism is, at its best, a form of nonterritorial federalism and otherwise a transitional political arrangement whose durability depends upon whether there is territorial federalism to give it a permanent anchor. In the past several years, the two schools have grown closer as they have gained a better understanding of both phenomena.

All told, some 32 percent of the world's population lives in states that, in one way or another, use federal principles, even though half of them either refuse to embrace the definition or do not wish to go all the way into a fully federal relationship.

Confederations. With the emergence of permanent multinational "communities," of which the European Community (EC) is the prime example, we are now witnessing a revival of confederal arrangements. Despite the hesitancy of the states involved regarding the transfer or even the delegation of national powers, the EC has acquired a very real existence and political personality.

For Europeans, confederal arrangements represented the original form of federalism, going back to the leagues of Greek cities in ancient times. Confederations disappeared during the modern epoch because confederal schemes could not mobilize sufficient political support to maintain themselves in an age of exclusive nationalism.[14] Confederations such as the Holy Roman Empire, the medieval city leagues of Germany, Belgium, and Italy, and the United Provinces of the Netherlands either disintegrated or were constituted as consolidated states. The Helvetic Confederation was transformed by the Swiss into a modern federal system. The German Confederation established on the ruins of the Holy Roman Empire was simply a way station toward the quasi-federal German Empire of the Second Reich.

The European Community presently embraces well over 300 million people. Moreover, seven of the twelve member states are either federal or use federal principles in their internal political systems. Add the populations of the others, and more than 75 percent of the world's population lives under some form of federal arrangement.

There are many indications that the European Community with its functional arrangements presages a revival of confederal government in other parts of the world as well, for example, in connection with the Association of the South East Asian Nations (ASEAN). Three confederations of this nature are functioning in the world today, of which the European Community is the best known. The former British West Indies, which failed as a federation, does function to all intents and purposes as a confederation of the newly independent microstates that emerged out of the wreckage of the West Indies Federation. There, too, the integration has been on a functional basis with a common supreme court, a common currency and bank, a common market, and a common university, among other institutions. Most recently, Senegal and Gambia have founded the Confederation of Senegambia for purposes of mutual protection and to overcome the illogical borders bequeathed the two states by their former local masters.

Southern Africa is also leaning toward confederation. Indeed, confederation is the solution proposed by the Republic of South Africa (RSA) to the problem of relations between the black and nonblack populations in that troubled part of the world. South Africa's president, Pieter W. Botha, has announced that this is the direction in which the RSA hopes to move now that it has its own internal consociational arrangement in place. Under Botha's plan, most if not all of the black homelands would be given independence but would be confederated with the republic. At present, the independent former homelands stand in an informal associated relationship to the RSA. The RSA also dominates a customs union, which embraces the three former British protectorates of Lesotho, Swaziland, and Botswana, now independent, as well as the independent homelands, in an overlapping protoconfederal arrangement. But although these arrangements exist de facto, they are not recognized as legitimate by the black leadership in the RSA and have been explicitly rejected by most of them.

The reemergence of confederation as a viable form of government is an important milestone in the history of federalism for several reasons. Its demise as a workable expression of federalism in the late eighteenth and early nineteenth centuries was related to the prevailing conception of statehood in the modern epoch. The idea of the nation-state possessing complete sovereignty and encompassing a single nation—potentially if not actually—had a negative impact on confederation as a form of polity because confederations violated or substantially reduced both dimensions of modern statehood.

It is only in the postmodern epoch, as notions of absolute national sovereignty diminish in the face of the reality of international interdependence and the myth of the nation-state gives way to the reality of the near universality of multiethnic polities, that new conceptions of political order which allow conceptual and operational space for confederation are emerging. The European Community is the first major expression of this transformation, in part because Europe has gone further than other regions toward revising its notions of statehood in practice, if not always in theory, as a result of its disastrous experiences with unlimited national sovereignty in the twentieth century. Today most of the states of Europe are linked within one of two supranational communities, either as satellite states in the Soviet empire or through the European Community. The only exceptions are Switzerland and Austria, whose middleman position makes neutrality attractive, and the peripheral states of Scandinavia, who have formed their own regional league on a more limited basis.

Because the countries of Western Europe had mature economies, economic integration was the most logical way for them to proceed. In doing so, they invented a new way to confederate, through the union of specific functions rather than through a general act of confederation. Within the sphere of each of those functions, union was substantial if not complete, with appropriate powers being given to the EC. Only after the number of functions grew to the point that more general institutions were demanded were such institutions constituted, in different ways for each class of powers. Adjudication was assigned to a high court, which functions as the constitutional court of a union within the spheres of its competence. Administration became the

province of the EC bureaucracy, which functions as the civil
service of a union within its functional spheres. Policy is
made by councils of ministers of the constituent states,
which function as instruments of a league. Budgetary review and approval as well as limited power to set long-term
policy guidelines rests in the hands of the European Parliament, which functions as the instrument of a confederation.
Thus the construction of common institutions proceeded in
such a way as to minimize the threat to the existing states,
which sought—and seek—to retain independence beyond
that normally allotted to federated states and at the same
time enabled the establishment of a sufficiently energetic
government in certain limited spheres with the means to
attain the ends for which it was constituted.

In part, this process was given theoretical expression
through the writings of the European functionalists in the
1950s. But because the functionalists were engaged in a
battle with the federalists, who sought a United States of
Europe on one hand, and the statists, who wanted to preserve as much of the status quo on the other, they played
down the federal elements of their theory and actively
moved it away from the sphere of federal theory. Although
useful at the time, at a certain point after the Common
Market was initially constituted and proved to be operational, their theory lost its relevance because it did not continue to evolve in line with the developments in the field. A
proper theory of this new-style confederation is still lacking, although the functionalists have provided a basis for its
development.[15]

Asymmetrical Federal Arrangements. Other applications of
the federal principle, which may or may not have existed in
the past, have also emerged in recent decades. One involves
small states with some necessary relationship to a larger
state, often a former colonial power. Rather than seeking
full independence, they have sought an asymmetrical fed-

eral association with the larger state power on the basis of internal autonomy and self-government, which enables them to share in the benefits of association with a greater power without being incorporated within it, even as a constituent polity. This phenomenon, sometimes known as free association, manifests itself in two forms: (1) associated statehood in which either the principal or the associated state may unilaterally dissolve the relationship according to procedures established in the constituting document; and (2) federacy in which any change in the relationship must be determined on a mutual basis by both parties. Table 2.3 lists the existing polities of both types.

Table 2.3. *Associated States, Federacies, and Condominiums*

Name (Form)	Federate Power	Population (thousands)[a]	Area (sq. mi.)
Aaland Islands (federacy)	Finland	23	572
Valley of Andorra (condominium)	France and Spain	34	179
Azores Islands (federacy)	Portugal	289	902
Bhutan (associated state)	India	1,296	18,000
Cook Islands (associated state)	New Zealand	19	90
Faröe Islands (federacy)	Denmark	44	540
Federated States of Micronesia (associated state)	United States	117	502

Greenland (federacy)	Denmark	51	840,005
Guernsey (federacy)	United Kingdom	53	25
Isle of Man (federacy)	United Kingdom	64	227
Jammu and Kashmir (federacy)	India	5,100c	85,805
Jersey (federacy)	United Kingdom	74b	45
Principality of Liechtenstein (associated state)	Switzerland	25	61
Macao (associated state)	Portugal	271	6
Madeira Islands (federacy)	Portugal	251	307
Marshall Islands (associated state)	United States	31	–
Monaco (associated state)	France	27.1	0.8
Netherlands Antilles (associated state)	Netherlands	251b	383
Nieu Islands (associated state)	New Zealand	4	100
Northern Marianas (federacy)	United States	17	185
Puerto Rico (federacy)	United States	3,188	3,421
Republic of Palau (associated state)	United States	12	127

San Marino (associated state)	Italy	21[b]	24
West Berlin (associated state)	German Federal Republic	1,899	185

[a]1979 or 1980 estimates.
[b]1978 estimate.
[c]1976 estimate.

The Netherlands Antilles and the Netherlands and Puerto Rico and the United States are particularly good examples of associated statehood and federacy, respectively. Puerto Rico has every power of internal self-government of any independent state and, in theory, more than any federated state of the American union. Its citizens are also citizens of the United States but do not have the right to vote in national elections. There are today more than twenty such arrangements in existence, including that between West Berlin and the Federal Republic of Germany. Because of its legal status under four-power occupation, West Berlin has evolved as an associated rather than a constituent state of the Federal Republic of Germany. It shares most of the prerogatives of a constituent state but has to maintain a certain distance because of the four-power agreements. As political arrangements, most examples of both are too new for evaluation. In some cases, they have been way stations toward absorption of the smaller state into the larger on a more fully integrated basis or its full separation from the larger one. In others, especially those that represent medieval arrangements transformed, such as San Marino and Italy, Monaco and France, and Liechtenstein and Switzerland, they have proved remarkably stable over centuries.[16]

Even less noted are condominiums, an unusual and rare species of federalism but notable for at least one great success and several lesser ones. Under condominium, responsibility for governance of a particular polity is shared with two or more external political entities. In the past, some condominium arrangements, such as that which prevailed in Tangier before World War II, were frankly colonial, with the external powers jointly administering the territory or polity in question. These, of course, were not truly federal because the residents of the polity did not have a reasonable measure of self-rule. On the other hand, a triadic arrangement such as that between Andorra, France, and Spain has survived for seven hundred years and has all the characteristics of federalism. Under that arrangement, Andorra has been able to preserve its independence between two large states known until recently for their voracious appetites for territory, maintaining internal self-government in the fullest sense even though ultimate authority is formally vested in a constitutionally restricted way, in the two external powers.[17]

Leagues. Leagues represent another, though limited, way of using federal principles. They serve to link entirely discrete polities in some lasting way. Among the most prominent manifestations of this form today are customs unions. The British Commonwealth can be considered a league for most purposes. The North Atlantic Treaty Organization (NATO) was founded as a league and not simply a military alliance but, like the British Commonwealth, has not developed its leaguelike characteristics to any great extent. One of the most long-lived leagues is the Arab League. Although it is limited in an operational sense, its members' view of themselves as parts of a common Arab nation has given it a permanence and reality lacking in other contemporary leagues.[18]

Yet another form of federalism may be emerging, which can be termed foralistic federalism whereby the relationship between the overarching government and the constituent governments is based on a network of bilateral agreements, each designed specifically for the constituent polity involved. The term comes from the Spanish *fuero,* the classic term for the negotiated charters between the king and his provinces in medieval Spain. The province of Navarre has maintained at least some of its foral rights up to the present time, and those rights are claimed by the Basque provinces. These *fueros* represent medieval constitutions, affirming traditional local liberties, which are independent of any grants by the overarching polity.

Although the present Spanish regime refuses to reaffirm the *fueros* as such, it has, in fact, adopted the foral approach as the basis for separate autonomy agreements with each autonomous region, adapting it to contemporary republicanism. Each agreement is authorized, drafted, and adopted through a complex process involving the consent of both the Spanish Cortes (parliament) and the population of the region involved. As a consequence, Spain is being transformed into a federal system through the network of foralistic agreements.[19]

The same term could be used to describe the relationship between the United Kingdom and its federacies, Jersey, Guernsey, and the Isle of Man. But since the concept of federacy embodies that bilateral principle of unique arrangements, foral federalism is better reserved for situations that are not asymmetrical but in which a common overarching government deals with constituent polities.

What is characteristic of all of the foregoing forms is that they are compound polities rather than unitary ones; two or more bodies politic are united in such a way as to preserve their respective integrities even as they form a third polity for certain purposes. The art and craft of compounding polities is the essence of the art and craft of federalism, and the study of compound polities is not only a legitimate branch of political science but one of growing importance. At least since *The Federalist,* the idea of the compound re-

Figure 2.4. *Varieties of Federal Arrangements (with Selected Examples)*

Basis

TERRITORIAL

Antigua-Barbuda Japan Solomon Islands Vanuatu	Argentina Australia Brazil Comoros West Germany Malaysia Mexico UAR United States Venezuela	Caribbean Community	Denmark-Faeroes India-Kashmir Portugal-Azores Portugal-Madeira UK-Guernsey UK-Jersey UK-Man	France-Monaco W. Germany-W. Berlin Italy-San Manno Switzerland-Liechtenstein		Arab League ASEAN Benelux NATO Nordic League
Italy Spain Sudan Tanzania United Kingdom	Austria Canada Nigeria Pakistan Switzerland	European Community Senegambia	Netherlands-Curacao Denmark-Greenland	Netherlands–Netherlands Antilles India-Bhutan	Andorra–France and Spain	British Commonwealth
Form UNION	FEDERATION	CONFEDERATION	FEDERACY	ASSOCIATED STATEHOOD	CONDOMINIUM	LEAGUE
Belgium Burma China Colombia Equatorial Guinea Netherlands Papau/New Guinea South Africa	Czechoslovakia India USSR Yugoslavia		Finland-Aaland US-Puerto Rico US-Normon Marianas	New Zealand-Cook Islands New Zealand-Nieu Islands US-Marshall Islands US-Micronesia US-Palau		
Israel Lebanon Namibia						

CONSOCIATIONAL

public has been tied to the new science of politics, to which it gave the first practical expression.

The variety of federal arrangements found in the world today is impressive, as Figure 2.4 reveals. Each of these forms can be classified as to whether its basis is predominantly territorial or consociational, although several may manifest characteristics of both. The number of polities or regimes that can be classified within this framework is impressive, and in every case the classification is either apparent or not difficult to justify. In other words, all do indeed partake of some aspect of federalism.

In Figure 2.4, the relationship of these various arrangements to one another is portrayed as a continuum, which is especially useful for contrast with the centralization-decentralization continuum descriptive of the other two models of the polity. It is equally useful to conceptualize the relationship in terms of the degrees of consolidation and symmetry present in each arrangement. Figure 2.5 does so schematically through a triangular model in which each plane affects the range of combinations of both dimensions.

Local and Nongovernmental Federalism. All these principles and arrangements are applied on the local plane as well and are growing in number and scope. Israel, for example, is a formally centralized state, organized de facto on a consociational basis with a minimal expression of political matters territorially. On the local plane, however, the country's rural settlements are linked through regional councils, which are classic federations in the modern sense. Cities in Israel's metropolitan areas are linked with one another in limited-purpose functional confederations. Federacy arrangements are common within governmental institutional structures, as when new schools are permanently attached to older ones. Most of the larger cities are unions of once independent neighborhoods or subdivisions and—in Jerusalem and Haifa at least—the terms of union provide for the

Figure 2.5. *Forms of Federal Arrangements*

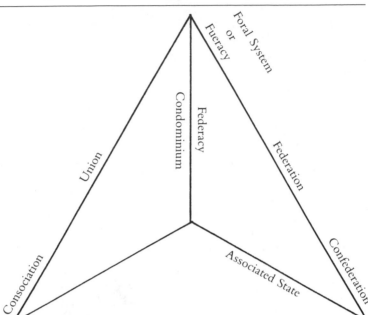

Interjurisdictional   League
Functional Authority

preservation of neighborhood control over certain policies affecting them. All the cities in the country are leagued together for certain clearly defined purposes in the Israel Union of Local Authorities.[20]

Federalism has been introduced as a solution to the problems of political integration in metropolitan regions. The Canadian experiments, particularly in Ontario (whose metropolitan Toronto is the best-known example), are good examples of the use of federal principles and arrangements on that scale. The United States has tried somewhat different arrangements based on federal principles in metropolitan Miami (Dade County), the Twin Cities metropolitan region of Minnesota, and other metropolitan regions.[21]

Many of the larger European cities, such as Paris and London, are examples of two-tiered quasi-federal arrangements.

The federal principle has also been used as the basis for nongovernmental associations, both public and private, that have become characteristic of the contemporary world. Labor unions in many countries are organized along federal lines in regard to the connections that form the basis for the great national labor confederations. So, too, are business and industrial associations, chambers of commerce, and health and welfare federations. When these public nongovernmental bodies use federal arrangements, they frequently do so on a functional rather than a territorial basis, thus adding another dimension to the use of federal principles.

The modern corporation has its roots to some degree in one variant of the compact idea that lies at the basis of modern federalism.[22] Pragmatically, as corporations have grown in size, they frequently have had to resort to the use of federal arrangements, if not to fully federal forms of organization, for many of the same reasons that have led polities in that direction—to manage very complex enterprises more effectively. In recent years, conglomerates have carried this use of federal principles further than ever.

Labor unions and businesses are frequently grouped together in sectoral federations. Such arrangements are particularly common in federal political systems, in which nongovernmental groups must accommodate themselves to a federal distribution of political power. They are not limited to such political systems, however, but are common in all modern democratic countries, adding a federal dimension ranging from symbolic to serious. Liberal democracy with its emphasis on pluralism creates an environment that is highly conducive to such arrangements. In fact, there is some reason to believe that coalition politics in mass-based, multiparty systems reflect a form of party federalism that stands outside of the "normal" patterns of federal government. These examples are not meant to suggest that everything is federal. Nevertheless, the pervasiveness of federal devices and arrangements does reflect the extent of the federalist revolution and its impact in developing a parallel system of human organization in our times.

Federalism as Unity and Diversity

One of the characteristics of federalism is its aspiration and purpose simultaneously to generate and maintain both unity and diversity.[23] This ambiguity is reflected in confusion over the very use of the term. People use the terms "federalism," "federalist," and "federalize" to describe both the process of political unification and the maintenance of the diffusion of political power. More than one discussion of federalism has foundered upon a basic misunderstanding by the parties involved as to which sense of the term is being used.

This ambiguity is real to the extent that federalism and its related terms do express both processes simultaneously. Federalizing involves both the creation and maintenance of unity and the diffusion of power in the name of diversity. Indeed, that is why federalism is not to be located on the centralization–decentralization continuum but on a different continuum altogether, one that is predicated on noncentralization, or the effective combination of unity and diversity.[24]

When discussing federalism, it is a mistake to present unity and diversity as opposites. Unity should be contrasted with disunity and diversity with homogeneity, emphasizing the political dimensions and implications of each. Figure 2.6 suggests the likely results if the two are correlated

Figure 2.6. Unity and Diversity in Selected Federal and Nonfederal Systems (mid-1970s)

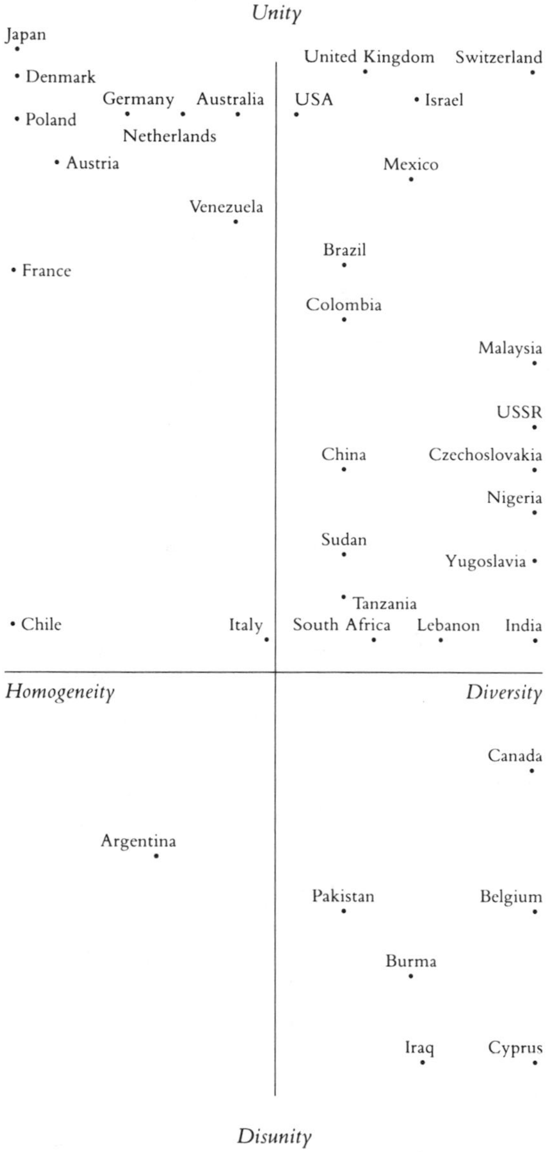

Unity

Japan
• Denmark

United Kingdom   Switzerland
•   •

Germany Australia   USA   • Israel
• Poland   •   •   •
        Netherlands
• Austria   Mexico
                                 •

Venezuela
   •

                          Brazil
• France   •

                        Colombia
                           •

                                     Malaysia
                                        •

                                       USSR
                                        •
                          China   Czechoslovakia
                            •   •

                                        Nigeria
                                          •

                        Sudan
                          •
                                    Yugoslavia •

                        • Tanzania
• Chile   Italy South Africa Lebanon India
                   •   •   •   •

———————————————————————————————

Homogeneity   Diversity

                                   Canada
                                     •

Argentina
   •

                  Pakistan   Belgium
                    •   •

                        Burma
                         •

                     Iraq   Cyprus
                      •   •

Disunity

Source: Daniel J. Elazar, ed., *Federalism and Political Integration* (Ramat Gan, Israel: Turtledove Publishing, 1979).

in this manner. The strong tendency of federal systems to reflect the existence of politically meaningful diversity is evident from the figure. Austria and Germany are the principal exceptions, and their federal systems constantly confront consolidationist pressures based upon homogeneity-related arguments. In some cases—Belgium and Canada, for example—use of federal arrangements is directly linked to the struggle to maintain sufficient unity. It is possible to have a strong federal system that combines a high degree of unity with a high degree of diversity (Switzerland, for example), just as it is possible for a high degree of diversity to lead to great disunity (in Iraq, for example, where the Arabs and the Kurds are in seemingly perpetual civil war).

Homogeneity does not always promote unity. Substantial ethnic homogeneity in nineteenth-century America did not prevent the clash of sectionally based interests from leading to civil war, just as the substantial ethnic homogeneity of Great Britain and her American colonies did not prevent the American Revolution in the eighteenth century. Moreover, various forms of unity and disunity are to be considered, as well as more varieties of diversity.

There is a difference between consolidated unity (for example, France) and federal unity (for example, Switzerland).[25] Diversity is manifested through nationality or ethnic, religious, ideological, social, and interest factors that may or may not gain political expression. Consolidated unity attempts either to depoliticize or carefully limit the political effects of diversity, relegating manifestations of diversity to other spheres. Federal unity, on the other hand, not only is comfortable with the political expression of diversity but is from its roots a means to accommodate diversity as a legitimate element in the polity. Thus consolidated polities can be diverse but, for them, diversity is not considered desirable per se, even if reality requires its reconciliation within the body polity. The question remains open as to what kinds or combinations of diversity are compatible with federal unity and which ones are not.[26]

Federalism as Structure and Process

In the earlier stages of the history of modern federalism, structural considerations were not only first and foremost but were essentially the be-all and end-all of the concern for federal arrangements, the assumption being that the introduction of a proper federal structure would create a functioning federal system. More recently, students of federalism have come to understand the limits of, as well as the necessities for, a structural approach to federalism. This recognition was born out of experience, which showed that many polities with federal structures were not truly federal in practice—that the structures masked a centralized concentration of power that stands in direct contradiction to the federal principle.[27]

Exploring matters further, they undertook to examine the processes of government in federal systems, and many came to the conclusion that federalism is as much a matter of process as of structure, particularly if process is broadly defined to include a political-cultural dimension as well. The elements of a federal process include a sense of partnership among the parties to the federal compact, manifested through negotiated cooperation on issues and programs and based on a commitment to open bargaining between all parties to an issue in such a way as to strive for consensus or, failing that, an accommodation that protects the fundamental integrity of all the partners. Only in polities whose processes of government reflect federal principles is the structure of federalism meaningful.

In the course of identifying the importance of process, the issue was posed in such a way as to question whether federalism was a matter of structure *or* process, with the two juxtaposed to make it seem as if an either/or proposition was involved. In fact, federalism must combine both structure *and* process. That combination, indeed, is what creates a federal system. If a federal structure exists without a correspondingly federal process, there is evidence to indicate that, although it may have some impact on the processes of governance even if the latter are not ultimately federal, in the last analysis, its impact will be secondary. This is the case in the USSR and in certain Latin American polities.[28]

The introduction of federal structures in a polity is a matter of concrete actions at specific times; we know relatively little about the introduction of federal processes and to what extent they are a prerequisite for the establishment of a federal structure or structures that can accommodate them. There is some reason to believe that a federal process can exist in a very attenuated way without a federal structure, but even there it must ultimately acquire some structural recognition. Figure 2.7 suggests a tentative classification of all currently extant federal polities, and selected others, with regard to their structures and processes based on assessment of currently available evidence. The figure illustrates that structure alone is not sufficient to determine the federal character of any particular polity. The groupings in the figure are of interest, with the Anglo-American, Western European, Communist bloc, Latin American, Afro-Asian, and Middle Eastern countries tending to concentrate in particular segments of the matrix.

Social, Territorial, and Cultural Expressions of Federalism

Social. Federalism as a political phenomenon, understood according to the modern meaning of "political," is essen-

Figure 2.7. *Structure and Process in Federal and Selected Nonfederal Polities*

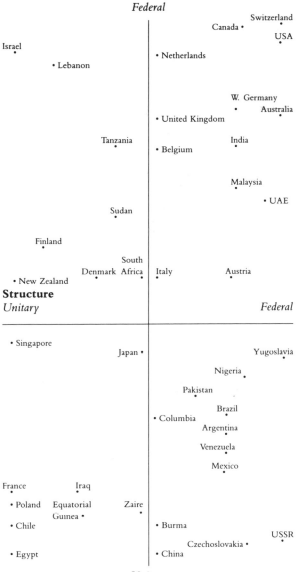

tially limited to relations among governments or polities. This conception of federalism is most widespread today, particularly in federal systems. (Premodern and, most particularly, classical thought understood "political" to include both the political and social dimensions because the polity was viewed as comprehensive.) At least since the nineteenth century, however, there has been a parallel conceptualization of federalism as what, in modern practice, is termed a social phenomenon. This conceptualization manifests itself in two ways. The first has to do with the proper relationships among people as individuals, or in families and groups, as well as in their capacity as citizens, whereby they relate to each other federally, that is, as partners respectful of each other's integrity while cooperating for the common good in every aspect of life, not just in the political realm. This latter emphasis was developed primarily by French and Russian thinkers, who did not live within federal polities but who sought federal solutions to social problems and saw in federalism the possibility to achieve harmonious social relationships as well as an appropriate form of political organization.[29]

The second emphasizes the existence of essentially permanent religious, ethnic, cultural, or social groups around which political life must be organized. Whether or not the polity is formally structured around those groups, they serve as its pillars. In recent years political scientists have come to refer to the latter as consociational arrangements.[30] Consociational arrangements usually emerge on a semiformal basis, then become institutionalized, usually through some form of legal and institutional adaption within the polity, thereby becoming constitutionalized. This latter step brings them into the realm of federalism.

Unless reinforced by federal structure in some way, consociational arrangements tend to be matters of regime rather than form, lasting from one to three generations before breaking down or being transformed into something else. Thus Dutch consociationalism, accepted as the classic example of the species, became the basis of the Dutch regime in the last generation of the nineteenth century and began to collapse in the last decade of the post–World War II generation. Belgium's consociationalism, introduced at the same time, is being transformed into a territorial arrangement. Lebanon's consociational "national covenant" broke down in civil war in 1975 after a generation. In Israel, the decline of ideological parties in all but the religious camp has greatly diminished its consociational character.[31] Pure consociational systems seem to have a limited life span because they lack the constitutional roots of territorial federalism.

Although most federal polities are not consciously informed by the idea of federalism as a social phenomenon and tend either to ignore or reject it, the most successful ones reflect the social dimension of federalism along with a federal political structure and a set of explicitly federal political processes. At the same time, there are nations and peoples that manifest the social dimension of federalism without its explicitly political dimension, although even in such cases the social phenomena require and obtain some political expression.[32] Figure 2.8 suggests a classification of selected federal and nonfederal polities on the basis of a correlation of these two dimensions. The assessment of the political dimension is based on the results of the classification in this figure. Thus the USSR scores low on that dimension despite its structure. The assessment of the social dimension is based on the degree of what can be termed consociational behavior present in a political polity.

Territorial. The existence of federalism plays a major role in shaping the geographic basis of social and political organizations in federal systems. One way it does so is obvious. The federal systems of today are based on fundamental ter-

Figure 2.8. *Federalism as Social and Political Phenomena in Selected Polities*

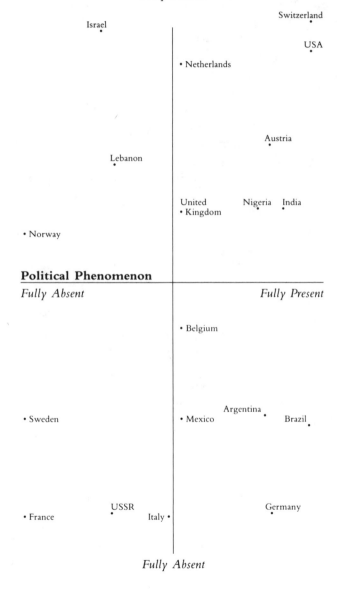

ritorial divisions of power, so that territory becomes the basis for political action. The essentially permanent boundaries of the major subdivisions serve as strong bulwarks for the diffusion of power. As permanent political units, they offer continued opportunities for diverse interests to find expression. Since every interest, new or old, is located willy-nilly in some formally defined political territory, every interest can gain some measure of expression more or less proportional to its strength, simply by making use of the country's political mechanisms.

Two examples from the American experience are illustrative. The state of Florida, once a typical representative of traditional southern interests, now speaks for pensioners from the greater Northeast and the pioneers of the space program. Detroit was a base of power for Yankee commercial and craft interests in the nineteenth century. With its economic transformation into an automobile center, it was politically transformed into a stronghold for ethnic and black auto workers without significantly having to alter its basic political structure or its institutions. In recent years, Detroit blacks have gained political control of the Motor City by virtue of their growing share of its total population. These changes have taken place without serious dislocations in the nation's political system because of the existence of territorial democracy.

Territorial divisions of power can also be used to protect minorities and minority communities by allowing them greater autonomy within their own political jurisdictions. Yugoslavia is an excellent example of the use of federalism to enable different nationalities to live together. India has used federal devices to serve the aspirations of linguistic minorities. Nigeria divided its original three states into nineteen to give each major tribal group a center of power while denying any of them a dominant position and has used local governmental arrangements within states to secure the positions of smaller tribes. Canada, Czechoslovakia, Switzerland, and the USSR offer other examples, each in its own way, not to speak of the examples that can be found in every federal polity on the local plane.

The geographic impact of federalism has another dimension as well. Federal polities are notably ones in which no single urban center is dominant. Within the federal matrix there is also a network of cities of relatively equal importance, often specializing in one or more functions. Contrast, for example, France and West Germany—two polities of relatively equal size. Life in highly centralized France is centered in Paris, whereas no single city can be said to dominate the German Federal Republic. Federal systems generally follow the German rather than the French model, whereas most unitary states reflect the French pattern.

In the days of colonialism, the French could talk about metropolitan France—that is, the French heartland as distinct from the French periphery—because at the heart of metropolitan France was metropolitan Paris. It would be inconceivable to try to define any fully federal system that way. In the United States, for example, Washington is the national capital, but it is no more than a governmental center and, recalling the matrix, not even central in the governmental sense in the way that Paris is. In economic and cultural affairs, one can name at least five cities that are more important than Washington, with New York holding preeminence. Boston is the academic capital of the United States, if there is one, and Los Angeles dominates in entertainment and shares dominance in mass communications. The country's popular music "capitals," for example, are New York, Los Angeles, Nashville, Philadelphia, and, most recently, Austin, Texas.

Canada reflects the same federal pattern, only more so. Ottawa, the capital, has even less national significance than Washington. The country's real centers are Toronto and

Montreal, which, between them, divide preeminence in all fields other than government. Montreal has no governmental preeminence because the capital of Quebec is Quebec City. Vancouver on the west coast and Winnipeg in the middle are both larger and economically more important than Ottawa.

True federal systems do not have capitals; they have seats of government. "Capital" implies a place at the top of the governmental pyramid, whereas "seat" appropriately suggests a place of assembly. Switzerland is the prime example of this phenomenon among federal systems. Bern is never referred to as the capital by the Swiss but is officially the seat of the federal government. In the United States, reference to Washington as the nation's capital is relatively late, introduced along with the changing conception of the role of federal government in American society. Washington was originally called the national city, the seat of the federal government, in the same way that the city or town where the county courthouse is located is referred to as the county seat. Usage is still mixed in the United States, with "capital" favored by the federal officials and media people who see the country and the world from a Washington-centered perspective.

In general, there is a clear relationship between the degree of centralization within a particular federal system and the extent to which a single national capital has emerged. Argentina, Mexico, and Venezuela, three federal systems in which the federal principle exercises a relatively weak influence on politics, reflect this relationship in the concentration of activity in Buenos Aires, Mexico City, and Caracas, respectively. The same factors making for concentration in Latin American federal polities are present in Brazil, but less concentration seems to have taken place for various political, social and historical reasons. This pattern is reflected in—and reinforced by—the broad sharing of urban preeminence between Rio de Janeiro and São Paulo, Belo Horizonte, Pôrto Alegre, and Brasília, the federal capital.

In Europe, the same principles are pronounced. Primary roles in Germany are divided equitably among Berlin, Hamburg, Frankfurt, Munich, and Bonn. Even little Netherlands, a consociational polity that has not had a federal structure since its conquest by Napoleon but maintains constitutional decentralization, has retained its three major centers in Amsterdam, Rotterdam, and The Hague. In Switzerland, Zurich, Geneva, Basel, and Bern are equally centers, depending on the purposes involved. Yugoslavia has Belgrade and Zagreb plus the other republican capitals. Even in the USSR, Moscow and Leningrad are longtime rivals for preeminence, not to mention the capitals of the union republics.

As part of their drive to unite and centralize Italy, first the risorgimentists and then the fascists made every effort to concentrate the political, economic, and cultural life of the new state in Rome. Nevertheless, Italy remained a congeries of regions and, since World War II, there has been a strengthening of other urban centers, particularly in the north, which, in turn, contributed to the establishment of regional governments under a constitutional provision, which for twenty-five years had remained a dead letter.

The one apparent exception to this general rule among European federal systems is Austria, where the magnitude of Vienna far outreaches that of the country's lesser cities. In the days of the great Hapsburg Empire, there were indeed as many principal cities as there were states under the monarch's authority. In theory, the reduction in Austria's size following World War I should have transformed the rest of the country into a hinterland of a powerful city-state. In fact, the closing of Austria's eastern border to substantial economic activity after World War II considerably weakened Vienna as a center and gave a boost to the smaller urban centers in the western and central *lander,* thereby initiating a redistribution in the country's internal balance of power.

The federal states of Asia reflect the same pattern. Bombay, Calcutta, Madras, and New Delhi hold equal rank in India, not to speak of the equal spread of cities of lesser size. Malaysia's urban hierarchy is even less defined because of the lesser role that urbanism plays in that country. Little consociational Israel divides its dominant urban roles between Jerusalem, Tel Aviv, Haifa, and Beersheba. In Australia, the relationship between Melbourne and Sydney, Perth and Adelaide, and Canberra is almost a mirror image of the Canadian situation without the internal ethnolinguistic division.

The Nigerian situation provides a particularly good case study of the special way in which federalism influences the pattern of political integration. Nigeria of today is one of the most ethnically diverse countries in the world. For that reason alone, it has remained strongly committed to federalism as the basis for nation-building. This commitment even weathered civil war and military rule. To avoid the implications of regional and tribal rivalries, the British built a new city, Lagos, on islands off the coast to serve as their base of operations. It is now the federal capital but will soon be replaced by a new city, specially built for the purpose, in the heart of the country. During the civil war, the military rulers divided the four then existing states into twelve and subsequently into nineteen better to accommodate ethnic and tribal demands for home rule. The capital of each was made the focal point for regional development, so that, rather than concentrating the nation's development resources in the capital, as has so often been the case in developing countries, the federal government is committed to spreading those resources among at least nineteen centers—and is doing so. The Nigerian experience points to one of the real benefits of federalism in the developing world—the increased opportunity potentially provided by federal arrangements for the spread of development beyond the capital region, thus avoiding the common phenomenon of confining so-called national development to a single metropolis at the expense of the rest of the country.

Cultural. True federal systems manifest their federalism in cultural as well as constitutional and structural ways. That is, the idea that society is made up of a series of interrelated covenants and compacts, which allow the parties to them to unite for common purposes while retaining their respective integrities, is deeply embedded in the national cultures of authentic federal systems. In this respect, federalism implies a posture and an attitude toward social as well as political relationships, which leads to human interactions that emphasize coordinative rather than superior-subordinate relationships, negotiated cooperation, and sharing among parties. Switzerland is a classic example of a polity that is federal to its core because its people "think federal" as a matter of second nature.[33]

In many respects, the viability of federal systems is directly related to the degree to which federalism has been internalized culturally within a particular civil society. The imposition of federal structures upon societies not thus attuned to federal relationships has rarely succeeded in creating genuine federal systems. On the other hand, some of the unions and consociations using federal arrangements sustain those arrangements despite seemingly inadequate constitutional guarantees because of culturally rooted support for them. The Netherlands is a striking case where a historical commitment to local self-government is embodied both constitutionally in the form of its union and culturally through consociational arrangements.[34] Belgium has maintained its federal characteristics through its culture for a century and a half, translating them into consociational arrangements for some two generations and, most recently, into more formally federal ones. Both arrangements reflect the adoption of measures to promote political integration appropriate to indigenous cultural conditions in light of changed circumstances.

Federal forms sometimes take root even in cultures emphasizing hierarchical social relationships, when the local cultures include strong traditional commitments to local autonomy within the constituent units, usually because the people have deeply rooted attachments to them. Germany and Austria in Europe and most Latin American federal systems offer good examples of the possibilities and limitations of this alternate form of achieving a cultural basis for federal arrangements.

Although in recent years there has been a growing interest in the question of political culture, little has been done to explore the political-cultural basis of federalism. One way or another, successful federal systems seem to require an appropriate cultural basis. Nigeria, for example, the one African nation where federalism has survived past the first few years of independence, offers excellent possibilities for such an exploration. Its multiethnic character has consistently encouraged the structural diffusion of governmental power in keeping with local realities. In addition, two of the three great Nigerian peoples, the Ibo and the Yoruba, have cultures attuned to noncentralization. The Ibo tradition is one of local self-government among equals, and the Yoruba maintained their traditional political institutions through a network of local oligarchies.[35]

3

Federalism as Means and End

Advocates of federalism as a theoretical formulation and as a way to resolve practical political problems have treated federal arrangements both as means and ends, with the distinction usually remaining implicit in their argument rather than being made explicit. Simply put, there are those who see federalism and federal arrangements as means to attain ends external to them, such as political unification, democracy, popular self-government, and the accommodation of diversity. They are not particularly interested in federalism as such but in the utility of federal arrangements to achieve what to them are larger ends. Their commitment to federal arrangements and principles will exist only as long as they conceive them to be useful in attaining those larger ends.[1]

Others, however, see in federalism—and most particularly in the realization of the federal idea—an end in itself. They hold that federalism is designed to produce the highest form of political and human relationships. To them federalism is not a tool for achieving other goals but embodies the goals themselves as well as the means for their attainment or realization. Those who see federalism as an end generally minimize the distinction between means and ends, at least in this context, holding that the ends must embody the means and that the two are interdependent. (This interpretation follows the temper of much of twentieth-century philosophy, which sees great importance in eliminating the means-ends distinction.)[2]

A few political theorists have posited federalism, political

Figure 3.1. *Varying Approaches to Federalism of Selected Political Theorists*

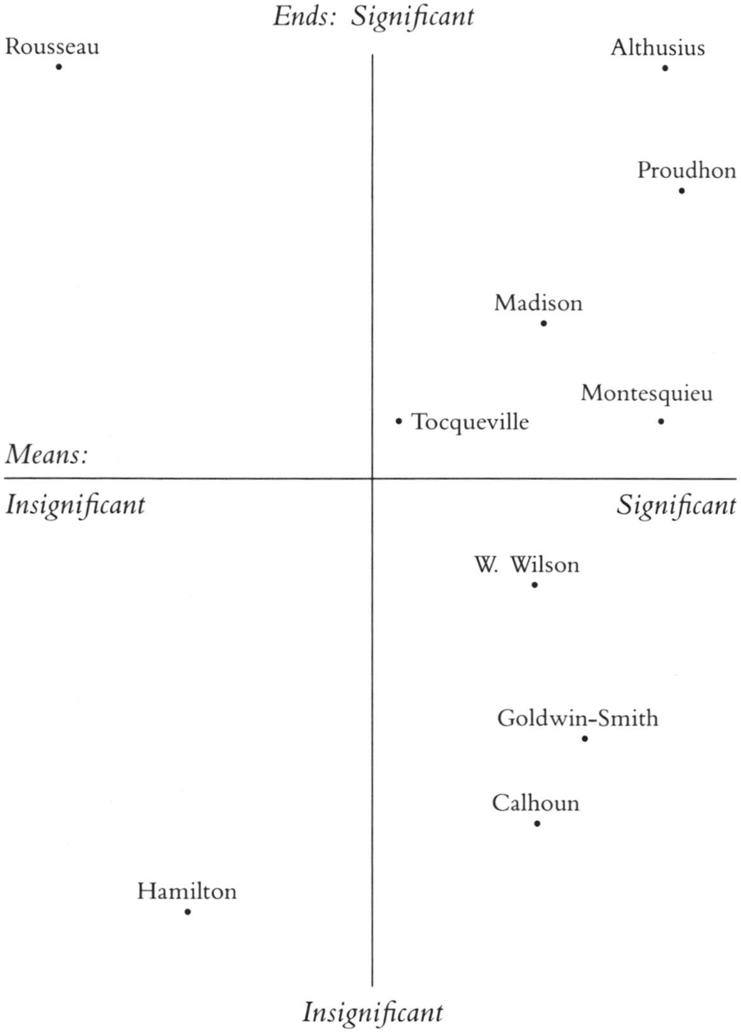

Ends: Significant

Rousseau
•

Althusius
•

Proudhon
•

Madison
•

Montesquieu
•

• Tocqueville

Means:

Insignificant   Significant

W. Wilson
•

Goldwin-Smith
•

Calhoun
•

Hamilton
•

Insignificant

or social or both, as an end but have not provided for it as a means. Jean-Jacques Rousseau may be the best example of this phenomenon.[3] Their theories have tended to emphasize the necessity to force men to be free and, hence, are extremely problematic. Figure 3.1 suggests a classification of selected political theorists who have paid significant attention to federalism, according to this dichotomy.

Federalism as Limited or Comprehensive

Closely connected to the ambiguities regarding means and ends, and federalism as a political or social phenomenon, is the question as to whether federalism is to be conceived of as limited or comprehensive in scope, which, to some extent, both cuts across and embraces the former two. Thus, even among those who view federalism as an end, there are several different perspectives. There are those who see politics as the sum and substance of human interaction, at least beyond the arena of the family, and federalism as the sum and substance of politics, so that for them, federalism becomes the comprehensive end.[4] Others see federalism as one among several ends to be weighed in relation to the others and balanced with them.[5] On the other hand, there are those who see federalism as no more than a means to achieve their particular ends in view but as the most comprehensive means.[6] They would be prepared to argue that a proper political system must be federal in its structure and processes but that the goals of federalism, as such, are directed (that is, limited) to achieving ends external to it. Still others would argue that federalism is simply one of several means to attain certain political ends, perhaps even a valuable one, but no more than that.[7]

Clearly, there is a close relationship between those who see federalism as a comprehensive end and those who perceive it as having both political and social dimensions (or comprehensive political dimensions, to use an earlier language). Similarly, those who see federalism as one comprehensive end may be more likely to emphasize the strictly political character of the federal principle—which is almost certain to be the case for those who see federalism as a limited means for achieving certain other goals. Undoubtedly there are some anarchists, for example, who, rejecting government as they do, see federalism as a comprehensive social phenomenon but of limited political significance. All this ambiguity only heightens the potential ambiguity in dealing with federalism, even as it enriches the potentialities inherent in the concept and, more important, in its operationalization.

Federal principles and arrangements have become so widespread precisely because they suit the modern temper. As basically covenantal arrangements, they fit a civilization governed by contractual relationships; since they place a premium on negotiation and bargaining, they are eminently suited to a civilization that seeks to maximize individual liberty and equality among the parties to the compact.

Considering the foregoing, some analysts have simply thrown up their hands and suggested that the concept of federalism has become meaningless as a result of the confusion that ensues in its wake.[8] I would suggest that, to the contrary, these ambiguities, and the variety of federal theories and arrangements resulting from them, demonstrate the richness of the concept and its importance in political life and thought. In this respect, federalism is analogous to other great concepts such as democracy, which offer a similar spread of ambiguities and variety of applications. Indeed, what is characteristic of a great political principle is both the essential simplicity in its basic formulation and the richness of the fabric woven around that simple base.

What Is Federalism Designed to Achieve?

Federalism is designed to achieve some degree of political integration based on a combination of self-rule and shared rule. Although its form may be used under other circumstances, it is appropriate only when and where that kind of political integration is sought. Political integration on a federal basis demands a particular set of relationships, beginning with the relationship between the two faces of politics, power and justice. On one hand, politics deals with the organization of power, in the words of Harold Laswell, with "who gets what, when, and how." Politics, however, is simultaneously concerned with the pursuit of justice—with the building and maintenance of the good polity, however defined. All political life represents some interaction of these two faces of politics, whereby the organization and distribution of power are informed by some particular conception of justice, whereas the pursuit of justice is shaped (and limited) by the realities of power.[9]

Federalism in its most limited form is usually defined as having to do with the distribution and sharing of power, but even in that limited form there is an implicit commitment to a conception of justice that holds, among other things, that a distribution of powers is necessary and desirable. On the other hand, federalism in its broadest sense is presented as a form of justice—emphasizing liberty and citizen participation in governance—but one which is inevitably linked to political reality because it must still be concerned with the distribution of powers. One of the primary attributes of federalism is that it cannot, by its very nature, abandon the concern for either power or justice but must consider both in relationship to each other, thus forcing people to consider the hard realities of political life while at the same time maintaining their aspirations for the best polity.

It is not unfair to say that one purpose of federalism is to achieve this linking of the real and the ideal—or the prosaic details of who does what and gets what on a daily basis—with the messianic aspirations for justice. This effort to require humans constantly to grapple with both the prosaic and messianic in relation to each other, never allowing the human pursuit of ideal states to bring people to ignore the hard realities of politics and never allowing people's concern for the hard reality of politics to give them an excuse for ignoring considerations of justice, can be seen as the pedagogic dimension of federalism.

Federalism's emphasis on structure *and* process, on the necessity to organize governing constitutionally in a certain way and then to live up to the constitutional demands, provides both governors and governed in federal polities with a continuing seminar in governance in which they must constantly ask the questions: Is it possible? Is it right? Is it good? Such diverse devices as the opinions of the American federal Supreme Court and the Swiss referendum process represent continuing forums for discussing the philosophy and practice of government, replete with considerations of the possible, the right, and the good from the different perspectives present in each civil society at any given time. In short, by providing a continuing stream of constitutional questions that require public attention, federalism generates a continuing referendum on first principles. The advantages of this continuing seminar for civic education are not to be minimized, and federal arrangements may be sufficiently justified for this reason alone.

With regard to both faces of politics, federalism leads to a concern with the distribution of power. *The Federalist* puts the matter as follows:

> In a single republic, all the power surrendered by the people is submitted to the administration of a single government; and the usurpations are guarded against by a division of the

government into distinct and separate departments. In the compound republic of America, the power surrendered by the people is first divided between two distinct governments, and then the portion allotted to each is subdivided among distinct and separate departments. Hence a double security arises to the rights of the people. The different governments will control each other, at the same time each will be controlled by itself.[10]

Federalism tries to take people as they are—"warts and all," in Abraham Lincoln's felicitous phrase—assuming humanity to have the capacity for self-government but the weaknesses that make all human exercise of power potentially dangerous. So the first task of federalism is to harmonize human capacity with human weakness, to create institutions and processes that enable people to exercise their capacity for self-government to the maximum and even grow in that capacity. At the same time federalism attempts to prevent the abuse of power derived from inherent deficiencies in human nature and, wherever possible, direct the results of those deficiencies to useful ends.[11]

Although there are federal theories that begin with the assumption of the goodness or unlimited perfectibility of human nature, all successful federal systems have been rooted in the recognition of man's dual capacity for virtue and vice and have sought to respond accordingly. Their success as political systems is attributable in no small measure to that realistic sense of both the limits and possibilities of man as a political animal. Hence it is from their experience that a proper understanding of the ends of federalism must be derived. Even those who see in federalism a possibility for the reconstruction of all human relationships and their reconstitution on the basis of coordinative rather than hierarchical arrangements need to see as the first end of federalism the effort to grapple with the dynamic and mixed character of humanity.

Federalism and Pluralism

Federalism differs from pluralism because it bases its efforts to deal with the realities of human nature on a firm constitutional structure and does not leave so vital a task to chance, that is, to the possible existence of cultural or social phenomena which, within the right environment, manifest themselves politically as pluralism. The federalist argument is that pluralism in one form or another may indeed be a safeguard of liberty, but that it cannot be relied upon by itself unless properly institutionalized constitutionally. Some proponents of federalism argue that it is important primarily as a means to institutionalize pluralism and thus guarantee (insofar as it is possible to guarantee) the latter's continued existence; this role often goes unrecognized by pluralists in federal systems, who take pride in the pluralism to be found in their polities, but who assume that this pluralism continues to exist in and of itself.[12]

Pluralism is more likely to sustain itself in polities in which strongly rooted primordial groups continue to dominate political and social life. Unfortunately, where such groups exist they are likely to make political integration—federal or otherwise—more difficult, as in Yugoslavia. Modern pluralism is something else again. The United States of America is often considered to be the post-traditional pluralistic commonwealth par excellence, in the sense that plural ways of social, religious, and to some degree political and economic expression are accepted as part of the natural order.[13] American pluralism does not and never did follow a single model. Indeed, the variety of models of pluralism in the United States is, in certain respects, paradigmatic of modern pluralism in general and the relationship between pluralism and federalism. Five models of pluralism have emerged in the United States, each initially in a different state and each spreading throughout particular regions or sections of the country.

The United States as a fully modern polity from the first was founded on the basis of strictly territorial communities, in contrast to Europe, where modernism emerged from a society that was divided into corporations and estates which, while occupying and sharing the same territory, were each governed by their own institutions and leaders. This form of corporate pluralism was already declining in Europe when the first settlers came to British North America, giving way there to the territorial organization of civil society.[14] The Americans adopted territoriality as the only legitimate basis of political organization from the first, but they expressed that commitment in two different ways. The first, developed in New York and Pennsylvania, was based on neutrality of territory. Whichever groups came to settle in a particular territory would gain the rights of citizenship and exercise a share of political power according to their size and strength. If one group replaced another, then so be it.[15]

Pluralism in New York evolved almost by default, as the pluralism of the marketplace, whereas that of Pennsylvania was deliberately introduced by its founder, William Penn, as an extension of the Quaker religious doctrine that every individual is guided by his or her inner light. In both cases, whoever was willing to abide by the rules of the game could participate in the marketplace and be rewarded according to their success in it.

The second face of territorial democracy was that represented by Massachusetts and most of New England, whereby different groups were expected to settle in different territorial entities which they then could use to build polities that would express their separate visions and protect their separate group interests.

The Puritan founders of Massachusetts sought to build a homogeneous commonwealth based on the purity of their religious ideology and its common forms of expression. They had no objection to non-Puritans going to other parts of the wilderness and founding their own commonwealths, as long as they did not try to settle in Massachusetts. There could even be cooperation between commonwealths motivated by different visions as in the case of the New England Confederation, directed toward maintaining common security against the Indians and common rights against England. Territory became a basis for maintaining separation on the basis of mutual respect and cooperation rather than an arena for determining the relative power of different groups.[16] Although the first face became the most widespread in the United States, and indeed has been made normative by recent decisions of the United States Supreme Court if not by the federal and state constitutions, the second face has continued to exist on the American scene and has an ancient and honorable place in American society.

Pluralism of caste, separating whites and blacks and rooted initially in human slavery, was a third model introduced into colonial North America. Never considered fully legitimate in the United States, it represents the dark side of pluralism. Pluralism of caste received its first full expression in Virginia in the late seventeenth century, when the white population of that commonwealth transformed indentured servitude for blacks (as distinct from whites) into permanent bondage. This pattern was to spread throughout the South even as slavery ceased to exist in the North during and after the revolutionary war and indentured servitude for whites disappeared throughout the country.

As a result of the Civil War and the emancipation of the slaves, a hierarchical pluralism of caste was reinstituted by southern whites and remained the dominant pattern until the civil rights revolution of the 1960s. During that time, each racial caste developed a complete society of its own. Many of the most overt aspects of this caste division have since disappeared, but it remains a factor in southern society and beyond.

A fourth model is the pluralism of associations whose mother state was Ohio and which is associated in American popular culture with the Midwest—a region of small cities dominated by networks of associations, whether the various fraternal bodies or civic associations or even the two major political parties that became foci for multigenerational commitments. What counts most in this form of pluralism is not one's primordial group but the associations one joins. One's links with particular associations are not matters of the moment; one joins for life, as it were, and in many cases one expects one's children to follow into the same network. But they are associations nonetheless, reflecting personal choice in joining, and not inheritance. Intergenerational patterns of associationalism in particular communities or areas might lead to the emergence of what Ellsworth Huntington has termed a kith, a multigenerational group united by a common culture, but even if ties are intergenerational, the association determines the kith in the Midwest, whereas in the first models the kith determines the patterns of association.[17]

In our own times, a radical pluralism of individuals has emerged as a fifth model, clearly identified with the state of California, in which every individual is so singularly separate that he or she need not maintain permanent ties with any other individual or group. Not only are primordial ties such as ethnicity and associational ties such as church and political party no longer sacrosanct, but even marriage and family ties can be changed at one's convenience. This radical pluralism of individuals has spread rapidly throughout the United States since the late 1960s.[18]

Two points are significant here. On one hand, each form of pluralism emerged in relation to a political base that either stimulated it or gave it the requisite support and grounding. On the other, the existence of federalism allowed the development of a variety of forms of pluralism side by side within the same civil society. The political base for pluralism is particularly important in post-traditional societies.

Federalism and Liberty

The central interest of true federalism in all its species is liberty. All forms of federalism begin with the assumption that government in some form is necessary and that the development of appropriately effective government is a major human task. In this respect federalist theories are realistic. The other "given" of federalism is that humans are born free and that good government must be grounded in a framework of maximum human liberty. The task of constitution-makers is to develop a regime for each people which secures liberty even while recognizing and allowing for government in its coercive aspects.

In the last analysis, political federalism is designed to secure good government based on liberty or, put in other terms, to maintain effective government under conditions whereby the liberties of the partners to the federal bargain are maintained. It seeks to do so, in part, by restricting and dividing governing powers and, in part, by giving the partners to the federal compact (whether individuals, communities, or polities) a participatory role in the exercise of those powers. Yet it seeks to do so, not out of a desire to prevent governing, but to allow governance to the maximum extent required. The combination of ends—liberty, participation (or citizenship), and governance—and the relationship between them is one of the defining characteristics of federal systems.

To say that liberty stands at the center of federalist striving is to open the door to the question of what constitutes liberty in the federal context and how federalists deal with the problematics of liberty. Each of the five models of pluralism reflects its own conception of liberty. The first emphasizes the liberty to maintain group identities within a shared polity, with its corollary of the market model based upon shared rules of the game. The second emphasizes the liberty to build communities, each with its own way of life and the necessity to make distinctions as to who can build what and where. The difference between them is that one emphasizes the moral foundations of civil society and the other emphasizes civil society as a marketplace, pure and simple. The third emphasizes the liberty of one group at the expense of another and hence has been judged severely wanting when measured against federal ideals.

The fourth, like the first, emphasizes the liberty of the marketplace based on common subscription to the rules of the game but goes beyond it in emphasizing the liberty of the individual to choose his primary as well as his secondary associations. This liberty is limited only by the shared recognition that it is necessary to have binding, long-term, primary associations, however free one is to choose them. The fifth model rejects even that, seeking radical liberty for every individual, even to the point of raising questions with regard to the extent to which individuals are bound by shared rules of the game.

Pluralism is a necessary concomitant of democracy, American style. It may not be a concomitant of every democracy. Indeed, strong arguments have been made by various political philosophers and others that true democracy can function only under conditions of social homogeneity. It is a concomitant of federal democracy, almost by definition. The United States, as a nation of immigrants, has gone down one such path, which is fraught with its own problems as well as blessed with its own virtues. Every federal system is informed by its own pluralism, which it must confront and conciliate. It does so through some conception of liberty that relates to the form or forms of pluralism that inform it. Switzerland, for example, was founded on the principle of communal liberty; Yugoslavia on that of national liberty; and Canada on the often clashing principles of ethnocultural and individual liberty.

These questions lead us to what may be the decisive difference between various species of federalism. Take, for example, confederation and federation. Federations are communities of both polities and individuals and emphasize the liberties of both. The American federation has placed even greater emphasis on the liberty of individuals than on the liberties of its constituent polities, an emphasis that has grown more pronounced over the generations. Confederations, on the other hand, are primarily communities of polities, which place greater emphasis on the liberties of the constituent polities. It is the task of the constituent polities to protect individual liberty, more or less as each defines it, although the constituent polities of confederations of republics must conform to at least minimum standards of individual liberty to preserve the republican character of the whole.

In the case of the United States, Article III of the Articles of Confederation sets forth its ends:

> The said states hereby severally enter into a firm league of friendship with each other, for their common defense, the security of their liberties, and their mutual and general welfare, binding themselves to assist each other, against all force offered to, or attacks made upon, them, or any of them, on account of religion, sovereignty, trade, or any other pretense whatever.

Contrast it with the Preamble to the Constitution of 1787:

> We, the people of the United States, in order to form a more perfect union, establish justice, insure domestic tranquility,

provide for the common defense, promote the general welfare, and insure the blessings of liberty to ourselves and to
our posterity, do ordain and establish this Constitution for
the United States of America.

Following Madison, the distinction between the two regimes can be summarized as follows: the Constitution of
1787 provided a government that was partly national and
partly federal to replace the Articles of Confederation,
which established a regime that was partially federal and
partially a league. The first combination came to be known
as federation and the second came to be known as confederation. The tension built into the former is between the
national and the federal elements, whereas the tension built
into the latter is between the federal and the league elements. Since federal arrangements always involve one or
another set of built-in tensions, the character of the tension
of each particular arrangement is the major clue as to the
species of federalism involved.

Thus to understand a confederation it is necessary to understand, first and foremost, what constitutes the liberties
of its constituent polities and how those constituents see
confederation as protecting those liberties. American pluralism has strayed far from the concept of group liberties to
become almost exclusively individualistic in character. This
is not surprising, given the character of American society.
No doubt one of the reasons why it was possible to con-
vince a majority of Americans voting by state to abandon
confederation for federation was because, even in the revolutionary era, the states were not able to command a level of
identification stronger than that of individual self-interest
and the growing common perception that Americans were
Americans, first and foremost.

Had the states been perceived by a majority of their citizens to be primary organic communities as John C. Cal-

houn was later to argue, there is little doubt that the Constitution of 1787 would have been rejected on behalf of state liberties. As it was, the challenge to that document revolved around the protection of individual liberty—the need for a bill of rights. Not that the principle of state liberties was totally rejected—the political liberties of the states were deemed to be very important, as witness the Tenth Amendment—but they were not primary in the American scheme of things.

Because of this special character of American pluralism, Americans have a very difficult time understanding the issues of group rights. For that reason, federation was easy for them. But for much of the world, group rights—variously defined as national, local, or ethnic liberties—are of the essence. For them confederation may be the most viable way to attain the combination of liberty, good government, and peace which federalism promises.

Thus liberty has a variety of meanings within the federal context. It may reflect the desire to maximize individual liberty (as in the United States and the Latin American federal systems); it may reflect the desire to maintain the liberties of the constituting units in which the individual's place in the community is what counts (as in Switzerland and French Canada); and it may reflect the desire to establish what was termed by John Winthrop of Massachusetts "federal liberty," namely the liberty of the partners to act in accordance with the moral principles embodied in God's covenant with humanity (as in biblical Israel and colonial New England). In whatever form, liberty is the key, and it is assumed that other human values are best maintained through the maintenance of liberties.

The concept of federal liberty goes beyond Winthrop's narrow definition and is vital for understanding the proper relationship between federalism and liberty. It can be juxtaposed to the idea of natural liberty, its principal rival in the modern epoch. John Adams told the story of an encounter he had with a horse jockey in Boston at the outbreak of the Revolution. The jockey indicated to Adams how grateful he was that the Patriots had liberated them all so that every man could do as he pleased. Adam's response was to express shock at this misinterpretation of the meaning of political liberty, rejecting the jockey's equation of liberty with anarchy. He sought a more secularized version of the federal liberty of his Puritan ancestors—that is, liberty limited by political covenant or compact. That liberty is both morally grounded and mutually agreed upon, hence it is the liberty to do what is right from a moral sense and according to the rules of the game in a consensual one.[19]

Adams was to give his views operational embodiment in the Constitution of Massachusetts, which he wrote and which was ratified by the people of that commonwealth in 1780 to remain its fundamental law to this day:

> The end of the institution, maintenance and administration of government, is to secure the existence of the body-politic, to protect it, and to furnish the individuals who compose it, with the power of enjoying in safety and tranquility their natural rights, and the blessings of life: And whenever these great objectives are not obtained, the people have a right to alter the government, and to take measures necessary for their safety, prosperity and happiness.—The Body-Politic is formed by a voluntary association of individuals: It is a social compact, by which the whole people covenants with each Citizen, and each Citizen with the whole people, that all shall be governed by certain Laws for the Common good. It is the duty of the people, therefore, in framing a Constitution of Government, to provide for an equitable mode of making laws as well as for an impartial interpretation, and a faithful execution of them; that every man may, at all times, find his security in them. WE, therefore, the people of Massachusetts, acknowledging, with grateful

hearts, the goodness of the Great Legislator of the Universe, in affording us, in the course of his Providence, an opportunity, deliberately and peaceably, without fraud, violence or surprize, of entering into an Original, explicit, and Solemn Compact with each other; and of forming a New Constitution of Civil Government, for Ourselves and Posterity; and devoutly imploring His direction in so interesting a Design, DO agree upon, ordain and establish, the following *Declaration of Rights, and Frame of Government,* as the CONSTITUTION OF THE COMMONWEALTH OF MASSACHUSETTS.

Natural liberty is unrestricted, the freedom of the state of nature, whether understood in Hobbesian or Lockean terms. In the end, it is the liberty that leads to anarchy, or the war of all against all. According to federal principles, proper liberty is federal liberty, that is, the liberty to act according to the terms of the covenant (*foedus*) that calls the body politic into existence.

Every proper polity is established by a pact among its constituents which is covenantal insofar as it rests upon a shared moral sensibility and understanding and legitimate insofar as it embodies the fundamental principles of human liberty and equality. Behavior that does not fit within those terms is, in effect, a violation of the covenant and a manifestation of anarchy. Hence it can be stopped and its perpetrator punished by the appropriate institutions or government.

In sum, federal liberty is liberty established by agreement. The content of any particular agreement may and will vary. Thus John Winthrop could understand true liberty as that flowing from the covenant in which God dictated the terms of the agreement and which man pledged to accept. On the other hand, James Wilson of Pennsylvania, one of the authors of the Constitution of 1787, could understand federal liberty as a strictly secular expression of the compact establishing civil society. Today, when the Supreme Court of the United States holds the state and federal governments to standards of behavior based on the U.S. Constitution even when the implementation of those standards places heavy restrictions on individual behavior, in effect it does so on the grounds that the Constitution is a compact entered into by the people of the United States which, inter alia, delineates what constitutes federal liberty within the American system.

Federal liberty has had to contend with natural liberty throughout history. Natural liberty celebrates the "natural man," who is not bound by the conventions of civilization but is able to pursue true feedom in nature.[20] Much of the myth of the American West is associated with natural liberty and natural men, implicitly rejecting federal liberty, even though the reality of westering, whether in wagon trains or mining camps—not to speak of temperance colonies or settlements of sober farm folk—rested upon the introduction of federal liberty into the wilderness.[21]

This struggle between federal and natural liberty can be traced back to the earliest days of the modern experience, in the confrontations between the Puritan vision and the Rousseauian ideal of the noble savage. In an earlier generation of this century, natural liberty was expressed as "doin' what comes naturally" and today as "letting it all hang out." Natural men in the western wilderness were limited by raw nature, which they confronted daily and thoroughly respected. Hence they were no more unlimited in their freedom than those bound by covenant. When people in civilization seek to behave as natural men, however, it is another matter entirely. Even they are finally restrained by nature as reflected in the increased incidence of death among young celebrities and others from drug- or alcohol-induced causes.

Federalism, Pluralism, and Liberty

Here we come to the intersection between federalism, pluralism, and liberty. Democratic polities must both maintain and contain pluralism if democracy is to survive. Many elements in politics are necessary or useful in fostering a polity conducive to accomplishing both tasks, including the proper political structure and processes, embedded in a proper constitutional framework, and rooted in a proper political culture, while encouraged by appropriate social and economic conditions. An increasing number of people have found federalism, although they have not always recognized it as such, to be an extraordinarily important element in both the maintenance and the containment of pluralism.

In a classic but perhaps too little-known exchange, Martin Diamond made this point to Morton Grodzins.[22] Both were at the height of their work on the origins and operations of the American federal system. Grodzins, in the spirit of contemporary political science, argued that it was the American party system which preserved the pluralistic dimensions of the American polity. Decentralized parties, in his words, allowed the continuation of decentralized government, despite twentieth-century pressures toward centralization. Diamond responded that the decentralized parties existed in no small measure because of the constitutional structure of the federal system, which made the states the building blocks of the party system and hence prevented the creation of strong, centralized, disciplined national political parties that would have furthered centralization at the expense of territorial-based pluralism and perhaps other kinds of pluralism as well.

The events of the 1960s and 1970s have demonstrated that Diamond's argument was the stronger. Even as the two men were writing, in the late 1950s, the tendency to build

strong, centralized national parties in the United States was
increasing. It surfaced in both parties in the 1960s and succeeded to a degree, but only to the extent that the U.S.
Supreme Court interpreted the federal Constitution in such
a way as to enable the national party organizations to impose controls on the state parties by superseding state laws
on the subject.

In other words, pluralism is not enough because sentiments for pluralism are not enough. Only constitutional
barriers will overcome the natural propensities of ambitious
men to consolidate power. Even they may not be enough,
but at least they give pluralism a fighting chance.

The sources of the pluralist thinking which Grodzins partially reflected can be traced to Harold Laski, whose famous
1930s argument that pluralism had come to replace federalism as a means of maintaining liberty was widely quoted for
at least a generation.[23] Grodzins, recognizing the importance of federalism as a structure, attacked Laski for ignoring these selfsame human realities.[24] Laski, of course, was
not only a socialist but a British subject, and his thinking
reflected English views that emerged from a setting in
which powerful and deeply rooted traditions serve to en-
hance liberty and certain forms of pluralism.

Perhaps in a country such as England tradition is sufficient
—although it certainly has not been sufficient to maintain
territorial pluralism in the form of strong local government.
Once Parliament decided to exercise what, up to the mid-
nineteenth century, had been essentially theoretical powers
of unlimited sovereignty to transfer powers from the local
authorities to the center, there was nothing that could be
done about it except for the supporters of local control to
try to capture Parliament and reverse the tide, an act which
almost by definition is not likely to happen given Britain's
strong, centralized, disciplined party system. Only a constitutional revolution animated by an ideological vision

strong enough to go against the natural human instincts to hold onto power is likely to bring Parliament to devolve it voluntarily. That has certainly not happened yet; witness the future of all the devolution efforts of the past decade. Indeed devolution seems a dead issue in the 1980s. Laski himself seems to have had second thoughts in light of his disappointment with Britain's Labour government after it came to power in 1945.

For countries without the British tradition, formal constitutional guarantees are vital to the preservation of pluralism. Indeed, they are necessary but are not sufficient. Additional institutional barriers are required in the form of checks and balances and, for many, federal arrangements.

For the United States it can fairly be said that federalism has been of the utmost importance in the maintenance of pluralism. Federalism has worked in both directions at various times, that is, in the ability of the states to resist federal encroachments and in the ability of the federal government to assault state-fostered or sanctioned encroachments on legitimate pluralism. What is important about federal arrangements is not the simple matter of power devolved but the more complex matter of power shared, allowing different avenues of recourse for injured parties or for those who wish to protect themselves against injury. This is what Grodzins referred to as the multiple crack, in the double sense of the opportunity to take many blows or cracks at the system and the existence of many fissures or cracks through which to hammer home those blows.[25] This notion considers the dual possibility of state protection and federal intervention that has made federalism in the United States a major bulwark of pluralism.

Every form of federalism can be used to gain those ends. Is pluralism not advanced when Puerto Rico enters into a federal arrangement with the United States as a federacy (commonwealth is the accepted American term), allowing it more internal autonomy to preserve its own language and culture than the fifty constituent states? Is liberty not advanced because Puerto Rico, a part of the United States, is spared the black plagues of revolution, dictatorship, and authoritarian government which are characteristic of most independent Latin American states forced to maintain standing armies, ostensibly for their security?

Students of the European Community will certainly attest that, as the member states have developed the EC into a confederation with a high constitutional court responsible for the maintenance of the common market and common standards of human rights, both pluralism and liberty have been advanced. At the other end of the scale, little Andorra has preserved its liberty for more than seven hundred years even though it is a tiny speck between two great and imperialistic powers, France and Spain, which for most of that period pursued policies designed to eliminate both liberty and pluralism within their own territories. Their joint rule of the little state through a federal arrangement known as condominium gave Andorra the space it needed to survive and be free while all the states around it that were independent when Andorra was founded were absorbed by one or the other of the two powers and lost their liberties and much of their ability to maintain anything resembling pluralism.

Here, too, the ability of federal systems to encourage experimentation without overcommitment to the results of the experiment is relevant. Although California-style pluralism has had a certain nationwide influence in the United States, its impact is much diminished in states that are influential as civil societies in other directions. In politics, for example, one need only look at the contrast between the mass-based, amateur-dominated politics of California and the amateur-dominated politics of Minnesota to note the differences in political culture and style between the two and the limits of California's influence as long as Minnesota maintains its own political system and party politics. If this is less true in other spheres of human activity in the United States, it is because American federalism has been weakened and no longer provides sufficient barriers.

The argument here rests on the assumption that various kinds of pluralism are appropriate in a large, multifaceted polity. If there is any kind that is not acceptable, it is one that violates the spirit of federal liberty, that is, seeks to elevate "doin' what comes naturally" at the expense of the bonds of covenant. Implicit here is the argument that without the bonds of covenant there can be no decent civil society. Natural man can function only in the wilderness, where his contact with others is limited, and, moreover, where nature provides sufficient checks to control his behavior.

This leads to the second part of the argument, that liberty is served by having different varieties of pluralism, provided that the extended republic is so structured as to allow them to find expression and to reach different syntheses in different parts of the polity. Federalism is an excellent way to make that possible. Hence for those who believe that pluralism is a significant dimension of liberty, the maintenance of a proper federal system should be high on their agenda.

It should be apparent by this point that federal theory assumes that dialectical relationships—diadic, triadic, or even quadrilateral—are of the essence in human relationships and that it offers an alternative to monism in the human sphere. Government itself is one element in a network of dialectical relationships. For federalists, a key dialectical relationship is that between government and liberty. In this respect, federalists differ from anarchists, who emphasize liberty as the central principle to the exclusion of government as a legitimate phenomenon. Similarly, federalists are necessarily opposed to hierarchs and authoritarians, who see government as the central principle and reject or strongly limit claims of liberty.

Modern federalists also differ from other democrats in that, although they see substantial equality as a necessary precondition for the establishment and maintenance of liberty, they also see liberty as taking precedence over the striving for absolute equality. Hence they are willing to sacrifice a certain amount of equality for the sake of liberty as distinct from those who would sacrifice liberty on behalf of equality. Most federalists would argue that, operationally, the best way to attain meaningful equality is through the maintenance of liberty, even though that means the rejection of the attainment of absolute equality as a goal. They argue that absolute equality (in itself a problematic concept) is not attainable in any case (it is contrary to human nature in certain crucial ways) and that attempts to sacrifice liberty for equality tend to lead to the loss of both. Federalism, by its nature, is based on the recognition of the reality and legitimacy of distinctions and the desirability of maintaining legitimate distinctions, something that goes against the grain of modern conceptions of absolute equality.

Four Levels of Ends

Federalism has been applied to achieve political ends on four different levels. They are, in ascending order, (1) to institute workable political arrangements, (2) to create a workable polity, (3) to establish a just polity, and (4) to achieve a just moral order. In part, the variety of federal forms can be correlated with these four ends.

The most modest of these goals is the use of federalism to institute workable political arrangements. By and large, confederations and leagues in their federal dimension are designed for these limited ends. In such cases, existing polities, complete in and of themselves, find the necessity to

create lasting but limited links with other polities for purposes of defense or the prevention of military aggression, to
deal with a limited range of common governmental problems, or to create a common market, and they do so
through arrangements using federal principles. The leagues
of ancient Greece and medieval Italy, the German confederations, and the European Common Market exemplify
this use of federal principles.

The difficulties—often fatal—of confederation flow from
a basic tension between the comprehensive ends of the constituting polities and the limited ends of the confederation
itself. Can this confederal tension be sustained in a polity on
a long-term basis? Under what conditions? This is a real
issue in the European Community today. Following the
definitions and distinctions presented here, the EC is more
likely to succeed because it does have limited ends. The
Western European states that constituted it deliberately rejected the larger ends of federation and sought the more
limited linkage of confederation, then described as
"functionalism." Hence the EC has the appearance of a
league to some but in fact has been able to develop real
powers in specific spheres that far transcend those of a
league. In doing so, it has strengthened its own framework,
its federal dimension, not as a station on the way to a United
States of Europe as anticipated by the evolutionists, but in a
clearly confederal way.[26]

The creation of a workable polity represents the application of federal principles a step beyond simply seeking
workable arrangements. What is characteristic of this end is
that units that may or may not be preexisting polities not
only seek better political arrangements to link them with
one another, but seek to create a new polity, usually an
overarching one, but one that is no less a polity than any of
its constituent elements and may be more of one. Modern
federations generally fall into this category. It has already

been suggested that the adoption of the federal Constitution in the United States was such an attempt.[27]

With respect to the United States, for example, the principal difference between the Constitution of 1787 and the Articles of Confederation was one of means rather than ends. In this respect, the Preamble to the 1787 Constitution specified that what is proposed is the establishment of "a more perfect union," not a new one. What was changed were the means for effectuating the union, which required the expansion of the powers granted to the federal government even to attain already agreed-upon ends. The nineteenth- and twentieth-century federations that followed in the footsteps of the United States, and were influenced by that first modern federation, reflect the same intent.

Both of the foregoing goals reflect the employment of federalism to achieve limited ends. The remaining two involve the use of federalism to achieve more comprehensive ones. The terminology should suggest the difference between the goal of creating a workable polity and that of creating a just one. Obviously the two are not mutually exclusive, especially in the light of the understanding of politics as having two faces, as suggested above. Nevertheless, there is a big step between the effort to achieve a polity whose major purpose is to handle certain tasks in an efficient manner and one whose central concern is the pursuit of higher levels of justice per se.[28] It is possible to argue that certain of the proponents of federalism in the United States also saw the use of federal principles as a means to create a just policy and not simply a workable one.[29] The most pronounced manifestation of this goal, however, is probably to be found in the Latin American federalist movements, which sought to introduce federal arrangements into polities without preexisting traditions of federalism on the grounds that political justice demanded it.[30]

Even the search for a just polity, however, is limited in

comparison to the final goal for which federalism is sometimes suggested, namely the search for a just moral order. In
effect, the search for a just polity suggests that federalism
offers the way to achieve justice in all its forms. French
federal theorists tend to emphasize this last goal. The Paris
Commune was an example, albeit a fleeting one, of the
effort to implement it.[31] The kibbutz movement in Israel is
a more long-lived attempt.[32] Related to this end, federalism
is not just a set of arrangements but a way of life that informs the entire civil society and establishes the basic
character of human relations within it.

That federalism can be directed toward any of these ends
in useful ways is another reflection of its flexibility. The
choice as to how federal principles and arrangements are
best used becomes wide-ranging and is not predetermined
by the federal idea itself, but rather remains in the hands of
individuals and groups to choose.

Federalism, Republicanism, and Democracy

Federalism by its very nature must be republican in the
original sense of *res publica*—a public thing; a federal polity
must belong to its public and not be the private possession
of any person or segment of that public, and its governance
therefore requires public participation. That, indeed, is a
primary source of the difference between federalism and
feudalism, another form of government based on contractual arrangements. Feudalism essentially involves a series of contracts among private fiefdoms, in which
authority is arranged hierarchically and power is usually
organized oligarchically. True federal arrangements must
invariably rest upon a popular base. The American federal
Constitution recognizes this in providing that the federal
government must guarantee republican forms of govern-

ment to the states. Its framers rested their case on their understanding of history, in which attempts to federate republican and nonrepublican polities invariably failed, usually to the detriment of the republican polities involved in the effort.

The American federal system was the first modern federal polity clearly to link federalism and popular government, or democracy, in the words of *The Federalist,* to seek to provide "republican remedies for republican diseases." It set the tone for the federal polities that came after. Since then, no federal polity has been established in which the case for federalism has not been argued on democratic grounds.

Not only do all modern federal systems claim to be democratic and seek democratic legitimacy, but there is likely to be general agreement among true democrats that the great majority of those polities held up as models of democracy (France is the great and important exception) are either federal in form or extensively use federal principles. Moreover, the minimal significance of formal federal structures in undemocratic political systems offers negative testimony in the same direction. This, in all honesty, must be recognized as a possible limitation on the uses of federalism for purposes of political integration where there is an insufficient republican basis among the peoples and polities involved. Like all tools, federalism as a tool of political integration can be used only in appropriate situations.

It is important to reiterate that one of the characteristics of federalism that flows from its popular base is the reduction of the question of political sovereignty to an incidental one. Sovereignty in federal republics is invariably vested in the people, who delegate powers to their respective governments or combine to exercise those powers directly as the government (as in the case of the traditional Swiss cantons). Powers can be divided and delegated by the sovereign people as they see fit, but sovereignty remains their inalienable possession. Hence in the discussion of federal governments, the question of sovereignty does not figure—only the question of powers does. No government (or, by extension, office) can claim to be sovereign and hence have unlimited, residual, or final powers, nor is there any theoretical limit to the number of governments that can receive delegated powers, although some practical limitations may arise. This characteristic also adds to the flexibility of federalism, as well as to the possibility of combining different federal arrangements to serve the same people.

Thus the federal principle represents an alternative to (and a radical attack upon) the modern idea of sovereignty. The latter idea became so much a part of the scheme of things than even discussions of federalism came to be couched in terms of sovereignty, particularly in the nineteenth century—so much so that our very understanding of the federal idea was distorted. In the postmodern era, however, the sovereignty that modern states exercised has become obsolete. No state can claim to be the sole master of its own affairs; rather, all are more or less dependent upon others. As a result, the original federal conception of power sharing is becoming even more relevant than before.

The Worldwide Federalist Revolution

The beginning of modern federalism can be found in the steps taken by the Dutch and Swiss on the threshold of the modern era to create larger political entities without consolidating their traditional polities and in the parallel work of political theorists such as Johannes Althusius and Hugo Grotius involved in or familiar with those efforts. It achieved full form toward the end of the eighteenth century with the establishment of the American federal system and went through a period of radical expansion in the nineteenth and twentieth centuries.[33]

The emergence of the federalist revolution rests on three basic phenomena of modern political life. First is the emergence of the modern nation-state encompassing, of necessity, relatively large territories and populations to maintain itself under modern conditions in the world of power politics. In turn, problems of the internal distribution of power within those newly enlarged polities were generated.[34] Second, modernism brought with it the breakdown of the premodern community with its "organic" lines of authority based on essentially fixed social relationships. With it came the concomitant need for the creation of new forms of local attachment and self-government. Finally, modernism led to the breakdown of the old aristocratic principles in favor of a new commitment to equality, with its concomitant demand for the creation of a more democratic social and political order.[35]

The federalist revolution emerged in response to all three of these phenomena and the problems they raise, suggesting itself as an antidote to them that is in keeping with the modern temper. Federalism has been used to enable nation-states to concentrate power and authority in large, energetic general governments, while at the same time diffusing the exercise of powers so as to give most, if not all, segments of civil society a constitutionally guaranteed share in their governance. Federal ideas have made possible the development of new forms of community, with new instruments for local self-government, by making it possible to build new societies through contractual relationships rather than relying on kinship or other traditional ties. Finally, the federalist revolution has been directed toward serving the cause of equality by creating better instrumentalities for citizen involvement in public affairs through the development of governmental arenas of differing size and scope, ranging from the immediately local to the most general. These three important trends are especially significant from the perspective of political integration. The necessity for even larger units of government, of production, and of association to achieve certain common goals is, for the present, a fact of life. So is the reassertion of the human desire for the maintenance of small-scale units for their humanistic value.

To take a simple example, to be a superpower today, a nation must have two hundred million people or more. Perhaps a very talented and aggressive nation of one hundred million could come close to the fringes of superpowerdom, but even that number probably is not sufficient. At the same time, it is clear that a nation of two hundred million people will contain a great deal of diversity, hence it will be under tremendous pressures for the development of units on a smaller scale to accommodate that diversity and to link its citizens to the body politic on an intimate basis, so that they can feel that they have some relationship to it or some control over their own particular individual or communal destinies.

This probably is as true in Communist China as it is in the United States. That China has had to adopt federal arrangements, at least in theory, to the extent of providing for autonomous regions and tribes, plus the recent struggles for power in that country which seem to have unfolded province by province, serve as evidence on behalf of this thesis. Stated as a hypothesis, in organizational terms every time an entity is made larger, a parallel need is generated for some aspect of it to be made smaller. And so the necessity to combine larger and smaller leads directly to the use of federal arrangements—we go back to the Jimmy Durante definition of federalism—the feeling that one wants to (or has to) go and at the same time that one wants to stay, to have one's cake and eat it, too.

On the other hand, the likelihood is growing greater that even small independent states in the world of the future are going to have to combine, if only for certain economic purposes. Once again, federal arrangements offer a way to balance larger and smaller and will be used even more as time goes on. The European Community and the Association of Southeast Asian Nations represent two different regional aggregations of medium-sized and small states that use federal principles to reach the two hundred million plus mark for limited common purposes. The first is already a confederation and the second a league in the classic sense.

The growing necessity for accommodating ethnic, linguistic, religious, and ideological heterogeneity leads to another set of reasons for the spread of federalism. As the world becomes more interdependent, these differences have not disappeared—rather, contrary to earlier predictions, they have intensified. If this is true in Europe, where all of history and high culture for centuries has pointed people in the other direction, where for three or four hundred years and more there has been conscious and deliberate suppression of such differences using both the carrot and the stick, what are we to expect in Asia and Africa, where such phenomena are so much closer to the surface?

In the early 1920s, a conference of stateless ethnic minorities (then called nationalities) was held in Brussels. Who remembers that conference? It was a peripheral event in post–World War I Europe. Even a few years ago, who would have forecast a Europe in which Bretons and Jurassiens, not to speak of Basques and Catalans, were actively seeking an ethnic place in the sun? Today as the integration of Western European states into a politico-economic community progresses, a "Europe of ethnics" is a real possibility. The development of international regionalism, involving northwestern Switzerland, Alsace in France, and southwestern Germany, has been advanced in the past decade by the common recognition on the part of the people on various sides of the international borders that they are all Allemanic—an ethnic group seemingly long forgotten.

Federalism in the Communist world, in particular, seeks to respond to this problem.

A third element affecting the spread of federalism is that it is part of a secular trend toward the stabilization of states. For the immediate future, the "sovereign states" of this world are striving to fix virtually all the state boundaries that exist as permanent, either to protect themselves or to protect the world order, such as it is. Consequently, if there are going to be changes in the world political order in the future, they will have to come through linking or dividing existing states in such a way that at least the formal integrity of each is maintained in some way. This situation, too, lends itself to federal solutions to deal with those problems in areas that require changes in the present political framework, either through the aggregation of existing states or their division to enable groups within them to obtain greater self-expression. As a result, the federalist revolution has come out of the closet and will become a matter of continuing and growing concern.

In light of the foregoing, it should not be surprising that the use of federal principles and processes has become so widespread. Even polities such as the Soviet Union, which are ultimately committed to a totalitarian centralization of power, or those such as Brazil, which are committed to a reliance upon personal leadership as repository of ruling power, have felt it necessary to affirm and reaffirm the federal basis of their constitutions and civil societies. Even polities such as France that are culturally far from being predisposed toward federalism have had to enter into federal relationships (through the European Community) to meet the demands the contemporary world places upon them. The federalist revolution, then, speaks directly to the problems and aspirations of modern popular government. That is why it is honored even in the breach as well as where federalism is meaningfully implemented.

In the past few years, we have entered the second generation of a postmodern era whose future form or shape is not precisely clear to any of us. It does seem certain, however, that the new era will be based upon some extension of the principles of modernism, particularly the principles of equality and liberty as manifested in the well-nigh universal commitment to the ideal of popular government—however that ideal is understood. The virtual completion of the task of modernization in certain Western countries has given us a glimpse of the direction we may be heading. In those countries there has been distilled out of the three central political phenomena of the modern era a dual political interest, first in creating more viable units of government (however understood) to undertake vast new responsibilities and, second, in enhancing citizen participation in government to foster democracy (however understood). The federalist revolution is precisely addressed to these twin interests, which is why experimentation with federal arrangements is on the increase in a variety of new settings and ways.

4

Federal Ideas and Forms

The History of Federalism and the Federal Idea

In its original form, the federal idea was theopolitical, defining the relationship between God and man as one in which both were linked by covenant in a partnership designed to make them jointly responsible for the world's welfare. First formulated in the covenant theory of the Hebrew Bible as the basis for God's relationship with Israel, this conception of federalism was revived by the Bible-centered "federal theologians" of the sixteenth- and seventeenth-century Protestant Reformation, who coined the term "federal"—derived from the Latin *foedus* (covenant)—to describe the system of holy and enduring covenants between God and humanity which lay at the foundation of their world-view. This covenant was as much a liberating device as a means of binding people to God's commandments. By restricting His otherwise omnipotent powers under the terms of the covenant, God granted humans a significant measure of freedom (from whence the Puritans developed the concept of "federal liberty").[1]

The federal idea was secularized in the late seventeenth and eighteenth centuries. The development of the compact theories of Thomas Hobbes, John Locke, and others marked the first step in that direction.[2] But it remained for Montesquieu and Madison to transform the federal idea into a fully secular political principle and technique.[3]

In the nineteenth century, still in keeping with its theological roots, federalism was developed as a principle of social organization by various French and German social theorists who wished to find a proper basis upon which to build human relations in the just commonwealth of the future.[4] Related closely to the various theories of social contract, federalism in this sense was characterized by the belief that the good society must be built on the basis of coordinative rather than subordinative relationships, emphasizing partnership among parties with equal claims to legitimacy seeking to cultivate their diverse integrities within a common social order. One of the most recent exponents of the federal principle as a basis of proper social organization was Martin Buber.

Federal institutions have developed in response to two different situations. On one hand, federalism has been used as a means to unite a people already linked by bonds of perceived nationality or common law by constitutionally distributing political power among a general government and constituent units so as to secure greater local liberty or national unity. In such cases, the polities that constitute the federal system are unalterably parts of the national whole, and federalism invariably leads to the development of a strong national government operating in direct contact with the people it serves just as the constituent governments do. The United States is a good example of this form.

On the other hand, federalism has been used as a means to unify separate peoples for important but limited purposes without disrupting their primary ties to the individual polities that constitute the basic units of federation. In such cases, the federal government is limited in its scope and powers, functioning through the constituent governments, which retain their plenary autonomy and, to a substantial degree, is dependent upon them. Yugoslavia exemplifies this form.

Ancient Expressions of Federalism

Both uses of federalism evolved from early federal experiments (Table 4.1) and, contrary to the views of some, both are of equal antiquity. In both, however, the early experiments were flawed for lack of a sufficiently advanced political technology to invest the institutions appropriate to the task.

The principles of strong national federalism were first applied by the ancient Israelites beginning in the thirteenth century B.C.E. to maintain their national unity by linking their several tribes under a single national constitution and confederal political institutions. The record of and rationale for their effort is presented in the Bible, the first great classic of humanity and the first to deal with federal models, particularly in the Pentateuch, Joshua, Judges, Samuel, and Ezekiel.[5] Although the biblical discussion is couched in historical and religious rather than theoretical terms, it does lay the foundations for the federal idea in its transformation of covenant from its origins as an ancient West Asian vassal treaty into a morally grounded pact among partners who are fundamentally equal, at least in their responsibility for common tasks.[6]

The biblical covenant was not simply designed to create a dependent entity linked and owing fealty to the imperial ruler but a partnership between the parties involved. Of course, the relationship between God and the human covenanting parties was not one of equals, but it was one of equal partnership in a common task (the reformation of the world) in which both parties preserved their respective integrities even while committing themselves to a relationship of mutual responsibility. According to the biblical account, God graciously limits Himself through His covenants so that humans may become His free partners. This

Table 4.1. *Exemplary Premodern Federal and Protofederal Systems*

Polity	Duration	Location	Form
Israelite Federation	13th century–722 B.C.E.	Israel	Federation of tribes
Achean League	First: 6th century–338 B.C.E. Second: 281–146 B.C.E.	Greece	Confederation of cities
Boeotian League	4th century B.C.E.	Greece	Confederation of cities
Aetolian League	4th century–189 B.C.E.	Greece	Confederation of cities
Decapolis	ca. 106 B.C.E.–C.E. 117	Roman Palestine	Confederation of cities
Holy Roman Empire	C.E. 800–1806	Central Europe	Imperial league
Lombard League	C.E. 1167–1250	Italy	League of cities
Hanseatic League	C.E. 1158–1669	Germany	League of cities
Swiss Confederation	C.E. 1291–1848	Switzerland	Confederation of republics
Aragonese-Catalan Empire	1200–1350	Spain	Dual monarchy
Castile Aragon and Navarre	C.E. 1469–1134	Spain	Dual monarchy
United Provinces	C.E. 1567–1798	Netherlands	Federation of provinces
Imperial Spain	1479–1716	Spain and Europe	Multiple monarchy
Iroquois Confederacy	ca. C.E. 1600–1760	North America	Confederation of tribes
Creek Confederacy	formal ties established in 18th century C.E.	North America	Confederation of tribes

audacious idea meant that subsidiary covenants linking human agencies or entities would perforce be covenants between equals in partnership. Hence federal partnership is not like that created in private law in which the partners have very limited obligations to one another but is a public law partnership that creates community and thereby involves a more extensive set of mutual obligations.

When carefully read, the Bible also gives us close insight into the operations of the Israelite tribal federation, describing its constitution, political institutions, and some of its central political problems, all within the framework of covenant theory. The Israelite federation survived for nearly six hundred years, through several changes of regime, before being destroyed by external conquest. During that time, constitutional changes in the Israelite polity were introduced through covenanting, and even after the introduction of the monarchy, the federal element was maintained until most of the tribal structures were destroyed by external forces. Its history was to have a profound influence on the political principles of later generations. The various founding covenants of the peoples, churches, or communities known to us as federal usually make clear reference to their biblical origins. Hence we can talk about the biblical source of the federal idea in much the same way that we talk about Greco-Roman sources of natural law.

Finally, the biblical grand design for humankind is federal in three ways. First, it is based on a network of covenants beginning with those between God and man, which weave the web of human, especially political, relationships in a federal way—that is, through compact, association, and consent. In the sixteenth century, this world-view was recreated by the Reformed wing of Protestantism as the federal theology from which Johannes Althusius, the Huguenots, the Scottish Covenanters, and the English and American Puritans developed political theories and principles of constitutional design.

Second, as indicated above, the classic biblical common-wealth was a fully articulated federation of tribes instituted and reaffirmed by covenant to function under a common constitution and laws; the biblical vision of the restored commonwealth in the messianic era envisages the recon-stitution of the tribal federation. The American Puritans and many Americans of the revolutionary era, among oth-ers, were inspired by the biblical polity to seek federal ar-rangements for their polities.

Third, the biblical vision for the "end of days"—the mes-sianic era—not only sees a restoration of Israel's tribal sys-tem but what is, for all intents and purposes, a world confederation or league of nations, each preserving its own integrity while accepting a common divine covenant and constitutional order. This order will establish appropriate covenantal relationships for the entire world. It is the antith-esis of the ecumenical world-state, although it seeks many of the same positive goals. Many important modern grand designs for world order, including those of Immanuel Kant, Martin Buber, and Woodrow Wilson, have drawn on that vision.[7]

The Israelite example represented federalism in its most complete form: a people founded by covenant and a polity organized on federal principles. Although federal arrange-ments often are used to link peoples that do not have a covenantal base and, conversely, some peoples founded by covenant or compact do not establish federal systems of government, federal systems are strongest when both are combined. That has continued to be the case throughout history.

Several centuries after the demise of the Israelite tribal federation, the Greek cities experimented with federal-style institutions as means for promoting intercity harmony and cooperation, primarily for defensive purposes, through as-sociations like the Achean and Aetolian Leagues that were

the forerunners of what are today defined as confederations.[8] Polybius and Strabo discuss the leagues they
knew, the former in his *History* and the latter in his *Geography*. It is not unfair to conclude that the Greeks were the
originators of confederation just as the Israelites were the
originators of federation.

The Greeks left some descriptions of specific leagues but
no theoretical discussions of the league as a political system.
Except for Aristotle's implied criticisms in the *Politics,* the
great Greek political theorists ignored federalism as a political principle because the very idea contradicted their conception of the small, unified, organic polis as the only basis
upon which to build the good society. In some cases, however, the polis apparently was a union of tribes or extended
families.[9]

Much earlier than both, beginning with the third millen-
nium before the common era, several West Asian empires
expanded by combining conquest with vassal treaties
forced upon the rulers of the conquered polities which guaranteed the latter a substantial measure of internal autonomy.
(The ancient Israelites adapted the device used by those
empires, the covenant, and transformed it as an instrument
for linking equals as well as unequals.) This system of decentralized imperialism, which emphasized religiocultural
home rule, was adopted by several of the later great empires, notably the Persian and Roman, which structured
their political systems around similar principles, using similar devices. Since political life was virtually inseparable
from the religious and cultural aspects of society in the
ancient world, imperial recognition of local constitutions
offered a measure of contractual devolution of political
power but, as in more recent examples of this form of imperialism, such home rule was not a matter of local right but
represented a conditional grant subject to revocation by unilateral decision of the imperial rulers. Hence, although they

used what in a sense are federal principles, they violated the essence of the federal idea in other ways. Modern imperial systems used many of the same mechanisms through such devices as protectorates, home rule, limited responsible government, and the like.

There are some cases, such as the early Roman Empire, the British Empire, and contemporary France, where the imperial power is itself republican, and home rule is constitutionalized and extended into the political realm. These cases usually involve protectorate or associated state arrangements (*foederae* in Latin) either in the early or later stages of the empire. Thus the Greek city-states were Roman *foederae* after their initial conquest, and Gibraltar has internal autonomy under British suzerainty today.[10]

Although the Romans introduced the word *foedera* to describe the bilateral relations between Rome and states absorbed into its expanding empire on the basis of equality (the *foederatii*), given their imperialist orientation, they paid no more attention to the federal idea than did the Greeks. In practice, the Romans promoted such bilateral federal ties, confederations and leagues of cities within the empire, particularly in the early period, and various forms of constitutional home rule over the long course of imperial history. One can speculate that they did not develop a parallel theoretical understanding because of their commitment to the canons of Greek thought. In short, they found the practice useful so avoided conflicts between theory and practice by avoiding theory altogether.[11]

The Jews, on the other hand, having lost their independence and been exiled from their land, retained their aspirations for the restoration of an ideal polity built on federal lines. Those aspirations were embodied in a series of speculative works beginning with the prophecies of Ezekiel (Chapters 34–48) during the Babylonian Exile (ca. 593–571 B.C.E.). The Talmud includes extensive and detailed constitutional-legal discussions of the governance of the to-be-restored twelve-tribe federation in its various folios. Although the matter has not been fully studied, it appears that it offers the oldest extant operational blueprint for a federal system.[12]

Medieval Efforts

Feudalism is often seen as a manifestation of certain federal principles because of its emphasis on essentially immutable contractual relationships permanently linking the contracting parties while guaranteeing their rights. But the hierarchical and essentially private character of those relationships coupled with the lack of practical mechanisms to maintain the terms of the contract drastically limited any association between feudalism and federalism. The Holy Roman Empire was the embodiment of this constitutionalized feudalism, which was additionally strengthened by medieval corporatism and the perennial weakness at the top of the imperial hierarchy.[13] Modern Latin American federalism, with its foundations in the often hierarchical linking of *caudillos,* is, in many ways, a contemporary echo of such feudal arrangements.

A more authentic movement in the direction of federalism grew out of the development of medieval commercial towns in central Europe, which formed leagues for mutual defense and assistance within the loose framework of the Holy Roman Empire. Their leagues followed the Greek model, but unlike the latter, the towns were also founded on a compactual basis. These medieval municipal corporations were founded by compacts among guilds, which were themselves partnerships. They acquired a formal place within the feudal system by means of charters obtained from the appropriate imperial or regional ruler,

which guaranteed their status and local liberties and were
subject to renewal or reaffirmation upon the succession of a
new ruler. Over time, a formal ceremony evolved whereby
the ruler approached the city gates and was invited in only
after agreeing to reaffirm the city's charter.[14]

In their adoption of the corporation form of internal organization, the cities paralleled the Jewish communities of
Europe and the Mediterranean world that organized themselves on federal principles throughout their history. All
Jewish communities were considered partnerships in Jewish
law, created by *askamot* (articles of agreement). Beginning in
the twelfth century, these Jewish communities frequently
joined with one another in leagues similar to those of the
new towns.[15]

The most important development in the medieval period
was the first confederation of Swiss mountain republics in
1291 for mutual aid in defense of their independence. This
effort was successful in no small measure because of its
connection with popular government on a covenantal basis
from the first. The Helvetic Confederation grew over the
centuries by addition of other Swiss republics through a
network of multilateral and bilateral covenants renewed
regularly.[16]

These embryonic federal experiments all proceeded pragmatically while federal theory was confined to juridical discussions of the corporate relationships between polities in
the Holy Roman Empire. Some medieval political philosophers, including Dante *(De Monarchia)*, discussed a system akin to imperial federalism. Most turned their attention
in other directions.

Ultimately a fusion of contractual elements from
feudalism with political mechanisms from the commercial
and agrarian confederacies gave rise to the immediate antecedents of modern federalism. The Christian states on the
Iberian Peninsula created a political system that in its most

advanced stages came very close to authentic federalism. During the years of the Reconquest, most of the peninsula was reorganized under the *fuero* system, which established local governments with relatively liberal political institutions to encourage resettlement. New states were formed through feudal-style contractual relationships designed to protect local rights. Three of these states joined in a quasi-federal arrangement under the Crown of Aragon, each of them (plus several in Italy added later) retaining its own constitution and governing institutions as well as acquiring representation in the overall Aragonese government. Unification of Spain under a multiple monarchy in 1469 left most of these federal elements intact for the next two and a half centuries, but the demands of the monarchy ultimately subverted them, transforming Spain into a precariously centralized state.[17]

The central constitutional characteristic of multiple (or dual) monarchies is that union exists only in the person of the sovereign and is maintained only through the exercise of executive power in his name. No other significant common institutions exist to unite the constituent polities—no common legislatures, no common legal system, and little in the way of a common political substructure. On the contrary, each constituent polity maintains its own political system, which the monarch guarantees to support under the terms of his compact with the realm.

Multiple monarchies have historically been less than democratic regimes. Even where there have been tendencies toward democratization, the very fact that union exists only by virtue of the common sovereign has tended to elevate the position of the monarch to one of real power. Attempts to transfer sovereignty or the attributes of sovereignty elsewhere by their very nature stimulate the division of this kind of association of civil societies into separate polities. Thus the Austro-Hungarian Empire was held together by

the Hapsburg emperors and disintegrated when that family
ceased to rule. The dual monarchy of Sweden and Norway
ceased to function when democratic government was introduced, transferring the attributes of sovereignty from the
monarch to the nation(s). In Spain, on the other hand, the
inability to transform a multiple monarchy into a federal
system in a locale that demanded some form of peninsular
union led to the consolidation of the constituent polities
into something approximating a unitary state, which became highly unstable once the monarchy lost power because of the localistic barriers toward consolidation that
could neither be accommodated nor eradicated.

Multiple monarchies have been transformed into stable
and integrated polities through legislative union. The
United Kingdom is a case in point, uniting in Parliament
England, Wales, Scotland, and Northern Ireland, as well as
certain smaller polities. The centrifugal tendencies of the
seventeenth-century dual monarchy linking England and
Scotland were finally eliminated through a legislative union
of the two nations in 1707.

The Federalist Revival in the Reformation

In the sixteenth century, certain emergent civil societies,
influenced by the Reformation, particularly its Calvinist
and Zwinglian formulations, to return to Scripture as a
source of political inspiration as well as by local necessity,
began to apply federal principles for state-building purposes. In the interim, the Hapsburg heirs to the Spanish
crown had applied Iberian principles to organize their other
European possessions. Their governmental reforms in the
Netherlands provided an organizational basis for the partly
Calvinist-inspired federation of the United Provinces in the
late sixteenth century. When that country gained its inde-

pendence, it established a political system that was unable to solve the most crucial technical problems of federalism but maintained itself in federal style for two hundred years until Napoleon put an end to its existence, leaving a residue of noncentralization that marks the Netherlands to this day.[18]

The Swiss, in the meantime, were developing their own techniques for combining agrarian and commercial elements to create a loose confederation of small republics, influenced by the Calvinist and Zwinglian understanding of the Bible and, perhaps negatively, by contacts with Hapsburg Spain. Achieving full independence in 1648, the Swiss Confederation remained loosely united for two centuries (except for an interlude of Napoleonic conquest) until it adopted a modern federal constitution in 1848.[19]

The Reformation in Switzerland, Scotland, the Netherlands, and England plus parts of France and Germany gave impetus to the development of federalism as a social principle. The assumptions of the Reformed Presbyterian and Puritan churches were manifested in the formation of communities of "saints" who covenanted together to create congregations and, in some cases, polities which they could govern as partnerships. The Swiss and the Dutch created federal states; the Scots reestablished their national identity through the Scottish national covenant; and the Puritans created the federal theology and organized their New England colonies and churches on federal principles. The French term for their Protestants was *Huguenot,* a corruption of the German *eidgenossen,* literally "oath-based association" or federation.[20]

The rise of the nation-state in the sixteenth and seventeenth centuries stimulated the search for federal solutions for the problems of national unification. Yet in all but a few countries on the peripheries of Western Europe, the application of federal principles foundered on three problems: (1) the reconciliation of feudally rooted hierarchies with a system demanding fundamental social equality to facilitate the sharing of power; (2) the reconciliation of local autonomy with national energy in an era of political upheaval that required most nations to maintain a state of constant mobilization basically incompatible with the toleration of local differences; and (3) the problem of executive leadership and succession, which was not solved until the United States invented the elected presidency.

Federalism, Centralization, and State-Building in the Modern Epoch

The history of modern federalism is intimately linked with that of the modern nation-state. In a very real sense, the federal principle stands in opposition to the centralized, reified nation-state, which is the principal product of modern nationalism. At the same time, modern federalism was invented to provide either an alternative or a corrective to the classic nation-state model but one that would still be within the parameters of modern state-building.

The modern nation-state was born, or invented, in Europe in the century and a half between the revolt of the Netherlands against Spain (1567) and the Treaty of Utrecht (1714). Building upon the centralizing, hierarchical, statist principle of absolutism in combination with the new trend toward national identity on a territorial basis, modern nationalism led to the abandonment of corporatism that characterized late feudal or postfeudal civil society. It was based on the notion of a single entity commanding universal loyalty on the part of all subjects or citizens and possessing full authority or sovereignty within its territorial limits. The classic modern nation-state was based on the principle that its sovereignty was indivisible and, indeed, to be properly exercised, that sovereignty had to be concentrated in a single center. This idea was a natural outgrowth of the circumstances of its birth, which involved the bringing of ever wider territories under the control of a single center, usually a single individual—a monarch—through conquest or dynastic merger.

France was the first of the modern nation-states; hence it is not surprising that a Frenchman, Jean Bodin (1530–96), developed the theory upon which it rested, presented in full in his *Six Books of the Republic* (1576). The theory came along with the fact, if not after it, helping to shape men's minds so that they soon would come to see the world in terms of the nation-state and brook no other notion of political organization as legitimate. By the time Europe's age of revolution began in 1789, the revolutionaries sought principally to seize the center of sovereignty in the name of the people, or if no such center existed, to create one in their name. Absolutism gave way to Jacobinism, a more popular way of reified state-building. This became the pattern for the next century and a half, until the modern epoch's end.

In the first stages of the development of the reified state, federalism stood in apposition, if not in opposition, to it. The early federalists made their appearance in the same century and a half that saw the emergence of the sovereign state and its supporters. The federalists also recognized the necessity for constitutional change to adapt to the new age that was emerging, but they sought that change through adaptation of late medieval corporatism to the new territorialism, which was a principal feature of modern state-building, in such a way that at least the exercise of sovereignty would be dispersed among different territorial and corporate centers so as to preserve traditional liberties and prevent absolutism—a characteristic feature of the early modern state. Although many now-neglected theorists articulated this view throughout the period under discussion, particularly in the Germanic world, and continued to do so well into the nineteenth century, Johannes Althusius (1557–1638) was its most articulate spokesman and systematic theorist. Althusius presented a comprehensive model of this polity in his *Politica Methodice Digesta* (1603 and 1614) and worked to implement that model as syndic of Emden during the better part of the first generation of the seventeenth century.[21]

The struggle between these two conceptions of the polity and their articulators was paralleled and superseded by the political struggle between rulers and peoples which set its stamp on the epoch. Every nation in Europe that had the opportunity to achieve statehood and every state that emerged was forced at one point or another to choose between the federalist and centralist models. Most chose the latter. Some made their choice before the invention of modern federalism and were faced with the option of choosing centralization or a system that would preserve their traditional liberties but failed to provide them with sufficient security against the growing strength of the centralized states. Others were founded after the centralist ideology had become the European norm and chose accordingly.

From the mid-sixteenth through the mid-eighteenth centuries, France, England, and Prussia chose the path of the modern nation-state; Switzerland and the Netherlands chose the path of traditional federalism or confederation; and the other German and Italian states tried to preserve their independence through a modernized version of medieval personal rule.[22] Russia and Austria were transformed into modernized empires with certain organizational characteristics of modern states but still were multinational medieval autocracies in conception. They remained such until World War I.[23]

While the first group waxed strong, the second ran into difficulties. The French Revolution and the Napoleonic Wars that followed threatened the regimes of both confederations, altering that of the Netherlands to bring it into line with the new statism but failing to do so in Switzerland, succeeding only in bringing an end to its traditional federalism. The German and Italian states were also weakened, and the stage was set for the transformation of their regimes in the nineteenth century. After 1784, Austria was plagued by nationalist revolutions. Only Russia was able to preserve its old order intact until the twentieth century.

In the end, Switzerland, Germany, Austria, and Russia chose federalism and stayed with it. Switzerland did so with full heart because its political culture and situation combined to make federalism a universal desideratum. Germany begrudgingly adopted federalism because it was the only way that Prussia could secure that country's unification. Austria's transformation into a modern nation-state came almost at the end of the modern epoch under circumstances similar to those that elsewhere were to create the postmodern federalist revolution.[24] Russia also chose a federal structure after its 1917 revolutions as the only feasible means for integrating the old empire under Bolshevik rule.[25]

While those changes were taking place in Europe, the newly independent American states were busy inventing modern federalism. Like other modern nations, the new American nation rejected medieval corporatism. Indeed, in British North America, corporations never took root. The American colonies were territorial republics from the first, and, with some early and transient exceptions, citizenship went with the territory. At the same time, Americans were congenitally opposed to absolutism or the centralization of power in any form. Even so, having fought a revolution against a superpower, Americans soon came to realize that the country's security needs alone required an appropriately strong and energetic general government.[26] In a brilliant invention, the Founding Fathers came up with the answer to their problem, transforming the sovereignty question into one of powers and their exercise—who has the power and authority to do what?[27] The new federal government of the United States of America served a community of states, each of which had full powers in the spheres delegated to it by the people through its own written constitution.[28]

Shortly after the Americans had invented modern federalism, the Dutch, under Napoleonic pressure, abandoned their traditional system for a centralized Jacobin republic, later to be reconstituted as a unitary, decentralized monarchy (in the words of the Dutch constitution). The Swiss, however, managed to recoup and learn from the American experience so that in 1848 they transformed their traditional federal system into a modern federation, borrowing heavily from the American model.

The German states went through a period of political change, each step taken in the wake of a war. The Thirty Years' War (1618–48) effectively ended the traditional confederation of German states known as the Holy Roman Empire. Although its shell survived until 1806, the rise of Prussia and Austria as modern states destroyed that basis of its existence. The Napoleonic Wars brought about regional leagues of princes and a general customs union (the *Zollverein*), which led to an all-German confederation established in 1815 by the Congress of Vienna. The body, always weak, was finally destroyed by the Austro-Prussian War of 1866. In its place there arose a Prussian-dominated federation of kingdoms established by Bismarck in 1871. World War I destroyed that regime, which was replaced by the reluctantly federal Weimar Republic. Needless to say, Hitler abolished federalism along with all other German liberties, all of which were restored to western Germany in the aftermath of World War II with the constitution of the present German Federal Republic in 1949.

Elsewhere in Europe, the Scandinavian countries moved

out of their quasi-federal medieval frameworks to become fully independent states, statist in form but emphasizing local home rule in fact. The Scandinavian countries always had a strong localistic tradition, which was constitutionalized in the twentieth century to devolve most internal governmental functions to their respective municipalities. At the same time, all retained their power to reorganize the local government system unilaterally, to the point of being able to consolidate local authorities at state discretion. Indeed, all have done so since the mid-1960s.[29]

Despite a strong tradition of local liberties and noncentralization, Belgium was forced to adopt the reified state model, within which it effectively developed a quasi-federation of internally decentralized provinces.[30] Spain and Portugal eliminated all but vestiges of the medieval *fueros* that had once kept those countries noncentralized.[31] Indeed, both were among the earliest centralized states. In Spain, this step could be taken only at the price of repressing regionally based nationality groups, which contributed to the state of almost constant civil war that plagued that country in the nineteenth century. Italy was unified by force in the middle generation of the century and opted for full centralization.

To the east of the German states, Ottoman imperial rule was reduced by force, allowing the rise of the nation-states of Greece, Bulgaria, Romania, and Serbia, each of which was based on a preexisting nationality group seeking its place in the sun.[32] The transformation of the Russian and Austro-Hungarian empires came at the very end of the epoch. The new Bolshevik regime in Russia, desirous of preserving as much of the old empire as possible, reluctantly turned to a federal structure to accommodate the various nationalities seeking independence but minimized the reality of federalism by extending the dominant role of the highly centralized Communist party throughout the USSR.

Austria lost its empire, which was replaced by a number of unitary states, some of which such as Yugoslavia tried— and failed— to impose a single artificial national identity on a multinational polity. Austria proper, although no longer a multinational state, became a federal republic, a reflection of the German leaning toward federalism.

The case of the Hapsburg Empire from its medieval beginnings to its collapse during World War I illuminates the situation in central Europe. That empire, long the greatest of the Germanic polities, was at the fulcrum of the conflict. Its ancient traditions were corporatist with a tendency toward the kind of structured pluralism that could have encouraged federalist expression in the Althusian mode while its political culture made it prone to absolutism. As a result, its history involved halfhearted efforts at federalist accommodation, which were unfulfilled because of stronger commitments to absolutism. Its struggle to achieve a modus vivendi was frustrated in the end because it embraced so many different nations, peoples, and ethnic groups, each seeking its own place in the political sun through modern statehood. Hence the pressures for dissolution of the empire in the name of national self-determination was constant as soon as the nation-state was born.[33]

In the seventeenth century, the Hapsburgs inherited the Spanish throne and gained control of the Lowlands, whose northern provinces became the second league of polities successfully to revolt against Hapsburg domination (the first was the Swiss Confederation). As already indicated, they formed a traditional federal system, what we would style a confederacy, known as the United Provinces of the Netherlands. They enjoyed a golden age during the seventeenth century, then dissipated their strength in contests with their great, powerful, and increasingly centralized neighbors, foolishly seeking to compete with them as an equal power on the international scene.

After two hundred years, certainly a substantial length of time and one which prevents us from judging the Netherlands confederation a failure, the weight of its medieval institutions did indeed become too great to resist the popular demands for greater participation in the governance of the body politic. Having become overly oligarchic and not very effective, the regime was swept away in the tide of the French Revolution. Nevertheless, its principles retained sufficient momentum and the political culture which it both reflected and fostered was sufficiently entrenched among the Dutch that, after a brief experiment with a Jacobin-style republic and then a Napoleonic-style monarchy, the Dutch adopted a constitution establishing a regime that was both unitary and decentralized. The old provinces retained substantial powers and the communes, real local liberty.

In the nineteenth century, the pluralism that was characteristic of the Netherlands took a new turn, expressed not through medieval corporations or territorial jurisdictions but through religious and ideological communities. The Dutch drew upon their own political cultural heritage to integrate this new pluralism into the regime through what a century later would be termed consociationalism by the Dutch political scientist Arend Lijphardt.[34]

One of the last European states to be established and to adopt the ideology of modern nationalism was Italy, in 1860, considerably after the invention of modern federalism. There the struggle between centralists and federalists was open and explicit, with the centralists winning but never being able to consolidate their victory.[35] Italy today is still engaged in trying to find a way to accommodate the regionalist impulses that first gave rise to the federalist movement.

If modern Europe's attitude toward federalism is at best mixed, North America is the federalist continent par excellence. All three North American countries, Canada, the United States, and Mexico, are formally federal and, certainly in the first two, federalism is truly the form of the polity. Canada is a twentieth-century carryover from late modern state-building efforts. Settled at the very beginning of the modern epoch by both French and British, two peoples—the Quebecois would argue two nations—developed in its vast territories, one anglophone and other francophone. The political fate of Canada in that epoch was determined by the struggle between the mother countries of both, one of the crucial struggles of the epoch's first half.

The second half of the modern epoch was devoted to a continuing effort on the part of Canadians to reach a modus vivendi, political and otherwise, between those two peoples within a common polity. For a while, it seemed as if such a modus vivendi was reached in the climax of the middle generation of the nineteenth century with the formation of the Dominion of Canada as a federal polity (in Canadian terms, a confederation). Indeed, that resolution did not undergo serious challenge until the first generation of the postmodern epoch. Only after Quebec's quiet revolution of the 1960s was Canadian nationhood seriously called into question.[36] By the mid-1980s, the threat of the dissolution of Canada had receded. Two founding events of the second postwar generation are manifestations of this turn: the rejection of the secession-oriented referendum of the Parti Quebecois by Quebec voters and the patriation of the Canadian constitution.[37]

It already has been noted that state-building in the modern epoch has been strongly associated with centralization, or at least strengthening what in the United States is often referred to as the national government. Since modern federalism was invented to make possible the existence of a national government that would be at one and the same time energetic and limited, this is a built-in problem in modern federations. In the United States over the years, this has led to a concentration of power in the federal government within the framework of a noncentralized political system.[38]

Recent American experience reaffirms what we already know, that the decisions of founders, once made, have a lasting impact but not the last word. Politics remains the civilized vehicle, not only for founding but for building and rebuilding civil society. To the extent that the form or constitution (in the largest sense) of a polity shapes its politics, we are bidden to take those forms and the decisions made in choosing them seriously.

The major polities of South America adopted federal structures for reasons that reflect the differences between the American and European situations. These polities deserve extensive treatment in their own right. Suffice it to say that in all there was a struggle between centralists and federalists, with the latter equating federalism with liberty, reflecting the clash between European and American theories of state and nation-building.[39]

Similar struggles are still taking place in the twentieth century in Africa and Asia with the decolonization of the Third World.[40] There, too, European and American theories of state-building are struggling with each other for control of the hearts and minds of people as reflected in the structures of their new polities.

This struggle and its results in each of the world's polities is a matter that should be of concern to students of federalism and comparative politics generally. Why did each nation or state make the choice it did? What are the consequences of its choice? Where there was a struggle, what echoes remain of that struggle after its initial resolution? For example, given the weak performance of federal systems in Latin America and their obvious incompatibility with the authoritarian regimes so prevalent in that region, why have

federal forms been considered critically necessary in the
major countries of the region? Why has only one country—
Colombia—formally abandoned federalism? Why have the
boundaries of the constituent states remained essentially
unchanged since they were established generations, if not
centuries, ago? Or, to take a different case, both India and
Pakistan opted for federalism when they became independent in 1947. Why has federalism taken root in the former
while remaining virtually a paper arrangement in the latter?
These questions of original constitutional choice are tied up
with issues of culture and circumstance, of external security
and internal power alignments, all of which deserve serious
consideration.

Modern Federal Theory and New Federal Experiments

The protofederalism of the United Provinces and the
Helvetic Confederation, coming at the outset of the age of
nationalism, also stimulated the first serious efforts to for-
mulate federal theories based on modern political principles. Distinctive theory for federal polities was born in the
late sixteenth century, first emerging in the work of
Johannes Althusius, whose *Politica Methodice Digesta* outlines the possible organization of a federal state and connects
the federal principle with the idea of popular sovereignty.
His work, which was the product of applied study, was
aimed at transforming the Holy Roman Empire, or at least
its Germanic states, into a federal union. It delineates the
principles of federalism and distinguishes between its principal species, what we today would refer to as leagues,
federations, and confederations. Moreover, since, as a student and teacher, Althusius studied the Swiss Confederation at first hand, his work clearly benefits from an
empirical grounding absent in previous efforts.

The main problem of Althusius's work stems from the admixture of older hierarchical notions and ideas that hint at the corporate organization of society with his attempts to delineate federal principles. These, of course, reflect the environment in which he lived. Althusius expanded his work in subsequent editions and ultimately laid the foundations for theoretical consideration of federalism as a form of political organization.

Althusius was strongly influenced by the federal theology that had become the intellectual foundation of the Reformed wing of Protestantism during the course of the sixteenth century. It can hardly be a coincidence that the federal theology sprouted from the four intellectual centers of Switzerland, Basel, Bern, Geneva, and Zurich, in the very first days of the Reformation. It achieved its fullest theological and political expression in the last two, through John Calvin in Geneva and Ulrich Zwingli and his successor Heinrich Bullinger in Zurich. Both city-states became covenanted republics under the magistries of those figures and their colleagues. The writings of Calvin and Bullinger not only contributed directly to the "new federalism" of Althusius but inspired an entire political thought that strongly influenced modern republicanism and shaped the two federal polities of the time, Switzerland and the Netherlands, both of which were dominated by Reform Protestants.

With the concurrent emergence of the concept of sovereignty, however, federal principles were challenged by a powerful new theory that denied the empirical reality as well as the legitimacy of truly federal polities. Jean Bodin, the principal formulator of the modern theory of the state, was the key intellectual figure in this development. He analyzed the possibilities of federalism in light of the problem of sovereignty, concluding that the necessities of maintaining indivisible sovereignty within states of a proper scale rendered federalism impossible. Greek-style leagues for defensive purposes were not incompatible with this new doctrine of national sovereignty. Bodin used the term *foedera* to describe cooperative relationships between states but ended up by emphasizing their incompatibility with the principle of sovereignty.

In the years following, Hugo Grotius and Samuel Pufendorf examined federal arrangements as aspects of international law. In their works they advanced the theoretical conceptualization of federalism from the statist perspective. Both observed existing federal (read: confederal) systems at close hand, Grotius in the Netherlands and Pufendorf in Germany. Grotius, with the Dutch experience before him, concluded that closely knit leagues could prove viable while Pufendorf held that federalism and sovereignty were so incompatible that even perpetual leagues were infringements upon the latter.

Thus a modified form of the Greek view was adopted by the early modern continental theorists of the state and international law who held that federalism could be no more than a permanent league of states united through a perpetual covenant, binding as international law, in which the constituent states delegated limited enumerated powers to a common governing council while retaining full rights of internal sovereignty. Their conception became the accepted one among most political theorists until the foundation of the American federal system.

In the eighteenth century the Baron Montesquieu advanced the discussion a step further in his work *L'esprit des loix*. Attempting to delineate the virtues of federalism in the promotion of republican government and the conditions conducive to the creation of federal systems, he then laid the theoretical foundations for modern confederation.

Jean Jacques Rousseau apparently considered federalism to be a vital aspect of popular government. Unfortunately, his major work on federalism was accidentally destroyed during the French Revolution, but fragments of his ideas survive in *Du contrat social*. What was left was of an entirely different spirit, and Rousseau became the spiritual father of Jacobinism.

Immanuel Kant was the last of the great European political theorists to deal exclusively with premodern federalism. In *Principles of Politics* he followed the spirit of his predecessors, discussing the federal idea as a means to achieve international order.[41]

With the possible exception of Althusius, Ludolph Hugo, and a few others who wished to reconstitute the Holy Roman Empire along modern lines rather than have it replaced by the new system of nation-states, prerevolutionary Continental federal theorists all treated federalism as a species of international law, that is, as a means to achieve limited unification of sovereign states not necessarily governed under republican constitutions.[42] In Britain, on the other hand, federal theorists began from the premise that polities were brought into being through political compacts, hence it was an easy step for them to envisage that a single nation or state could be divided into subsidiary polities—equally contractual in formation but with political rights stemming from ancient traditions of local self-government and individual liberties. Most referred to biblical sources to support their theories before the public. Hence in the perspective of the history of ideas, it may not be too simple to state that the continental theorist looked first to the Greeks for federal ideas and that the British theorists looked first to the Jews.[43]

None of the great seventeenth-century British political theorists discuss federal systems per se, but all deal with federal ideas out of their commitment to the compact theory of the polity. For example, Thomas Hobbes emphasized the foundation of all civil society through covenant, and John Locke used the term "federative" to discuss the political powers of citizens carried over from the precompact period—that is, the naturally vested political powers of every individual.[44] The only English political philosopher to approach the issue of noncentralized government was James Harrington, who suggested strengthening the autonomy of English county government so that the counties would be analogous to the Israelite tribes in their federation.[45]

Parallel to the secular philosophers, the English Puritans and Scottish Covenanters produced their own speculative thinkers whose political thought grew out of the federal theology. They were directly concerned with polity-building from the initial covenanted community to larger arenas.[46] Their work was to bear its greatest fruit in North America, where their colonies were established on federal principles, from the town through the New England Confederation.[47]

The eighteenth century opened with a public discussion of federal questions in Britain proper incident to the legislative union of England and Scotland in 1707. There was no further discussion of federalism until the eve of the American Revolution, when the problem of imperial relations within the British Empire brought it once again to the fore. Adam Smith called for transformation of the imperial relationship into a "general confederacy" and proceeded to analyze its prospects from that point of view.[48] Edmund Burke, as a practical political leader, opposed this idea as impractical because of geography.[49] Jeremy Bentham was the only British theorist to treat federalism as such analytically.[50]

In the interim, the British had provided the framework for the establishment of the requisite popular institutions in their colonization of North America, and the biblically influenced colonists had created the social basis and theoretical justification for those institutions. The theoretical ambiguity of the quasi-federal imperial system led Americans to assume that their relationship to the British government was federal even though London entertained no such notion. The Americans' response to the imperial system as they viewed it helped them to develop the federal ideas they were later to use so creatively.[51]

The founders of the United States of America can be said to have transformed the principles of federalism into a practical system of government. They were able to do so in part because their nation developed without the disadvantages that plagued earlier federal systems. As an entirely modern (that is, postfeudal) society, the United States had no serious problem of coping with existing social hierarchies with differential political rights. Because it was a relatively isolated nation, external pressures for centralization were not present for nearly 150 years. American political inventiveness took care of the internal problems of applying the federal principle though a major civil war had to be fought to resolve some of them.

Almost every other nation attempting the federal solution to the problems of popular government in pluralistic civil societies attempted to imitate either the forms or the principles of federal organization developed in the United States, though not necessarily successfully. The creation of the theoretical framework for those principles was part and parcel of the invention of federalism. That framework was developed in the debate over ratification of the Constitution. At its core was *The Federalist,* the classic formulation of the principles of modern federalism, by Alexander Hamilton, John Jay, and, principally, James Madison.[52] Equally important to the definition of federalism were the often neglected arguments of the Antifederalists, who wished to preserve even greater state autonomy, many of which were transformed into tools to promote extraconstitutional decentralization in the United States during the nineteenth century.[53]

In essence, the Americans took biblical and British notions of covenant and compact and, through hard thinking about federalism, combined them into a federal theory. *The Federalist* addresses itself to the problems of modern popular government, proposes a federal solution to those problems, and justifies its proposal. The formulation of the principles of modern federalism (or, to paraphrase its authors, national federalism) provides the basis for defining the concept, and its discussion of those principles remains the most insightful and comprehensive treatment of the character and utility of federalism available. Writing for a new society in a new world, its authors were not deflected by the confusion of the federal principle with feudal or corporate arrangements as were their predecessors. By separating the older idea of confederal arrangements from the concept of federalism, they launched a new political concept.

When the American federal system was created in the late eighteenth century to become the prototype for other modern federal systems, its architects developed a conception of federalism much like that of ancient Israel, a conception already rooted in American soil as a result of earlier federal experiments. Although that influence is not mentioned in *The Federalist,* the general debate over the new constitution emphasized that linkage more than any other. The Bible was cited as precedent more than any other source. The number of citations from the book of Deuteronomy alone equalled that from all other sources.[54]

From the first, American federalism functioned to serve a people with a single national identity and was constituted with a strong general government to serve that people on a countrywide basis. In advocating ratification of the American Constitution, the authors of *The Federalist* felt it necessary to describe the system it created as "partly national and partly federal" in deference to the then accepted view. The successful efforts of the proponents of that Constitution to appropriate the term "federalist" for their own use restored to common usage the older conception of federalism as a noncentralized national union having a general government with supremacy over the governments of the constituent states in those spheres assigned to it.

The Federalist was but one of a substantial body of works on the problem of federalism to be published as a consequence of the struggle over ratification of the Constitution. Speakers and writers on both sides of the issue contributed to the elucidation of the federal principle because both sides accepted the principles of federalism and argued only about the best manner of applying them. This literature, one of the largest bodies of material on federalism, has been largely ignored though it has recently been rediscovered by students of political theory.

From the first, American contributions to federal theory—even those of the few theorists not actively involved in politics—have been rooted in the practical concerns of maintaining a federal system. Most of these contributions have, accordingly, been formulated as discussions of constitutional law. The courts, particularly the federal Supreme Court, have conducted a continuing debate on the meaning and character of federalism through the medium of case law. Leading political figures such as Albert Gallatin, John C. Calhoun, Abraham Lincoln, and Woodrow Wilson have made important contributions through their state papers, and presidents such as the two Roosevelts, Dwight Eisenhower, Lyndon Johnson, Richard Nixon, and Ronald Reagan have stimulated contributions of theoretical interest through their advisers. The pragmatic orientation of those contributions, however, has tended to obscure their more lasting theoretical importance.[55]

The French Revolution also stimulated the development of popular government but was essentially hostile to the spirit and institutions of federalism. Jacobin democracy, the major alternative to federal democracy, drew its inspiration from Rousseau's concept of the general will as interpreted by the revolutionary leadership. Unlike federal democracy, which views the constitutional sharing of power among multiple centers (noncentralization) as the keystone of popular government, Jacobin democracy is committed to centralized majoritarianism whereby a single elite guides the state by interpreting the general will of its citizens as a matter of public opinion simply expressed or manipulated.[56]

Centralized France rejected federalism during the struggle between the Girondists and the Jacobins in the early days of the French Revolution. Once the French people embraced Jacobinism, which was far more in tune with French political culture, they never seriously reconsidered the federal option. The immediate heirs of the French Revolution tried to destroy existing federal institutions in Western Europe in the name of democracy, and the subsequent bearers of its tradition have proved equally hostile to federal ideas—except insofar as some of them have equated federalism with decentralized government. The minority tradition among the revolutionaries, which endorsed federalism as a more moderate means of instituting popular government, was later to emerge as an intellectual force in the works of Alexis de Tocqueville and as a political movement among the twentieth-century exponents of integral federalism based on the ideas of Pierre-Joseph Proudhon.[57]

Just as the American system became the prototype for other modern federal systems, the American conception of federalism became the generally accepted one in the modern world. After a period of some confusion, it was generally accepted that the other conception would be described by the word "confederation." The two systems described by these different terms reflect, in part, the distinctions implied in the German terms developed in the mid-nineteenth century, *staatenbund* (confederation) and *bundesstaat* (federation). In French and Spanish the meaning of the terms is often reversed.

Theoretical discussions of federalism blossomed in the nineteenth century under the impetus afforded by the existence of functioning federal systems and in response to the ideas and practices of modern federalism, particularly in the United States. These discussions took a practical turn after the European revolutions of 1848.

German schools of federal theory that arose in the latter half of the nineteenth century in response to the efforts of the Germanic states to federate offered the most abstractly theoretical inquiry, fully in the German intellectual tradition. The intellectual impetus to discuss federalism came from Alexis de Tocqueville's work on the American federal system, but rather than attempt to analyze the political behavior of federal nations and states insightfully as did Tocqueville, the Germans turned to doctrinaire and metaphysical analyses of problems of nationalism, sovereignty, and popular consent. Their works have lost much of their appeal in the twentieth century. Only Otto Gierke has attracted and maintained an international reputation.[58]

Pierre-Joseph Proudhon, the French utopian theorist, presented an equally abstract, if linguistically more elegant, federal model as the basis for his ideal society. Abstraction flowed from the necessarily utopian character of his thought, given the antipathy to federalism common to all French regimes. Proudhon represents a continuing minor federalist chord in French intellectual life beginning with Benjamin Constant (a Swiss by birth) on the eve of the Revolution and continuing to the present. In the 1920s, Proudhonian federalism reemerged as integral federalism, now a functioning school of federalist thought centered in France and its francophone peripheries. Its principal representatives are Alexandre Marc and Denis de Rougemont, and it maintains an organizational network which since World War II has focused on the building of a federal Europe on the basis of that continent's primordial groups.[59]

Most other Europeans analyzed federal questions on a

directly political level after first observing federal systems in operation. Most of these writers were Englishmen and Frenchmen who came to observe the American political system and write about it from a reasonably dispassionate and theoretical point of view, although a few observed continental systems. The best-known of this group, whose works have become classics, were Tocqueville and James Bryce, both of whom were reservedly predisposed toward popular government and wished to understand its operations so as to overcome its defects. Tocqueville, indeed, can be said to have laid the foundations for the scientific-empirical study of federalism.[60]

Johann Kaspar Bluntschli, of Switzerland, built a theoretical analysis of federalism upon his observations of the formation of the Swiss federal union. Because of its concern with a real situation, his work was perhaps the most impressive contribution to modern federal theory in the German language, clarifying the operational distinctions between confederal leagues and federal systems. Unfortunately, the style of his work is heavily Germanic.[61]

During the late nineteenth century, a school of British theorists and men of affairs emerged to advocate the transformation of the newly won British Empire into an imperial federation. Their thought had a distinctly practical bent, generally directed toward solving colonial and imperial problems. The discussions of these theorists consisted principally of arguments about the utility of federal organization and specific constitutional proposals. They were accompanied by the successful introduction of federal systems in certain colonies and the failure to achieve the federal reorganization of the empire. Canada and Australia were given federal constitutions and dominion status in 1867 and 1901 respectively, the foundations were laid for the federal unification of India, and an attempt to give New Zealand a federal form of government was abandoned only at the New Zealanders' request.

British political theorists such as Bryce and Edward A. Freeman, interested in imperial unity and internal devolution, explored contemporary and historical federal experiments and presented arguments regarding the utility and proper organization of federal systems to create a peculiarly British contribution to federal theory, no less distinctive than that of the Americans, Germans, or Swiss. The form Freeman and W. Jenkins gave to the theory of imperial federalism gained many adherents in Britain and the dominions and led to the formation of the Imperial Federation League in 1884.[62] The league's foremost theorist was F. P. de Lubilliere.[63]

The federalists lost to the liberals, who wished to establish self-contained governments in the dominions with a less formal bond of imperial attachment. The institution of federal systems in Canada and Australia did not produce any important theoretical works or federalism but did lead to the beginnings of a body of federal constitutional law through the decisions of the Privy Council as the federal court of last resort. Similarly, the movement toward internal reorganization of Britain along federal lines gained some limited tactical successes but failed of its overall purpose.[64]

Some British students of politics did approach the study of federalism from a more general interest in political systems, among them Bryce, Albert V. Dicey, John Stuart Mill, and Henry Sidgwick.[65] The thrust of their work was to avoid doctrinaire problems and to analyze the evolution and operation of federal systems. Their central conclusion, maintained by such contemporary British students of federalism as K. C. Wheare, was that federalism was no more than a technique for political integration—occasionally useful, transitory in nature, and ultimately to evolve into a more simple form of decentralization within a strong unitary government.[66]

In the United States, the development of federal theory moved into a new channel closely connected with the day-to-day problems of government in a federal system. Notably lacking were theoretical studies by detached observers. The men who contributed to the development of federal theory in America were primarily political practitioners who were deeply involved in working out the issues of the day. Those with sharp intellects and serious theoretical concerns made real contributions; the others simply added to the mound of political clichés that replaces serious thought in every political system. Hence the American judicial system with the federal Supreme Court at its apex became the central instrument for theoretical debate about the questions of federalism.

Early in the nineteenth century, most of the new Latin American nations, following the Yankee example and also influenced by the federal elements in the Hispanic imperial tradition, experimented with federalism with distinctly mixed results. For them, federalism was part of the ideology of liberty, the proper political structure for a liberal polity, as well as a device for resolving the conflict between the capital city and the provinces, which was a common feature in the early years of independence in most Latin American countries. For some, this experiment was transient, unable to stand up to the pressures for unification or fragmentation. For others, it became a permanent feature of their political systems.[67]

Even where federalism survived in theory, the instability of Latin American governments and the frequent recourse to dictatorial regimes hampered its effective operation. The three largest Latin American nations, Argentina, Brazil, and Mexico, as well as Venezuela, retain federal systems of varying political significance, and some federal principles are retained in the political system of Colombia. Latin American federalism remains the primary modern manifestation of feudalistic federalism with *jefes* and *caudillos* replacing counts and dukes.

As a whole, in the nineteenth century federalism was used to abet ethnic nationalism, with demands for the creation or maintenance of federal institutions coming from ethnic groups seeking national unity and political autonomy but not in a position to achieve either in any other way. In the twentieth century it has been used as a means to unify multiethnic polities. Several of the ethnically heterogeneous nations created or reconstructed after World War I, including the Soviet Union, formally embraced federalism as a nominal solution to their nationality problems. The United Kingdom added a federal dimension at the same time to accommodate the Ulster Scotch-Irish. Modern federacy arrangements, such as the relationship between Finland and the Aaland Islands, were developed and introduced at that time for similar purposes.[68]

The post–World War II extension of nation-building activities to Asia and Africa, where ethnic diversity is even greater than in Europe, has led to new efforts in the same vein.[69] In nations outside of the totalitarian orbit, such as India and Malaysia, federalism has been used to secure political and cultural rights for their larger ethnolinguistic groups. In Africa, where the survival of separate ethnic groups has been called into question by the native nationalists, federalism has been far less successful, taking hold only in Nigeria and the Comoros Islands as a device for sharing political power more than as a way to maintain cultural autonomy. As yet, in neither case have these developments been accompanied by any serious federal theory in the polities involved, although Indian and Nigerian political scientists have produced a useful literature on the subject with a local focus.

Controlled experiments linking independent countries for economic and very limited political purposes emerged after World War II in various parts of the world. The European Community is the first of these in importance. It has developed into a true confederation. The Association of Southeast Asian Nations is moving in a similar direction in its own way. Although the British effort to federate their West Indies colonies failed, a confederal framework is emerging, out of sheer necessity, to link the newly independent microstates in the region. Any number of regional common markets have been established in the Third World, with varying degrees of reality and prospects for success.[70] Finally, federacy and associated state arrangements—two asymmetrical forms of federalism—have become much more common from Puerto Rico to Macao.

These new developments require new theory-building to give them theoretical expression. Such theory-building can only enrich our understanding of federalism as idea and reality and help us go beyond the slender theories of modern federation which neither explain that phenomenon adequately nor allow us to see the full meaning of federalism as a political genus.

Federalism: The Present State of the Art

The long line of ancient, medieval, modern, and contemporary efforts to "think federal" and build federal institutions testifies to the endurance of federalism as idea and form. As an idea, federalism has been treated by many eminent political philosophers, although it was not particularly popular among the towering figures of political thought until the beginning of the modern epoch. The disposition of ancient and medieval philosophy to see the universe as organic militated against a serious concern with federalism. It was left to theology to consider the possibilities of covenantal systems. At the same time, there were numerous efforts to implement a variety of federal arrangements, even in the bailiwicks of philosophers who ignored them. Thus the beginnings of federalism reflect its subsequent history—considered by philosophers to be too practical to be worthy of the highest level of philosophic concern and by statesmen as too demanding of cooperative effort to be used in building polities of other than free men.

The convergence of theology and political thought at the outset of the modern epoch, which led to the philosophic revolution of the seventeenth century, opened up the possibility of serious federalist thought while the accompanying republican revolution made federalism possible as a workable form of political organization. In the modern epoch, new federal institutions were invented, which became the necessary artifacts for successful federal government. There was a flowering of federal theory as well, some of classic proportions. Thus federalism is a particularly modern device, albeit with ancient roots, inseparable from modern democratic republicanism. Ironically, despite its modernity, in the modern epoch federalism had to compete with statism at a disadvantage. But, there is every sign that the balance is shifting in the postmodern epoch to allow federalism to come into its own.

5

The Elements of Federalism

Federalism as a Basis of Political Association

Federalism involves a commitment to partnership and to active cooperation on the part of individuals and institutions that also take pride in preserving their own respective integrities. Successful federal systems are characterized not only by their constitutional arrangements in the narrow sense of the word but by their permeation with the spirit of federalism as manifested in sharing through negotiation, mutual forbearance and self-restraint in the pursuit of goals, and a consideration of the system as well as the substantive consequences of one's acts. Political institutions common to different political systems, when combined within a federal system and animated by federal principles, are effectively endowed by those principles with a distinctive character. For example, although political parties are common in modern political systems, parties in federal systems show unique characteristics of fragmentation along the lines of the major federal divisions in the system and a lack of central discipline that functions to increase the power of local groups within the system as a whole.

Federalism, it has been argued, is essentially a transitory phenomenon, which serves primarily as a means to bring unity to nations composed of highly autonomous polities where such unity can be obtained only by allowing the constituent units to retain substantial powers. As federal

154

systems mature, so the argument goes, power is increasingly concentrated at the center, and federalism remains only to promote a certain degree of decentralization within an otherwise highly unified political system. K. C. Wheare, the principal exponent of this view, argues that federalism is then gradually discarded (in fact if not in form) as an unnecessary encumbrance.[1]

This argument may have some validity in describing the history of nonfederal political systems that have used federal principles to promote national unity. For example, it may be used to describe the evolution of Spain from the fall of Granada in 1492 to the death of Francisco Franco in 1977. It cannot be applied, however, to any of the three exemplary federal systems—Canada, Switzerland, and the United States. Although aspects of their systems have changed, there is no evidence that federalism has declined in importance as those nations have matured.

Canada, indeed, has moved in the other direction. Its founders intended it to be a centralized federation; Wheare even questioned whether it should be considered a federal system at all. Instead, it has become a loose federation of highly independent provinces whose leaders negotiate as equals with the federal government on most policy issues.[2]

The Swiss federal system combines the medieval Althusian model of local communal republics compounded into cantons federated into the Helvetic Confederation, transformed into a modern federation in 1848 and strengthened in the constitutional revision of 1874. In the original medieval model, many of the communes were compounded of guilds—again echoing Althusius. The guild basis was jettisoned as a result of the conquest of Switzerland by Napoleon and replaced by consociational arrangements whereby the various confessions or religious groups, economic sectors, and linguistic groups have a continuing voice in policy making, which relies heavily on consensus rather than strict majority versus minority decision making.

In essence, something akin to John C. Calhoun's concurrent majority prevails as the basis for policy making in Swiss federalism. The Swiss actually refer to Switzerland as a "consensus polity." If policy making in this manner is relatively slow-moving, the Swiss are not in a hurry. They have been around for nearly seven hundred years as a confederation, and they expect to be around indefinitely. They are rooted in their land, in its soil, and in its institutions, and they see no reason to hurry. They are hardworking and deliberate but far from frenetic; for them, one thing at a time is enough. Government does what it has to; it does not seek out tasks, and it decides what it has to do only after the complex process of consensus-building is completed.[3]

Switzerland is well governed because its government does not seek to do more than it should or can. What it does, it does well. Visitors to Switzerland soon come to see the entire country as a kind of park, a preserve. But for federalists, too, Switzerland is a kind of a preserve, showing what federalism can and should be.

Even though many attempts to establish federal systems have ended in failure, such systems, once established, have proved to be most durable. No authentic federal system that has lasted for even fifteen years has ever been abandoned except through revolutionary disruption (as in the case in Germany) or foreign conquest (as in the case of Switzerland), and in most cases, including the aforementioned two, federalism—showing remarkable resilience—has ultimately been restored. Even Spain is now moving in the direction of federalism after nearly five hundred years of centralization, with a system very close to it enshrined in the Constitution of 1978 and being implemented.[4]

With the possible exception of Colombia, no federal system in history has ever "evolved" into a unitary one, nor has any established federal system been structurally consolidated by internal decision. On the contrary, federal devices to conciliate minority populations have been used increasingly in recent years in place of force to maintain unity even in consolidated systems. Differences between mature and emergent federal systems are more likely to relate to changes in the character of conflict and modes of negotiation between the general and constituent governments than to their relative strengths.[5]

The Requisites of Federal Systems

Wide functional differences can indeed be discerned in the various political systems that call themselves federal. Nevertheless, some basic characteristics and operational principles can be identified as common to all truly federal systems, which help define them as such. Three of these are essential for all, and a number of others are vital but supplementary.

Written Constitution. First, the federal relationship must be established or confirmed through a perpetual compact of union, usually if not inevitably embodied in a written constitution that outlines, among other things, the terms by which power is divided or shared in the political system and which can be altered only by extraordinary procedures. Every existing federal polity possesses a written constitution, as do most of the other nations incorporating elements of the federal principle. Juridically, federal constitutions are distinctive in that they are not simply compacts between the rulers and the ruled but involve the people, the general government, and the polities constituting the federal union. Moreover, the constituent polities often retain constitution-making rights of their own.[6]

The written constitution is a product of federalism, in-

vented as a political artifact to make possible the constitution or reconstitution of polities on a federal basis through
regularized processes of constitutional choice. All constitutions follow one or another of five basic models: the constitution as (1) frame of government and protector of rights;
(2) code; (3) revolutionary manifesto or social charter;
(4) (tempered) political ideal; and (5) modern adaptation of
an ancient traditional constitution.

*The Constitution as Frame of Government and Protector of
Rights.* This constitutional model is characteristic of the
United States and is the oldest of the modern constitutions.
As a frame of government, it delineates the basic structure,
institutions, and procedures of the polity, and as protector
of rights it declares certain rights to be basic and provides
means for their protection in civil society. It is not a code.
Hence it is not designed to be highly specific and is explicit
only in connection with such elements as must be made
explicit in order for the constitution to frame a government.
American constitutions frame governments and not states
because the American system lacks any sense of the state as a
preexisting phenomenon, a reified entity that continues to
exist regardless of how it is constitutionalized (or not constitutionalized) at any particular moment.[7]

Frame-of-government constitutions establish polities as
often as they establish governments. Indeed, in many cases
the two are inseparable. In fact, written constitutions of this
model often are designed to be devices for organizing new
societies founded in new territories, such as the United
States, Canada, Australia, and South Africa. In such cases,
they frequently begin with political covenants or compacts
that establish the body politic in question. For example, the
Preamble of the Massachusetts constitution (1780) specifies
that the people of that commonwealth both covenant and
compact to form a body politic. The Montana constitution
(1972) includes a compact with the land in its Preamble.[8]

Reform in such situations really amounts to keeping the

frame of government in tune with societal change. Often, the frame can be tuned up through such mechanisms as Supreme Court decisions, which will not be written into the fundamental document if everybody accepts that what the Supreme Court is doing is tuning. The tuning then becomes part of the constitutional tradition even if it is not written into the document itself. Only if reform requires changes in specific wording is formal amendment used. In the American states, such tuning is usually left to the people through an active amendment or referendum process.

The Constitution as Code. The frame-of-government model works best in political systems in which there is basic consensus with regard to the character of the polity, whereas the constitution as code model reflects the reality of polities in which the character of the regime is sufficiently problematic for changes in its authority, powers, or functions to require explicit consent. Constitutions as codes tend to be far more rigid and require precise and deliberate formal textual change to be tuned.

For most Western European states, the constitution is a state code designed to cope with an established order, with established preexisting constituencies, not to speak of a preexisting state. As the word "code" signifies, it is long, detailed, highly specific, and explicit, certainly by American standards. Constitutional change in the case of such constitutions reflects either a change in regime or the necessity periodically to adapt the constitution of the existing regime to reflect the specifics of governmental powers on the assumption that the state continues to exist a priori but that its regimes must be delineated and harnessed to the current specified ends of government. The constitutions of Austria and the German Federal Republic are classic examples of that highly rigid model, but so, too, is the 1978 Spanish constitution, introduced after Franco's death as the basis for a more liberal regime in that country.[9]

The Constitution as Revolutionary Manifesto or Social

Charter. The third model, most common in the socialist (Communist) states, is designed for the comprehensive revolutionary reconstruction of an established civil society, based upon the achievement of a fundamental social revolution with all of the attendant political manifestations and impact. Such a constitution is designed to root out the old order and to reorder its elements in their entirety. Thus Communist constitutions tend as much to exclude certain groups or classes from participation in the body politic as to define the rights, roles, and responsibilities of those who are entitled to participate. Moreover, the central feature of every Communist constitution is the location of power in the hands of the organized revolutionary cadres. Indeed, the constitution is used not only to establish the myth of the social revolution but as an instrument for fostering that myth and enhancing the power of the revolutionary cadres to make the revolution in the name of the myth.

If there is any constitutional reform in such systems, it involves bridging the gap between the constitutional myth and regime reality. Such constitutions establish certain myths about the Communist state and its society which are far from the realities of political life under such regimes. At some point, the gap between the constitutional myth and the regime reality becomes too great, and some attempt at reform has to be made. This has been particularly true in Yugoslavia, where the federal republican constitution has been rewritten several times since the regime was instituted at the end of World War II to reflect changes in the distribution of power between the federal government and the republics and between the various classes and groups within Yugoslav society. Another such change was the institution of a federal system in Czechoslovakia as a result of the 1968 revolt in the country. The sociopolitical liberalization sought by the liberals was rejected by the ruling Communist party, but federalism was introduced to accommodate the ethnic aspirations of Czechs and Slovaks.

The USSR has undergone the least constitutional change in this respect. Its most recent effort was launched by Nikita Khrushchev when he was in power, principally to eliminate the federal structure which he, following Leninist doctrine, held to be a temporary expedient to communize non-Russian nationalities and was no longer needed. After seventeen years of negotiations and long after Khruschev had passed from the scene, a new constitution was adopted with the federal structure intact. Even the Communist leaders of the national states in the USSR had refused to accept the change. Such changes as were introduced served to modify the ideal vision of the former constitution in line with the realities of the Soviet system.[10]

The Constitution as (Tempered) Political Ideal. This model is most closely identified with the Third World. It was pioneered in the nineteenth century by the Latin American countries, which must be considered part of the Third World in this as in many other respects. This model constitution combines an expression of what its citizens believe the regime should be with the basic structure of authority that will enable the current powerholders to rule with a measure of legitimacy. The former is presented without any serious expectation that the polity or regime will achieve that constitutional ideal, and the latter in anticipation of periodic change as rulers change, usually through revolution or coup. This model bears some superficial resemblance to the Communist model, but it has a political rather than a social revolutionary intent. In essence, then, Third World constitutions are designed to present an ideal picture of the institutional framework of the proper polity while simultaneously reflecting the character of already rooted power systems and the specifics of rule by the current powerholders.

Constitutional change in the Third World involves balancing regime realities with constitutional aspirations. Hence Third World polities seem to be constantly changing their constitutions in their entirety. Although each constitution is presented as new, usually there is a great continuity of basic articles from one document to the next, combined with changes in specifics to reflect each new regime.

The Latin American experience offers the best example of this fourth model because it has existed for the longest time. An examination of Latin American constitutions over the past 150 years or more reveals precisely this pattern: on the surface an apparently frequent change of documents but underneath substantial continuity in their contents. Each Latin American polity has had a "classic" constitution, usually adopted some time during or at the close of the first generation of independence, in which the fundamental tensions of the founding are sufficiently reconciled to enable the polity to continue to exist. Each subsequent constitution accepts this original reconciliation and adapts it to reconcile proximate regime reality with long-term constitutional aspirations. In most cases, after a revolution or coup, when a constitution is changed, the new powerholders will explicitly make the point that what they are doing is "temporary" or "interim," to make possible the achievement of larger constitutional aspirations. If this is so much rhetoric, as it usually is, it remains an important part of the Latin American political mythology.

The Constitution as a Modern Adaptation of an Ancient Traditional Constitution. Polities using this model have a deeply rooted commitment to what can only be characterized as an ancient and continuing constitutional tradition, rooted in their history or religion or both. This commitment frequently finds expression in what is conveniently referred to as an "unwritten constitution," which often encompasses a collection of documents of constitutional import, each of which marks (or purports to mark) an adaptation of the great tradition to changed circumstances.

No formally federal system relies upon such a constitution, but certain compound politics that use federal arrangements do. The United Kingdom is one example. The British constitution is celebrated for being just what is described above. Its piecemeal constitutional development has been uninterrupted at least since the Norman Conquest and perhaps even before if William the Conqueror's claims to the throne are recognized. The only time there has been constitution-writing in the United Kingdom or any of its constituent countries has been in connection with some strong necessity to clarify or adapt what are viewed as ancient principles, as in the case of the Magna Carta (1215), the 1689 Bill of Rights connected with the Glorious Revolution, and the 1832 Reform Act; and/or to establish new relationships among its constituent countries as in the case of the Act of Union between England and Scotland (1707) or the reconstitution of Ireland in the 1920s. Indeed, when this element has been lacking, efforts to change the British constitution in so formal a way have generally failed, as happened most recently in the attempted devolution of legislative powers to Scotland and Wales. At all times, constitutional change is achieved through ordinary legislative procedures, which are endowed by convention with constitutional status.[11]

Despite the tendency for each constitutional model to prevail in a particular geocultural area, the models should not be seen as strictly confined to a particular region. For example, India is an excellent example of a Third World country whose constitution is closer to the continental European pattern. The Indian constitution is not only more like a code than a frame of government, but it deliberately seeks to democratize the Indian political tradition through which the subcontinent has functioned for millennia as a decentralized empire with a relaxed system of governmental control that rarely penetrated beyond the elites.

Constitution-making brings us back to the essence of the political. However much extrapolitical forces may influence particular constitution-making situations or constitutional acts, ultimately both involve directly political expressions, involvements, and choices. In that sense, the dynamics of constitution-making have to do with questions of what Vincent Ostrom has termed constitutional choice.[12] Constitutional choice is more art than science. Scientific principles are involved in the making of constitutions, as the fathers of the United States Constitution of 1787 demonstrated in their reliance on the "new science of politics," which had discovered such vital principles of republican regimes as separation of powers, federalism, and the institution of the presidency.[13] But the combination of those elements and their adaptation to the constituency to be served is an art.

It is an even greater art to bring the constituency to endow the constitution with legitimacy. Constitutional legitimacy involves consent. It is certainly not a commitment that can be coerced—however much people can be coerced into obedience to a particular regime. Consensual legitimacy is utterly necessary for a constitution to have real meaning and to last. The very fact that, although rule can be imposed by force, constitutions can exist as meaningful instruments only by consent, means that constitutional documents cannot be treated in the abstract, divorced from the power systems of which they are a part and the political cultures from which they grow and to which they must respond.

It is well known, for example, that constitution-makers borrow from one another, not only within the framework of a particular constitutional tradition but across traditions as well—despite a general recognition by statesmen and political scientists alike that institutions cannot be simply transplanted from one political system to another. At an earlier time in the modern epoch, such borrowings were commonplace under all circumstances and were advocated by reformers as a matter of course. Through a process of trial and error, constitutional designers have learned the limits of borrowing. Constitutional architects and designers can borrow a mechanism here or there, but, in the last analysis, those mechanisms must be integrated in a manner that is true to the spirit of the civil society for which the constitution is designed.

At first glance, for example, the Spanish constitution of 1978 may seem to have certain consociational features, reflecting the influence of the Belgian constitution and its framers, but, in fact, Spain is not consociational because it does not give the nationalities within the country a real share in the national government as nationalities. Similarly, there are many apparently federal features of the Spanish constitution, in the sense that it constitutionalizes decentralization on a territorial basis, but, at the same time, it denies the autonomous territories a major role as territories in the national government. Indeed, the Spanish constitution deliberately rejects the constitutional principle that the territories have ancient rights (*fueros* in Spanish) other than those provided in the constitution itself, which is a matter of some contention in Spain's constitutional history.

The Italian constitution is closest to that of Spain with its system of regionalization, in which the regions are given certain autonomous powers of home rule without being involved *qua* regions in the general government. Indeed, the Italians borrowed their model from the pre–civil war Spanish republican constitution, and then Spain borrowed back some of the same ideas, very deliberately.[14] But Spain is not Italy, and its nationalities do not see themselves as merely regional expressions of a common Spanish culture as do those of Italy. Hence the reborrowing has involved a transformation as well.

The Spanish constitution of 1978 may have been the first step in the evolution of what, in Chapter 2 was referred to as foralist federalism—a combination of self-rule and shared-rule arrangements between the general government and the autonomous regional governments based upon bilateral negotiations between Madrid and each region, leading to special constitutional arrangements for each entity. This process offers the possibility of designing constitutional arrangements appropriate to the "personality" of each entity. Since each arrangement is then embodied in a constitutional document ratified bilaterally, the system is, in essence, a modern adaptation of the ancient Spanish system of *fueros* for a democratic state and hence is anchored in Spain's political culture.[15]

Noncentralization. The political system must reinforce the terms of the constitution through diffusion of power among a number of substantially self-sustaining centers, generally coincident with the constituent polities established by the federal compact. Noncentralization ensures that no matter how certain powers may be shared by the general and constituent governments at any particular time, the authority to participate in exercising them cannot be taken away from either without their mutual consent. Constituent polities in federal systems are able to participate as partners in national governmental activities and to act unilaterally with a high degree of autonomy in areas constitutionally open to them—even on crucial questions and even, to varying degrees, in opposition to national policies, because they possess effectively irrevocable powers.

Areal Division of Power. A third element that appears to be essential in any federal system is the internal division of authority and power on an areal basis, fully or partially, what has been called in the United States "territorial democracy."[16] It is theoretically possible to create a federal system whose constituent units are fixed but not territorially based and, indeed, such quasi-federal systems have existed. Protofederations of nomadic tribes have not been uncommon in history, and, as noted above, federal elements can be found in consociational polities constitutionally structured to accommodate social and political divisions along ethnic, religious, or even ideological lines. Nevertheless, it seems that federal systems require some areal basis for the federal division, though perhaps in combination with other elements.

As was suggested in Chapter 3, democracy has two "faces," one, the use of areal division to ensure neutrality and equality in the representation of the various groups and interests in the polity, and the other, in the use of such division to secure local autonomy and representation for diverse groups within the same civil society. Although seemingly contradictory, both faces are closely related to the purposes of federalism, and manifestations of both are frequently found side by side within the same federal systems. Territorial neutrality has proved highly adaptable to changing societies, allowing for the representation of new interests in proportion to their strength simply by allowing their supporters to vote in relatively equal territorial units. At the same time, the accommodation of very diverse groups whose differences are fundamental rather than transient within the same polity by giving them territorial power bases of their own has enhanced the ability of federal systems to function as vehicles of political integration while preserving democratic government.

Historically, constitutionally fixed areal divisions of power have been necessary to maintain noncentralization. In modern democratic theory, the argument between federalists and pluralists has frequently revolved around the respective values of areal and functional diffusions of power. Theorists who have argued the obsolescence of federalism while endorsing the values used to justify its existence have generally based their case on the argument that the areal division of powers is unnecessary to preserve liberty and, indeed, may interfere with its protection. Proponents of the federal-areal division argue that the deficiencies of territorial democracy are greatly overshadowed by the advantages of a guaranteed power base that it offers different groups in the political system coupled with the neutrality of areal representation of functional interests, arguing further that any other system devised for giving them power has proved unable to cope with the complexities and changes of interests endemic in a dynamic age while certainly limiting the advantages for local differentiation inherent in the areal system.

Studies of federal systems indicate the existence of other supportive elements that supplement the three basic ones. Although all of them are not always present in every federal system, their near-universality leads to the conclusion that they serve important functions for the maintenance of federalism in each. Similarly, although many of them are found individually in various kinds of political systems, it is their combination within a single system structured around the basic elements that is characteristic of federalism. They can be grouped according to their primary impact on the systems they serve.

Maintaining Union

Generally characteristic of modern federal systems are direct lines of communication between the public and both the general and constituent governments allowing the public to influence both governments directly and permitting the governments to exercise direct authority over a common citizenry. The people may (and usually do) elect representatives to all governments that serve them. All of the governments may (and usually do) administer programs so as to serve the individual citizen directly. The courts may serve both planes of government, applying the relevant laws directly to the citizens.

The existence of those direct lines of communication—one of the major features distinguishing federations from confederations—is usually predicated on the existence of a sense of common nationality or citizenship binding the constituent polities and people of federal nations together, another element requisite for the maintenance of a successful federal system. In some countries, this sense has been inherited, and in most it has had to be invented. Federalism in Germany has been based on a common sense of an inherited German nationhood. In the United States, Argentina, and Australia a sense of nationhood had to be at least partly invented. National consciousness soon became second nature in those countries because none of their constituent states (or sections) ever had more than a partially developed national consciousness of its own apart from the larger national ties. Canada, Switzerland, and Yugoslavia have had to invent a sense of common nationality or citizenship, or at least political identity strong enough to embrace "nationality groups" with intense national feelings rooted in the constituent polities. In such newly formed federal systems as India, Malaysia, and Nigeria, the future of the polity as such, as well as its federal system, is endangered by the absence of a common sense of nationality. Contrary to some theories, federalism has not proved to be a particularly good device for integrating diverse nationalities into a single political system unless it has been accompanied by other factors compelling integration.[17]

Geographic necessity has been a major factor promoting the maintenance of union within federal systems even in the face of strong pressures toward disunion. The Mississippi Valley in the United States, the Alps in Switzerland, the island character of the Australian continent, and the mountains and jungles surrounding Brazil have served as direct geographic influences promoting unity. More political than "natural" but no less compelling geographically have been the pressures for Canadian union generated by that country's neighbor to the south or for the federation of the German states generated by their neighbors to the east and west.[18]

Maintaining Noncentralization

The constituent polities in a federal system must be fairly equal in population and wealth or at least balanced geographically or numerically in their inequalities if noncentralization is to be maintained. The United States has been able to overcome its internal inequalities because each geographic section has included both great and small states. In Canada, the ethnic differences between the two largest and richest provinces have served to inject balance into the system. The existence of groups of cantons in different size categories has helped maintain Swiss federalism. Similar distributions exist in every other system whose federal character is not in question.[19]

The existence of a large polity dominating smaller states with which it is nominally federated on equal terms has often been a major reason for the failure of federalism. In the German federal empire of the late nineteenth century, Prussia was so obviously dominant that the other states had little opportunity to provide national leadership or even a reasonably strong hedge against the desires of its king, who was also the German emperor, and government. Similarly, even without the problem of the Communist party, the existence of the Russian Soviet Federal Socialist Republic occupying three-fourths of the area and containing three-fifths of the population of the USSR would have severely crippled the possibilities of maintaining authentic federal relationships in that country.

Successful federal systems have also been characterized by the permanence of the boundaries of their constituent units.[20] This does not mean that boundaries cannot be changed, but it does mean that as a matter of constitutional law such changes can be made only with the consent of the polities involved and that, as a matter of political policy, they are avoided except in the most extreme situations. Boundary changes have occurred in the "classic" federal systems—the United States divided Virginia during its Civil War, Canada has enlarged the boundaries of its provinces, and Switzerland has divided cantons—but they have been the exception rather than the rule and in every case except the division of Virginia were done with the consent of the constituent polities. Even the latter required and obtained Virginia's formal consent, however coerced.

Even in weaker federal systems, such as those of Latin America, state boundaries have tended to remain relatively secure. Indeed, one of the major bulwarks of federalism in Latin America has been the coincidence of state boundaries with major social and economic interests or ethnic-cultural groups that has given them an importance that transcends the periodic diminution of the political autonomy of their governments. When the boundary changes have been made as part of a founding or refounding, as in the postwar re-drawing of boundaries in West Germany to account for the diminished territory of the Federal Republic and the altera-tion of state lines to recognize linguistic unities in India, the historic heartlands of the polities involved have been pre-served.

In a few very important cases, noncentralization is both reflected and supported through the constitutionally guar-anteed existence of different systems of law in the constitu-ent polities. Though the differences in those systems are likely to be somewhat eroded over time—the extent of their preservation varying from system to system—their con-tinued existence as separate systems and the national mix-ture of laws which their existence promotes act as great bulwarks against centralization. In the United States, each state's legal system stems directly and to a certain extent uniquely from English (and in one case French) law while federal law occupies an interstitial position, binding the systems of the fifty states together insofar as necessary. The resulting mixture of laws keeps the administration of justice even in federal courts substantially noncentralized. In Canada, the existence of common law and civil law systems side by side is one constitutional guarantee of French-Canadian cultural survival.

Noncentralized legal systems are a particularly Anglo-American device, often used in legislative as well as federal unions (the Scots, for example have preserved their own legal system in Scotland under the terms of the Act of Union). They are rare in other political cultures and have become less common in all federal systems established since 1900. More common is the provision for modification of national legal codes by the subnational governments to meet special local needs, as in Switzerland.[21]

In caudillistic federal systems, noncentralization often is maintained through local jefes maintaining power bases in the constituent states. Very little attention has been paid to the relationship between political structure and military power in federal systems where the military is powerful. For example, in Brazil, up until the Vargas years, the military was organized on a state-by-state basis, so that Brazilian federalism meant something principally because the army, which was the equivalent of the party system in other polities, was organized along federal lines with various generals having their power bases in the states.[22] Apparently, a similar system exists in Nigeria under military rule.[23]

For bureaucratic states, it is necessary to examine how bureaucracies are organized. It is not accidental that in central Europe, where civil societies are highly bureaucratic in character, the tendency has been for the federal government to operate almost exclusively through the bureaucracies of the constituent units. Implicit in this arrangement is some sense—perhaps intuitive—that if a federal bureaucracy were to be created to perform federal functions, it would overwhelm the constituent units.[24]

The point is generally well taken that unless the constituent polities have substantial influence over the formal or informal constitutional amending process, the federal character of the system is open to question. Since many constitutional changes are made without recourse to formal constitutional amendment, the position of the constituent polities must be additionally protected by a constitution designed so that any serious changes in the political order can be made only by the decision of dispersed majorities which reflect the areal division of powers. This protection, which federal theorists have argued is important for popular government as well as for federalism, is a feature of the most truly federal systems.

Noncentralization is strengthened in all federal systems by giving the constituent polities guaranteed representation in the federal legislature and often by giving them a guaranteed role in the federal political process. In some federal systems, notably those of the United States and Switzerland, the latter is guaranteed in the written constitution. In others such as Canada and those in Latin America, certain powers of participation have been acquired and have become part of the traditional constitution.

The long struggle over the patriation of the Canadian constitution foundered more than once over the amendment issue. From the first, it was an accepted convention that no amendments of the British North America Act would be enacted by the British Parliament, its custodian, without the agreement of both Ontario and Quebec. This convention gave meaning to the theory that the Canadian constitution was the product of a compact between the two peoples of Canada. Subsequently, the smaller provinces were able to assert their veto over undesired constitutional changes through the Premiers' Conference, the regular meeting of the federal and provincial prime ministers in which most of the basic decisions of Canadian governance were made. This was another institution developed by convention rather than enacted into law. The latter body agreed to change the two-province veto system in 1981 for one involving a dispersed majority of provinces, thereby breaking deadlock and allowing patriation to take place.[25]

Students of federal systems have tended to focus their attention on the federal constitutions that frame the entire polity while neglecting the constitutional arrangements of the constituent polities. Concern with constituent state constitutions has tended to be an American phenomenon and even there confined to those interested in state constitutional reform. In fact, the constitutions of constituent states are part and parcel of the total constitutional structure of federal systems and play a vital role in giving the system direction.

The United States has a living and active tradition of constituent state constitutions and constitution-making going back to colonial times. That tradition is reinforced by the continuing processes of constitutional design: regular referenda on state constitutional amendments in most states, periodic constitutional conventions to achieve major constitutional revisions or comprehensive constitutional change, and state supreme court decisions that shape state constitutional law. As Albert Sturm points out, since 1776, the fifty American states have had 146 constitutions (although nineteen states are still served by their original documents as amended). They have held 230 constitutional conventions and have dealt with uncounted referenda on constitutional issues to develop what is perhaps the richest mine of constitutional experience of any people in the history of the world.[26]

In Switzerland, there has been an upsurge in cantonal constitutional revision efforts since 1965 in an effort to clarify cantonal-federal and cantonal-local relations to reflect the new conditions of cooperative federalism; better delineate the tasks (powers, in American terminology) of the three branches of cantonal government and the relationships among them; expand the list of cantonal tasks to take into account the welfare states; improve protection of individual rights vis-à-vis a more powerful government; provide greater citizen access and participation in the political process; and redefine the relationship between church and state (which are not separated in Switzerland).

The results of these efforts have been mixed—Swiss voters have rejected as many of the proposed changes as they have accepted—but it is fair to conclude that the art of cantonal constitutional design is being revived in Switzerland. All told, the Swiss experience would not be unfamiliar to Americans, even if the Swiss approach is more formalistic and the scope of cantonal constitutions greater.[27]

Each of the six Yugoslav republics has its own written constitution, as do the two autonomous provinces within the Serbian Republic. But, as one might expect in a Communist polity with a continental tradition of constitutional design, the federal, republic, and provincial constitutions are frequently changed to reflect regime changes and are always changed in tandem to maintain constitutional harmony and symmetry. As Steven L. Burg suggests, "The politics of constitution-making in Yugoslavia have been shaped largely by the impact of conflicts arising out of the coincidence of ethnonational, regional and economic differences; by the development of the Yugoslav ideology of self-management; and by the strong commitment of the Communist party leadership to unity" since Yugoslavia adopted its first federal constitution in 1946.[28]

Communist rule is a major element to be considered in

connection with constitutional design in Yugoslavia. Also, in the continental European tradition, Yugoslav constitutions are long and highly specific documents. Hence there is a need to change them as frequently as power distributions are changed in the political sphere. In contrast to the American and Swiss situations, the constitutional process in Yugoslavia is very centralized indeed; yet since 1967 the overall trend has been toward the individuation of the constituent state constitutions in reflection of the growing power of both the republics and the provinces as expressions of ethnonational aspirations within the federal system. As a result, despite the interlocking system of constitutional change, Yugoslavia is more like a confederation today than a federation. With its republics so strong, their constitutions take on added importance.

On the other hand, in the recently adopted Nigerian federal constitution, the now nineteen states relinquished their right to separate constitutions and instead accepted a reliance upon the appropriate articles of the federal document. The reasons for this were to assure greater national unity and intergovernmental comity.[29] This does not leave them entirely without individual constitutional frameworks but does establish their full dependence on common action in the federal arena to achieve major constitutional change. Under the previous federal constitutions, the states (or regions, as they were then called) had the right and obligation to draft their own constitutions but within clearly prescribed limits.

The 1979 federal constitution was designed to restore civilian rule to Nigeria. It was developed over a three-year period, first by the Constitutional Drafting Committee and then by the Constituent Assembly; the document was finally promulgated by the Federal Military Government. As L. Adele Jinadu points out, "In Nigeria, federalism is viewed primarily as a political device to protect ethnic interests which militate against unitary government." In this respect, Nigeria is like Yugoslavia rather than the United States. But whereas Yugoslavia has a single ruling party to hold together its diverse ethnic groups, Nigeria does not and is constantly threatened by centrifugal pulls as a result. The ethnic theme pervades Nigerian constitutional design, which included the establishment of seven new states in 1976 as part of the constitutional process. The new federal constitution was both more centralized in thrust than its predecessors and more explicitly designed to protect ethnic interests through the states and local governments.

These four examples highlight the three principal approaches to constituent state constitution-making. Looking at all nineteen formally federal systems (Table 5.1), in eleven the constituent states have their own constitutions, with at least two, Czechoslovakia and the USSR, following the Yugoslav model with even more centralization and less state discretion. The Latin American federal polities also tend to follow the Yugoslav model. Their military or highly hierarchical civilian regimes do not tolerate significant constitutional independence on the part of the states any more than they tolerate political competition. As in Yugoslavia, the less tolerant the federal ruling elite is of differences, the more it insists on de jure conformity in the constituent state constitutions. Austria and the German Federal Republic follow the Swiss model, combining detailed documents with their meticulous application and requiring formal amendment rather than interpretation to change existing arrangements.

India and Pakistan follow the Nigerian model of a common constitution for their federal and state governments. The Australian states and Canadian provinces are governed by constitutional statutes rather than true written constitutions. In all four cases, state fundamental law is of little significance. Constitutionalism is made manifest in other

Table 5.1. *Constitutional Arrangements of Constituent States in Federal Systems*

Separate Written Constitutions	Constitutional Statutes	Common Federal/State Constitutions
Argentina	Australia	Comoro Islands
Austria	Canada	India
Brazil		Nigeria
Czechoslovakia		Pakistan
German Federal Republic		United Arab Emirates
Malaysia		
Mexico		
Switzerland		
USA		
USSR		
Venezuela		
Yugoslavia		

political ways through parliamentary processes, all of which require more study.

In addition to these formally federal systems, many of the constituent units of other political systems using federal arrangements also have constitutions worthy of investigation. Table 5.2 lists selected examples that may be of particular interest because of their vitality or historical character. No doubt there are others worthy of inclusion.

Recent studies have shown that the existence of a noncentralized party system is perhaps the most important single element in the maintenance of federal noncentralization.[30] Noncentralized parties initially develop because of the constitutional arrangements of the federal compact, but once they have come into existence, they tend to be self-perpetuating and to function as decentralizing forces in their own right. The United States and Canada provide two examples of the different forms that can be assumed by a

Table 5.2. *Constitutional Arrangements of Constituent Entities in Political Systems Utilizing Federal Arrangements (Selected Cases)*

Separate Written Constitutions	Constitutional Statute/Federal Charters	Common Constitutions
Zanzibar–Tanzania	Andorra–France	Finland–Aaland
Puerto Rico–USA	and Spain	Islands
	Italy–5 special	UK-Scotland,
	regions	Wales
	Cook Islands–New	
	Zealand	
	Azores–Portugal	
	Spain–autonomous	
	communities	
	UK–Jersey,	
	Guernsey, Man	

noncentralized party system. In the United States, where party responsibility is minimal and virtually nonexistent on the national plane, a nationwide two-party system has developed with parties actually coalitions of the several state parties (which are, in turn, sometimes dominated by specific local party organizations) that function as national units only for the quadrennial presidential elections or for purposes of organizing the national congress. Party financing and decision-making functions are dispersed either among the state organizations or among widely divergent factions operating nationwide.

In Canada, on the other hand, the parliamentary form of government with its concomitant requirements of party responsibility means that on the national plane considerably more party cohesiveness must be maintained simply to gain and hold power. The noncentralized party system in Canada has developed through fragmentation of the parties along regional or provincial lines. The one or two parties that function on a nationwide basis are subject to great shifts in electoral support from election to election. Moreover, they are divided internally along provincial lines with each provincial organization more or less autonomous as in the United States and, at the same time, individual provinces are frequently dominated by regional parties that send only a few representatives to the national legislature. Very often, the party victorious in national elections is the only one able to expand its provincial electoral bases to momentarily national proportions.[31]

Federal systems in which parliamentary government is the norm resemble the Canadian model. Australia and Switzerland come closest to paralleling it, and traces of it can be found in the Federal Republic of Germany.[32] A more centralized variation of the same pattern exists in countries like India, which are dominated by a very large and diffuse national party held together nationally by personal leadership but factionalized in the states, which must share the governing power in one way or another with a host of other parties in the state arenas.[33]

Federal polities with less developed party systems frequently gain some of the same decentralizing effects through what the Latins call *caudillismo*—noncentralized personal leadership systems that diffuse power through strong local leaders operating in the constituent polities.[34] Caudillistic noncentralization is most characteristic of Latin American federal systems but apparently exists in such new federations as Nigeria and Malaysia as well.[35]

The importance to federalism of a noncentralized party system is well illustrated by contrast with those formally federal nations dominated by one highly centralized party such as the USSR, Czechoslovakia, Yugoslavia, and Mexico. In all four cases, the dominant party has operated severely to limit the power of the constituent polities in direct proportion to the extent of its dominance. Decentralization has taken place in one of them, Yugoslavia, as the League of Communists has been restructured along republican lines, with power passing to the leagues in each of the constituent republics.[36]

Ultimately, however, noncentralization is maintained to the extent that there is respect for the federal principle abroad within each federal system. Such respect is necessarily reflected in the immediate recognition by the decision-making publics that the preservation of the constituent polities is as important as the preservation of the nation as a whole. In the words of the American Chief Justice Salmon P. Chase, federalism looks to "an indestructible Union, composed of indestructible States" (*Texas* v. *White,* 7 Wallace [1869]). This recognition may be based on loyalty to particular constituent polities or on an understanding of the role played by federalism in animating the political system along certain unique lines. Thus those who value government by conciliation and partnership with emphasis on local control are likely to have respect for the federal principle.

Federalism can exist only where there is a considerable tolerance of diversity and willingness to take political action through the political arts of negotiation even when the power to act unilaterally is available. The usual prerequisite to action in federal systems is the ability to build consensus rather than the power to threaten coercion. Western federal nations can furnish many examples of the exercise of national self-restraint in dealing with difficult federal problems. Even in a federal system as centralized as that of India, the constitutional right of the national government to assume control of the state governments is exercised as little as possible and then only temporarily to promote regime stability.

The historical record indicates that the dual purpose implied in Chase's dictum has been at least as responsible for the creation of federal systems as the single interest in political unification. The Canadian confederation came into being not only to create a new nation out of the British North American colonies but to give Ontario and Quebec autonomous political systems of their own. Similarly, every move toward greater union in the Swiss confederation has been made to preserve the independence of the cantons from both outside encroachment and revolutionary centralism. A good case can be made that similar motivations were also important in the creation of most other federal systems.

Maintaining the Federal Principle

Several of the devices commonly found in federal systems serve to maintain the federal principle per se and are consequently supportive of both the federal government and the constituent polities. Two of these are particularly common and important.

The maintenance of federalism requires that the common polity and its constituent polities each have a substantially complete set of governing institutions of their own with the right—within limits set by the compact—to modify those institutions unilaterally. Both separate legislative and administrative institutions are necessary. This does not mean that all governmental activities must be carried out by separate institutions on each plane. It is possible for the agencies of one government to serve as agents of the other by mutual agreement. What is essential is that each government have enough of its own institutions to function in the areas of its authority without depending upon the other and to have the structural wherewithal to cooperate freely with the other's counterpart agencies.

Judicial review is another device widely used for surveying the maintenance of federal principles. A. V. Dicey, one of the first to observe federal systems systematically, suggested that they characteristically turn to litigation instead of legislation to resolve difficult policy problems. It has been said that in the American system, every political question eventually becomes a judicial one. Constitutional courts, then, are permanent institutions in many federal systems, serving as devices for maintaining both union and noncentralization.[37]

The United States Supreme Court remains the most prominent of the great constitutional courts. Its influence on the shape of American federalism has been decisive. The Australian Supreme Court has similar status and powers and has been instrumental in shaping Australian federalism. The German Constitutional Court has risen in prominence in recent years, and the Canadian Supreme Court is about to gain substantial power in the wake of the patriation of the British North America Act with the addition of a charter of rights giving that court great new responsibilities and opportunities to interpret federal rights and related questions. Even earlier, Canadian federalism was reoriented by judicial decisions of the British Privy Council.

Other constitutional courts such as those of India, the Latin American federal systems, and Malaysia have had somewhat less success because the traditions of judicial decision making vis-à-vis strong leaders have been less well established in those countries and the courts themselves have acted gingerly on issues which in other federal systems would have been tackled more vigorously.

The only federal system not to place great emphasis on a similar role for constitutional courts is Switzerland, where the referendum has taken the place of litigation in dealing with most federal questions.

Second federal chambers in which the constituent states

are represented are another device for maintaining federalism, offering the opportunity to protect constituent state
interests and also give the states an effective role in the
federal government. Perhaps the most effective second
chamber from this perspective is the German Bundesrat,
which clearly speaks for the *lander* in both respects. The
Yugoslav Council of the Republics approaches it in effectiveness. The United States Senate is one of the least effective federal chambers because its members are elected *ad
personum* and are not required to represent their states per se.
The decorative Canadian Senate does not even pretend to
perform a serious federalist function.[38]

In most federal systems, noncentralization and territorial
democracy are made operationally effective by intergovernmental partnerships that have grown up within the framework of their respective constitutions. In the United States,
Mexico, and Nigeria, this partnership is based on a well-
nigh universal sharing of functions among governments on
all planes, involving a complex of deep-seated governmental and political arrangements designed to recognize and
accommodate national and local interests and to preserve
the basic integrities of the several governments that participate in the system, while mobilizing sufficient energy to
maintain and develop positive public programs. In Canada
and Australia, it is based more on sharing of revenues coupled with a division of functions among governments. In
South American federal systems, the partnership is based
upon all governments providing the same services for the
same populations simultaneously but separately with coor-
dination through the political sphere.[39] In Switzerland,
Germany, and Austria, it is based on a relatively sharp de-
marcation of responsibilities coordinated through highly
structured legal and administrative formulas.[40] India relies
on a high level of administrative collaboration within the
content of a highly conflict-oriented political environment,

and Malaysia emphasizes negotiation among the rulers of the states. The United Arab Emirates divide common tasks among the constituent governments with each taking on the administration of particular responsibilities.

In this regard, the contractual sharing of public responsibilities by all governments in the system appears to be a central characteristic of federalism. Sharing, broadly conceived, includes common involvement in policy making, financing, and administration of government activities. In contemporary federal systems it is characterized by extensive intergovernmental collaboration. Sharing can be based on highly formal arrangements or informal agreements. In federal systems, it is usually contractual in nature. The contract—politically a limited expression of the compact principle—is used in formal arrangements as a legal device to enable governments responsible to separate polities to engage in joint action while remaining independent entities. Even where government agencies cooperate without formally contracting to do so, the spirit of federalism that pervades ongoing federal systems tends to infuse a sense of contractual obligation into the participating parties.

In any federal system, it is likely that there will be continued tension between the federal government and the constituent polities over the years and that different "balances" between them will develop at different times. The existence of this tension is an integral part of the federal relationship, and its character does much to determine the future of federalism in each system. The questions of intergovernmental relations which it produces are perennially a matter of public concern because virtually all other political issues arising in a federal system are phrased in terms of their implication for federalism as part of the public discussion surrounding them. In this way, federalism imposes a way of looking at problems that stands apart from the substantive issues raised by the problems themselves. This is particularly true of issues that affect the very fabric of society. In the United States, for example, the race question inevitably is a problem of federal-state relations as is the cultural question in Canada and the linguistic question in India.

In the last analysis, federalism is a form of popular government embodying elements of both republicanism and democracy. The federal structures occasionally adopted by nondemocratic systems must generally be considered "window dressing" except insofar as their injection may serve as a democratizing force. In Yugoslavia, for example, the existence of a federal structure specifically developed to maintain unity in a multinational state plagued by separatist tendencies proved useful in fostering such decentralization as the Communist party leadership wished to allow in the early days of the Tito regime. In recent years, federalism has played a major role in stimulating new decentralization tendencies and in fostering a truly noncentralized system of government in that polity.

Local Government in Federal Systems

In this connection, it is useful to examine the place of local government in federal systems, particularly in light of the massive urbanization that has characterized the modern world since the seventeenth and, most especially, the eighteenth centuries. From the very beginning of the modern era until the present time there has been more or less linear progression toward greater concentration of population in urban areas in all countries. This linear progression has followed an accelerating curve at least since the late eighteenth century (the halfway point in the three-hundred-year modern epoch when the world's population began its dramatic increase). Although this urban revolution is widely recognized and well documented, it is all too often treated as if it were of a single piece worldwide, without due regard to differences in local environment, culture, and social and political structures.

It has been noted that federalism orders civil societies, their politics and territories, in at least four ways: (1) by establishing a certain kind of constitutional and legal framework for them; (2) by encouraging certain geographic patterns within them; (3) by influencing their political culture basis; and, (4) by shaping the political behavior of their residents or citizens. Each of these points in turn may shape the patterns of urbanization and urban politics in distinctive ways.

The implications of a federal constitutional-legal framework for cities are many and varied. In most federal systems, the essential bargain is between a general government and state governments or their equivalent. In such cases, local government—even the local governments of major cities—occupies a constitutionally subordinate position. Some federal systems have made special accommodations to give local governments more constitutionally protected autonomy, and a few, like Yugoslavia, have built them into the constitutional framework on a basis of equality.[41] In the United States, for example, all local governments are legally the creatures of their states. At the same time, even in the United States, the states have acted in that direction although they have not been required to do so by the terms of the federal compact. What happens is that the basic noncentralized relationship between the federal government and the states has been extended de facto through the political process to the localities as well and has been affirmed in the overwhelming majority of state constitutions through local home rule provisions. American local governments have gained a substantial measure of entrenched political power because they have been able to capitalize on the spirit of noncentralization—the spirit of federalism, if you will—

in their day-to-day operations and in their bargaining with other governments.[42]

Noncentralization makes it possible for local governments to develop policies and programs of their own within systems that are often too complex to allow them the luxury of isolation, to acquire outside aids for carrying out those policies and programs, and to adapt those aids to their own needs. They are usually encouraged to do so by state and federal authorities, but they do so even without encouragement.

In sum, when federal principles are translated into political structures, real possibilities are opened up for governmental arenas of all sizes to maintain the ability to act freely within the complexities of the whole. Their success in doing so depends upon the interaction of the particular elements of political structure, culture, and process present in each civil society. For example, local autonomy is deeply embedded in the political cultures of both Switzerland and the United States but in significantly different ways. Localism in Switzerland is based on a commitment to the stability of local citizenship never present in the always highly mobile American society. Every Swiss is first a citizen of his commune, and only through that citizenship can he acquire a cantonal and federal citizenship. The idea of the commune as a self-sufficient political unit with regard to those tasks entrusted to it has diminished in the face of modern realities but remains strong.[43]

In the United States, on the other hand, the long tradition of intergovernmental cooperation has led to the expression of the commitment to local autonomy through the idea of local control; that is, a local community should be able to control, administratively or politically, the many state and federal programs that affect it and thereby maintain its integrity as a body politic.[44]

Even with the great expansion of the velocity of government in the United States in the twentieth century and the increased role of the state and federal governments in local affairs, the cultural bias toward local self-government has survived by adapting itself as a bias for local control of activities in the locality regardless of who stimulates or finances them. In both cases, cities have the "right" to demand great autonomy vis-à-vis the federal and state governments, on one hand, and vis-à-vis sister municipalities within a particular metropolitan area, on the other. The great growth of suburbs adjacent to the major cities in both countries has led to a division of governmental powers among many local governments within a single urban region, each of which has come to represent very real interests, ideological as well as material, that are preserved by the citizenry regardless of any patterns of economic integration that might prevail locally.

In Canada, on the other hand, the provinces have always been more important than the local governments, constitutionally and politically. Of all federal systems, Canada probably provides the least recognition of local self-rule, formally or in practice. (Nigeria provides almost no formal recognition of local self-rule, but its multiethnic character has functioned in practice as a localizing force.) Hence several of provincial Canadian governments have felt free unilaterally to consolidate metropolitan areas under single governments or to reorganize existing municipal jurisdictions into metropolitan federations. Such steps would not be tolerated in either the United States or Switzerland despite the legal powers possessed by many of the states and cantons to do so.[45]

Antecedent Influences on Contemporary Federal Systems

Federal systems or systems strongly influenced by federal principles have been among the most stable and long-lasting of polities. But relatively few political cultures have proved suitable environments for federal forms of government. Anglo-American civil societies have adopted them most successfully. Even those not fully committed to federalism have, without exception, included federal principles in whatever systems they have chosen, no doubt because both constitutionalism and noncentralization rate high on the scale of Anglo-American political values.

Of the nineteen formally federal polities and the twenty-three that use federal principles in the world today, twenty-one have a British connection (Table 5.3). These include all the nations established since World War II that have been able to maintain federal systems, and they provide most of the successful examples of federalism in operation.

Table 5.3. *Federal Systems and Arrangements: The British Connection*

Federal Systems	Federal Arrangements
Australia	Antigua and Barbuda
Canada	Union of Burma
India	Republic of Ghana
Malaysia	Israel
Nigeria	Papua–New Guinea
Pakistan	Solomon Islands
United Arab Emirates	Republic of South Africa
United States	South West Africa (Namibia)
	Democratic Republic of Sudan
	United Republic of Tanzania
	United Kingdom of Great Britain and Northern Ireland
	Republic of Vanuatu/New Hebrides

Of the eleven remaining federal polities and the ten others using federal principles, Argentina, Brazil, Colombia,

Mexico, Portugal, Spain, and Venezuela fall directly within the Hispanic political tradition, and Austria, Belgium, Czechoslovakia, Germany, Switzerland, and Italy fall within the political tradition of the Holy Roman Empire. Both political traditions have been influential in stimulating federal inclinations in many of the nonfederal nations, but they have been notably less successful in fostering lasting federal institutions. The Hispanic tradition has failed to combine federalism and stability, and the Germanic has tended toward authoritarian centralization. Federal arrangements or efforts in that direction in Yugoslavia, Iraq, Lebanon, and Cyprus represent adaptations of the millet system that has been a feature of the Near East since the Byzantine Empire, if not earlier, and Israel combines elements of the Jewish federal tradition with millet adaptations. The USSR and China use adaptations of older imperial systems with a minimal nod to authentic federalism.

The successful operation of federal systems requires a political environment conducive to popular government and with the traditions of political cooperation and self-restraint that are needed to maintain a system that minimizes the use of coercion. Beyond the level of tradition, federal systems operate best in societies with sufficient homogeneity of fundamental interests—or consensus—to allow a great deal of latitude to local government in political operations and to place primary reliance upon voluntary collaboration. The existence of severe strains on the body politic, which lead to the use of force to maintain domestic order, are even more inimical to the successful maintenance of federal patterns of government than to other forms of popular government. Moreover, federal systems are most successful in civil societies that have the human resources to fill many public offices competently and sufficient material resources to allow a measure of economic waste in payment for the luxury of liberty.

Thinking Federal:
The Role of Political Culture

In the last analysis, the maintenance of federalism involves "thinking federal," that is, being oriented toward the
ideals and norms of republicanism, constitutionalism, and
power sharing that are essential to the federal way. It has
already been noted that there are formally federal polities
that exist despite contrary ideologies, such as the Soviet
Union, where the force of geohistorical circumstance requires at least a nod toward federalism, but in the last analysis, such polities are federal in name only, reflecting the
tribute that vice pays to virtue. It is equally true that many
of the political systems that use federal arrangements deliberately abjure the word for reasons of their own, also in
response to particular geohistorical circumstances. On the
other hand, there is no federal system that is commonly
viewed as successful by the standards of federalism whose
people do not think federal, that does not have a federal
political culture and a strong will to use federal principles
and arrangements.

There has been much discussion about what constitutes a
federal political culture and how important having such a
political culture is in the animation of federal systems.[46]
Increasingly, however, students of federalism agree that
there is such a thing and that it is important. The Swiss may
well represent the most clear-cut example of a people with a
federal political culture. Their bearing and relationship to
one another are manifestations of such a political culture,
which is reflected in their music, art, and literature as much
as in their politics and in the constant cultivation of balance,
of collegiality, of the involvement of the widest variety of
groups in consultations surrounding decisions if not in actual decision making. On an individual level, there is the
noted Swiss ability to provide service without seeming in

the least bit servile. All of these elements are reflections of the Swiss federal political culture.[47]

Because culture in the United States is more dynamic and associated with changes in style than is the case in Switzerland, the specific federal elements in American political culture are perhaps harder to pin down. Like the Swiss, they are manifested in literature as well as politics and may reach their fullest expression in American folklore. In a sense, the American cowboy as the archetypal figure in American folklore is presented as the most prominent manifestation of federal political culture. He is able to work for and with others as a hired hand without surrendering an iota of his independence. It is culturally significant that the standard greeting of one cowboy to another was "pardner." Were Americans, for some unfortunate reason, to adopt a common salutation to express an ideological commitment on the order of the Communist "comrade," pardner would be it.[48] For that very reason, it is significant that most federal political cultures have equivalent terms, such as "mate" in Australia, and *haver* in Hebrew.

Even federal systems that lack a fully federal political culture usually have appropriate analogues. In Nigeria, for example, where three principal ethnic groups dominate the country, there is every evidence that the Ibo have a fully federal political culture and that the culture of the Yoruba, based on power sharing among oligarchies, is adaptable to federalism. Hausa-Fulani culture to the north, however, which is apparently hierarchical, is antithetical to federalism in the same measure that it is open to Islam, a hierarchical religious ideology. Thus Nigeria has a strong basis in federalism but also a strong culturally induced tension built into its federal system.[49]

India's political culture looks toward a kind of decentralized imperialism as the classic pattern of the Indian polity, going back well over twenty-five hundred years.

The great empires of Indian history were all of this character, possessing strong power centers but recognized peripheries exercising power legitimately and fully responsible for carrying out imperial decisions in ways adapted to local conditions. That no Indian imperial power before the British sought to improve internal communications within the country, even to build suitable roads, reflects this acceptance of institutionalized decentralization. The same political culture remains pronounced in contemporary India. The Indian constitution refers to India as a union and the government in New Delhi as "the centre," when, in fact, the constitutional system provides for the same kind of decentralized imperial rule on a republican basis that was familiar in prerepublican days of the subcontinent.[50]

It is surely no accident that the classic federal systems of the West serve countries in which ideas of covenant and compact were part of the common coin of the realm and provided the foundation for political thought. The federal theology of the Reformation originated in Switzerland and reached its fullest flowering there, in the United Provinces of the Netherlands, and in the United States. Theories of the political compact developed in Britain when the United Kingdom was a dual monarchy on its way to becoming a union. The synthesis between covenant ideas in religion and politics made the Rhineland the traditional heartland of liberal republicanism in Germany. The German Federal Republic has been successful at least partly because it represents the western third of Germany anchored in the Rhineland and does not include hierarchical Prussia (which is the heartland of the most efficient of the Soviet bloc dictatorships). Even in South Africa, where the relations between whites and nonwhites are hardly federal or covenantal, the relationship among whites remains so, a reflection of the federal political culture which the Afrikaaners brought with them from their Dutch and Huguenot backgrounds.

The will to federate, though almost invariably encouraged by the existence of a federal political culture, may exist for other reasons as well. It is usually a response to a particular situation that makes the introduction of federal arrangements the best and most acceptable solution to some difficult problem. A federal solution may be accepted reluctantly. In such cases implementation of the solution is usually problematic. Canada's primordial francophone and anglophone political cultures are both somewhat deficient in their federal dimensions—the first with its Gallic penchant for hierarchical centralization and the second with its English orientation toward the organic Westminster model of rule. Nevertheless, by the mid-nineteenth century, necessity brought Canadians to accept federation as the only way to attain national unity. Subsequent crises have led to the reaffirmation of that choice, also out of necessity. Consequently, Canada has developed a strong will to federate in its pursuit of national unity, which, in turn, has intensified the political cultural dimensions of its federalism.[51]

The will to federate involves just that—the desire to build a compound polity on the basis of republican principles, embodied in an appropriate constitutional framework and including power sharing as a fundamental element. Most attempts to establish federal systems fail because of a lack of sufficient will to federate, perhaps because of lack of a sufficiently federal political culture, perhaps for other reasons.

Federal polities that have undergone civil wars and have reemerged as federal systems are excellent examples of the will to federate. The United States, Nigeria, and Switzerland come to mind in this connection.

Although it has often been claimed that the American Civil War was a product of American federalism, in fact it was a product of two conflicting social systems that would probably have come into conflict even sooner under a unitary system of government with no mediating institutions to delay the confrontation. What is significant, however, is that once the North was victorious it was clear that the South had to be reintegrated on a federal basis. Even Radical Reconstruction never proposed doing away with the southern states as states, but only wished to reconstruct them in such a way as to ensure the triumph of abolitionist principles by destroying the remnants of the slave power. Moreover, because the southern states were returned to the Union as full-fledged states within hardly more than a decade after the war, there was no southern irredentist movement. The federal system functioned to co-opt the leaders of the South, including leaders prominent in the rebellion, and to reintegrate them into the body politic precisely because they could be elected to state offices and to national office from their own states.[52]

In the aftermath of the Nigerian civil war, there was a similar reconstitution on federal principles which involved the reintegration of the Biafrans into the body politic through the use of federal principles. After the end of the war, even the leaders of the rebellion resumed their involvement in Nigerian politics. In 1983 the Ibo former president of Biafra was elected to the Nigerian Senate on the ticket of the National party, which had been founded as an expression of Hausa-Fulani interests. Part of Nigeria's reconstitution involved the restructuring of the country, first into a twelve-unit, then a nineteen-unit federation in place of the unstable three- or four-unit federation of the pre–civil war period.[53]

In 1874 the Swiss avoided a civil war because of their will to federate, which led them to seek a constitutional compromise instead. Centuries of bilateral and multilateral intercantonal agreements, punctuated with occasional civil wars, always brought them back to the necessity for unity on a federal basis.[54]

More difficult problems occur when there is a will to

federate without the requisite federal political culture, which is the case in most of the Latin American federal systems. In such circumstances, a federal structure is usually found, which fails to live up to its promise but is retained because it reflects the ideal to which the civil society aspires.

6

Centralizing and Decentralizing Trends in Contemporary Federal Systems

The Complexities of Centralization in Federal Systems

Although the centralization-decentralization problem is common to all political systems, it takes on special characteristics in federal systems because of their noncentralized character. Students of federalism have long since learned that in federal systems what may seem on the surface to be a centralizing activity, such as the involvement of the federal government in a new program, may actually have equally strong decentralizing tendencies, such as liberating constituent governments from other pressures that have prevented them from acting.[1] To give two examples from the American experience, much of the New Deal legislation, which was attacked as centralizing, in fact freed the states from the grip of private interests that had prevented them from enacting social programs desired by the majority of their citizens by providing federal incentives and supports for such actions. Contrarily, much of what the Nixon administration hailed as the "New Federalism," designed to restore power to the states and localities, actually involved federal intervention into spheres previously left in state and local hands. Had Nixon been successful, the main result would have been to centralize policy making in Washington and establish federal administrative frameworks for enforcement of Nixon administration policies, while delegating the implementation of those policies to the selfsame states and localities, that is, to replace noncentralization with decentralization.[2] In sum, the existence of noncentralization as the basis of federalism means that more sophisticated instruments must be used to measure centralization or decentralization within federal systems.

The contrast between a simple centralization-decentralization continuum and noncentralization can best be conceptualized by the three contrasting models described in Chapter 2. The simple centralization-decentralization continuum is predicated on the existence of polities built upon the hierarchical or center-periphery models. In both, the opposing poles are clearly demarcated; it is also clear that initiatives are more than likely to come from the center or the top rather than the periphery or the bottom. Although some complexity may be introduced by considering the interests of the lower levels in top-level decision making on the pyramid model, or in the identity of interest between peripheral actors and those controlling the center, basically the relationship remains fairly clear-cut.

As indicated in Chapter 2, the basic characteristics of federalism are best reflected in a matrix model whereby the polity is compounded of a number of arenas or cells of different sizes with no single center and certainly no periphery. In the matrix model, the largest arena frames the whole and is the functional equivalent of the center or the top in the other two models. The smaller arenas which it encompasses are the functional equivalents of the periphery or bottom in the other two. Figures 6.1 and 6.2 illustrate this matrix in connection with the United States and the European Community.

The differences between them should be apparent. The first two models, in their very terminology, suggest that the center or the top of the pyramid is more important than the periphery or bottom. The third does not prefix importance because every arena, large or small, may be of impor-

Figure 6.1. *The American Governmental Matrix:*
Interacting Power Centers of General, State, and Local
Government

U.S. Supreme Court and Federal Judiciary

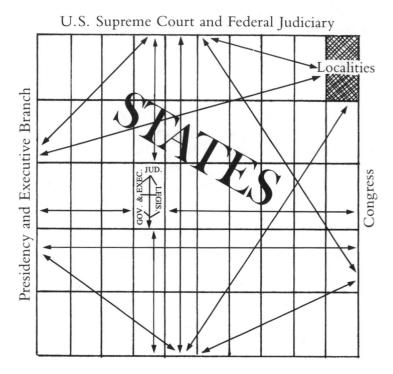

tance for some particular purpose. By conceptualizing relationships in federal sytems along the lines of the matrix model, it is possible to see why the issue of centralization-decentralization becomes far more complex and the effects of any particular policy or action murkier. The study of federal systems—not to speak of the understanding of federalism itself—has suffered because political scientists have generally accepted the center-periphery and hierarchical models as normative and have tried to force federal systems into their mold, not only their terminology (for example, when they speak of "levels" of government in the federal systems as in others—an obvious contradiction in terms) but, far more important, by obscuring accurate analysis.[3]

Figure 6.2. *The European Community as a Matrix*

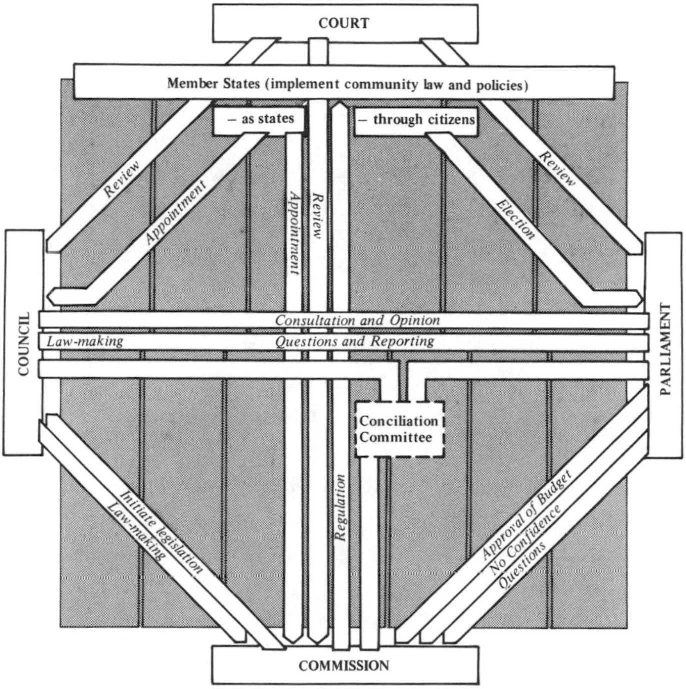

Overall Tendencies

Until very recently, the overall thrust of the twentieth century was toward centralization of power in most political systems, whether federal in character or not.[4] Indeed, a conventional wisdom emerged that centralization was an inevitable concomitant of the twentieth-century nation-state and indeed of the nation-building process.[5] Beginning in the late 1960s, however, contrary tendencies began to be noted. These tendencies increased in the 1970s so that by the mid-1980s, after crossing the threshold into a new historical generation, we must perforce make a different and less clear-cut assessment.[6]

Federations compounded of constituent units identified with particular ethnic groups (hereafter referred to as ethnic federations) have shown strong tendencies toward comprehensive decentralization in the past decade or so. Canada and Yugoslavia are the two most striking examples.[7] In both cases, pressures from ethnic groups identified with constituent polities have been accommodated by the federal government through the reduction or relaxation of federal control, intervention, or activity and the encouragement of additional activity, regulation, and control by the constituent units instead—all in an effort to limit secessionist tendencies and increase satisfaction within the federation so as to preserve its political integrity.

Although similar trends are not possible in the USSR, where the federal structure is at best a slight counterbalance to the overriding centralization of party and state, the success of the ethnic republics in preventing the revision of the Soviet constitution to eliminate federalism—a major policy goal of Nikita Khrushchev and his successors—after a seventeen-year struggle is a manifestation of the same tendency.

Federations not constituted along ethnic lines (hereafter called nonethnic federations) have tended toward selective decentralization in the past decade, either by design or by default. The United States and Australia are good examples of this trend, but so is Austria, which in the past was a highly centralized federal system. In Brazil, military rule, which had generated a very high level of centralization culminating in the constitution of 1969, was not only somewhat relaxed, but decentralization was made part of the government's policy and serious public discussion of federalism was revived. Officially, Mexico, too, has begun to promote "federalism," meaning greater decentralization to the states.[8]

In all of these cases, such decentralization as has taken place has involved both design and default. That is, the efforts of those in power on the federal plane consciously to reduce federal intervention were coupled with the weakening of those same elements for other reasons, leading to the necessity for the constituent units to assume a greater role, even in fields that would not have been decentralized by design. At the same time, centralization continued to occur in certain spheres despite the overall tendency.

These tendencies can be analyzed in greater detail by focusing on policies, policy-making structures, institutions, and parties. Each of those categories will be examined in turn.

Policy Making and Implementation

The theoretical tendency in the last decade as throughout the twentieth century has been toward the encouragement of centralized policy making; more recently it has been coupled with the principle of decentralized policy implementation or execution. Nevertheless, ethnic and nonethnic federations alike have tended to favor some measure of decentralization in policy making as well as in execution, de facto if not de jure. After the peaking of the drive toward centralization in the mid-1960s, there has been increasing pressure in that direction on the part of publics and even many interest groups, in large measure because of their dissatisfaction with the performance of federal governments, which in turn reflects the general dissatisfaction with the performance of governmental institutions throughout the world. This pressure is most intense in ethnic federations, where it is associated with ethnic demands for greater autonomy for the constituent units in which they form majorities, if not for outright secession.

At least in Switzerland and the United States, there is another ideological dimension to this demand. The dissatisfaction with the federal government's performance in the United States and the development of transnational ties by cantons in Switzerland has led to a reawakening of strong ideological leanings toward local control, which had never disappeared from either the American or the Swiss scenes, even when pressing problems encouraged greater public receptivity to national action.

By and large, decentralization through pressure has rested upon generalized dissatisfaction with "big government." There has been no substantial shift of the interest-group focus that initially led to centralization, whereby important interests came to the conclusion that federal intervention would best serve their purposes. If anything, the strongest interests in many federal systems remain predisposed toward securing federal intervention in specific areas even while they support decentralization as a general principle, mainly because the centralizing tendencies of previous generations have led to their reorganization along countrywide lines so as to compete better in what had become, for them, the most important and energetic governmental arena. Thus to the extent that interest groups are active they may still function as a counterforce opposing the overall tendency toward decentralization of policy making but supporting at least a measure of decentralization of policy implementation, if only because this helps them justify their demands for federal intervention to themselves and to others, when those demands fly in the face of ethnic or localist ideological positions. In short, decentralization of policy making through pressure is largely based on general rather than specific interests whereas decentralization of policy implementation is a widely shared goal.

Far more important is decentralization of policy making and execution by default. The perceived failure of general government institutions around the world, including federal institutions in federal systems, and the leadership vacuums that have become almost endemic have led to constituent governments acquiring policy-making and implementation powers by default. If nobody in the national capital has been capable of acting, at least in response to certain problems, energetic leaders in regional capitals have stepped in to fill the gap. Only in those formally federal systems which are in fact so highly centralized that federalism is no more than a modest modifier of centralist institutions and policies rather than a central fact of life, such as the Soviet Union and Czechoslovakia, has this not been true.

Even in countries such as Canada and Yugoslavia, when positive pressures for decentralization by design are great, default has played a role, especially since constituent state leaders in those countries already have come to see themselves as able to play such roles. This has been less true in the United States, where many state governors had come to accept a more hierarchical view of the system and preferred to await federal action. Nevertheless, beginning with the energy crisis of 1973 and the subsequent truckers' strikes in 1974 at the height of the Watergate scandal, even they began to move to fill leadership vacuums. More recently, the states of the United States have undertaken a wide range of initiatives from use of the tax-exempt status of their bonds to raise funds to stimulate the availability of new housing to major refugee resettlement efforts.[9]

In borderline cases such as India and Pakistan the same process has been at work, although less intensively. In Pakistan, problems of changing national leadership have tended to paralyze the national government and increase the scope for provincial activity; in India the experience of Indira Gandhi had much the same effect. Significantly, during her period of absolute rule, Mrs. Gandhi did not try to change the federal system, being content to exercise a stronger hand in the policy-making sphere but for the most part leaving implementation to the states, even when it came to imprisoning opposition leaders. Thus the extent to which political arrests were made varied from state to state, as did the length of imprisonment and the prison conditions for political prisoners. Only in a few cases did Mrs. Gandhi go so far as to impose presidential rule on states noted for the intensity of their opposition to her.[10]

The one great effort to centralize policies in this period was that of Prime Minister Gough Whitlam in Australia.[11] Representing the Australian Labor party, which has traditionally opposed federalism in that country, even within his party Whitlam was noted for his strong ideological commitment to centralization throughout his career. After his party won power he attempted to implement his program in two ways: by centralizing more power in Canberra and by developing direct federal-local relations to bypass and thereby weaken the states, a practice that in Australia had not been the norm. In essence he was following the classic pattern of trying to replace the noncentralized federal-state relationship with a decentralized federal-local relationship.

Whitlam ran into serious problems in this and other areas, which finally led to a constitutional crisis, the intervention of the governor-general, new elections, and the return of the Liberal party by the voters in place of Labor, which ended the effort. His successor, Liberal Prime Minister Malcolm Fraser followed the ambivalent pattern of most federal government heads since the late 1960s, talking decentralization and even encouraging it in practice, while moving toward more centralized policy making in specific fields. He, too, had mixed success, but there has been a great deal of decentralization by default in Australia as in other countries. As a result, Australian federalism, which was considered to be weakening drastically in the postwar generation, is probably stronger now than it has been in decades.

Policy-Making Bodies

Two principal trends can be noted with regard to policy-making bodies: (1) a general movement toward collegial decision making, and (2) a movement toward the establishment of special-purpose authorities and mixed public-private bodies as policy-making and implementation devices. The movement toward collegiality has had mixed impact with regard to the flows of centralization and decentralization. On one hand, it can be argued that intergovernmental collegiality has involved constituent units in fields in which federal policy making was more or less unilateral except insofar as the constituent units were represented in the legislative body that established the broad policy outlines. On the other, the same result has been obtained in reverse, with federal government representatives sitting in with state and local decision makers in fields in which it either had no direct involvement before or indirect involvement through grants-in-aid or transfers of payments.

Although collegiality is not a violation of federal principles, it has not been a prominent element in modern federalism, in which the idea of administratively separate institutions has been the norm.[12] Even in cooperative programs, which have been more of a feature of all modern federations than the original federal theories may have suggested, the sharing has been principally manifested through separate actions on the part of each different institution involving a series of steps with interchanges at the "joints," as it were—the points at which the separate institutions have come together to coordinate with one another.[13] Collegial decision making, on the other hand, involves a single body in which the separate institutions are represented but which takes its decisions on a collective basis.

The examples of collegial bodies in federal systems are fast becoming legion. In Canada, the first ministers' conferences have become important collegial devices.[14] Yugoslavia has reorganized its presidium on a collegial basis.[15] Malaysia and the United Arab Emirates are governed by what are in effect colleges of princes.[16] Switzerland has no similar grand institution of the cantons (its federal executive is a collegial body on a consociational rather than a federal basis) but has traditionally resorted to collegial decision making in specific functional areas as part of its orientation toward decision making through consensus in any case.[17] Austria and Germany have developed similar collegial mechanisms.[18]

The separation of powers in the United States, coupled with the large number of constituent units, has limited efforts to develop any general-purpose institution equivalent to the first ministers' conferences. Neither the president of the United States nor the governors of the fifty states can make decisions and then make them stick as prime ministers can in parliamentary systems. Nevertheless, collegial bodies to undertake specific tasks have become widespread in the United States on a federal-state, federal-state-local, federal-local, and state-local basis. The Appalachian and other regional commissions were among the first prominent examples of this trend.

The spread of collegial decision making is a function of the necessity in increasingly complex and interrelated systems to have single policy-making or coordinating mechanisms in an even greater number of fields. The collegial method may indeed allow for the preservation of the basic principles of federalism while achieving collective decision making, as some have argued.[19] If so, it is a useful addition to the arsenal of federal arrangements, even if it is not precisely what federal theorists had in mind. There is every reason to believe that there will be a continued and increasing use of collegial decision-making arrangements and the development of collegial bodies on an intergovernmental basis in the future to accommodate continuing tendencies toward decentralization, just as they were originally developed to accommodate tendencies toward centralization.

Similarly the development of special-purpose authorities, quangos (quasi-nongovernmental organizations), and mixed public-private bodies represents a continuing and increasing trend.[20] The United States is unique in this respect because it has always relied heavily on such bodies as means to supplement general-purpose governments to assure the goals of federalism,[21] but today even unitary systems that are ideologically and constitutionally committed to concentrating power in a relatively few institutions have found it necessary to develop special-purpose bodies to accomplish tasks that do not easily fit into existing jurisdictional frameworks, that require special expertise, or that involve the public-private mix which general-purpose governmental institutions cannot permit themselves to engage in directly.

Although no proper comparative research has been done on the subject, there is reason to believe that federal systems have an even greater tendency in that direction than unitary ones, with compound polities that are not federal in character, such as the United Kingdom, falling somewhere in between. In those federal systems for which data are available, the number of such special-purpose bodies has been increasing steadily since the early twentieth century (except for isolated phenomena such as school district consolidation in the United States). In some countries they are known as special districts, in others as authorities, in others as quangos (an acronym attributed to Americans, which has not gained currency in the United States but is becoming standard usage in other English-speaking countries). This phenomenon, like the phenomenon of collegiality, begs to be studied by political scientists.

Since the governance of special-purpose bodies tends to be in the hands of boards, commissions, or committees, they became another reflection of collegiality, though in this case they arose less from a desire to create joint decision-making forums in areas of general interest than to focus decision-making forums on problems of very specific concern. In other words, this is another example of how the same trend may lead to movement in what seems to be two different directions to accommodate differing but equally important political trends.

Institutional Responses

In the last analysis, developments in the field of policy making and implementation and new forms of policy-making bodies relate to the way in which the principal institutions of federal systems and modern government generally have responded or failed to respond to the demands placed upon them. The problem of institutional response is shared by both federal and nonfederal polities. It is the way in which the institutions within the polity have responded to the problem that marks federal systems as different. Since the mid-1960s the Western world in particular has been witnessing a failure of the governmental institutions that were developed in the eighteenth, nineteenth, and early twentieth centuries and the political arrangements that were built around them to make them work. This failure has affected federal and nonfederal systems alike. But it may be cautiously asserted on the basis of the fragmentary data available that federal systems have been more resilient in responding because they offer built-in institutional alternatives—in cybernetic language, fail-safe mechanisms—that have prevented paralysis when the overreaching institutions within the polity fail.

What is characteristic of these institutional failures is that each is in itself a failure of an attempt on the part of a particular institution to reach beyond its intended purposes or to interpret those intended purposes in such a way that it overextends itself. This is blatant in the case of the overreach and consequent failures of the three traditional branches of government: executives and their administrative hierarchies, legislatures, and the courts.

Bureaucracies. For most federal systems, as for all but the more autocratic polities of the Western world, administrative hierarchies only emerged in the late nineteenth and twentieth centuries. They were introduced as a part of the managerial revolution that accompanied the growing complexity of government and society as a result of the several industrial revolutions that have engulfed the world. It is not generally noted that in most of the polities in which federalism is the organizing principle, even bureaucracies were not hierarchically structured until relatively recently, being organized in such a way as to be responsible both to the executive and legislative branches or to special publics.[22] This was done deliberately to make them more permeable and hence more responsible. Administrative hierarchies in authoritarian systems are older precisely because they are designed for just the opposite purposes—to support the continuing effort on the part of authoritarian leaders to impose hierarchical control throughout the systems they govern.

At one time certain of the preindustrial bureaucratic polities such as Prussia and France were viewed as being in a better position to weather the transition from premodern to modern governmental organization than the anti-bureaucratic federalist models. They were even seen as models for the latter to follow, but whatever promise they had in that direction has not proved to be without very great costs.[23]

Most federal systems developed their administrative hierarchies reluctantly. At the very least, their legislative bodies, political organizations, or *caudillo* networks were reluctant to transfer power to this new phenomenon, which, from the first, meant a reduction of their powers, at least relatively.[24] Reluctantly accepting the necessities of the new age, the nonhierarchical institutions of the polity increased the power of hierarchical ones and reorganized bureaucracies so as to make them more so, while trying to find new ways to keep general control over them. In the United States, Switzerland, Canada, Australia, and the Latin American federal systems, the struggle to hierarchize the bureaucracies involved a series of political and administrative conflicts of considerable magnitude.

Only in federal systems such as Germany and Austria, which were erected on the ruins of empires, and the Soviet Union, Czechoslovakia, and Yugoslavia, with a similar imperial past plus the added dimension of Communism, were hierarchical bureaucracies already in place. Third World federations, which emerged only in the twentieth century, adopted hierarchical forms as a result of their exposure to modern ideas and to serve what were usually autocratic systems in any case. They tended to do so, however, within their own traditional context. Bureaucracy has become extremely problematic for them as well, but not because of Western styles of hierarchical control.

In any case, the administrative hierarchies continued to grow, and as they did so, they continued to specialize, develop greater strength, and become capable of mobilizing greater resources, human, technical, and financial. At some point, each became capable of generating new growth through its own resources by creating perceptions of new problems or calling attention to problems hitherto ignored, thereby generating responses from legislatures and publics that tended to strengthen the powers of those selfsame bureaucracies. Frequently this was done for the best of motives, sometimes in the simple desire for self-aggrandizement, and usually for some combination of both.

As a result, the administrative hierarchies in most political systems, including federal ones, began to reach beyond their capabilities. First, they convinced the public that bureaucracies actually functioned according to the hierarchical model, namely that power was controlled at the top and could be best coordinated there. In fact, the more they expanded the less control there was at the top, since the top itself became more complex and in effect ceased to exist altogether.

What emerged in reality was an inverted pyramid in which the distance between offices, departments, and decision makers at the top was far greater than the distance between their counterparts at the bottom of their own organizational charts.[25] Consequently, it became well-nigh impossible to produce results within the pyramid because lack or slowness of communication and political infighting disrupted the intended communication process. Soon hierarchies began to fail to deliver on commitments they had made.[26]

Despite rising public anger, the bureaucracies continued to persist through inertia. Because the inertia was oriented toward growth, they also continued to grow on a self-generating basis, which meant that costs accelerated and benefits declined. This result has led to an antibureaucratic reaction, which has discredited almost all bureaucratic structures in federal systems and others, even in cases where such judgments are unjustified. Even hierarchies that deliver as well as an objective observer would expect have failed because they cannot deliver what they promise. Consequently, even good administrators have failed to maintain public confidence. Excessive reach has led to excessive distrust.

Legislatures. Legislatures, which gained power in the seventeenth through the nineteenth centuries, are also viewed today as failures by the publics they serve. In some respects this is because the growth of complexity in general government has reduced legislatures' ability to cope. But beyond that, they, too, reached too far and generated or acquiesced to demands that they cannot meet. As a result, they, too, are suffering from the failure of overreach.[27]

In parliamentary systems one aspect of the failure has been manifested in the way that governments are able to control parliaments, rather than vice versa, with the legislative body becoming a rubber stamp to an executive presumably responsible to it. In congressional systems, the intervention of legislative bodies into more and more aspects of public life, leading them to expand the scope of bureaucracy as a concomitant of increased governmental activity, has redounded to overcommit their own members and at the same time reduce their power vis-à-vis the executive branch. Thus in both cases legislatures have lost public confidence, even legislative bodies like the United States Congress and many American state legislatures, which have attempted to build staff capabilities that can respond to their bureaucratic counterparts. That growth in turn has led to problems of internal bureaucratization.

Courts. Finally, the constitutional courts, at least in federal systems in which they have substantial powers of judicial review, have also reached too far and have failed. The United States is by far the leading example of this phenomenon, since its federal Supreme Court has by far the most highly developed powers of judicial review of constitutional and federal questions. It is fair to say that the overwhelming majority of the centralizing steps that have occurred in the American federal system in the past two generations have been as a result of federal Supreme Court decisions.[28] Once the United States Supreme Court abandoned judicial self-restraint, adopted an activist role, and coupled that activist role with a positivistic view of jurisprudence, it became inevitable that the Court majority would decide cases on the basis of its preferences, unlike most earlier Courts (excepting the Fuller Court) which were reluctant to introduce substantial political change without clear-cut constitutional grounds. Since the preferences of the majority followed the intellectual trends of the twentieth century, the result was foreseeable.

The move from judicial self-restraint to judicial activism came in the interwar generation. The move to unrestrained activism came with the Warren Court in the 1950s. During the years of the Warren Court, the United States Supreme Court almost unreservedly functioned to nationalize standards in the United States. In most cases its efforts have produced mixed results at best. The one great exception is in the first round of the civil rights cases, about which a national consensus was waiting to be formed. But in other fields—criminal justice, obscenity and pornography, the second round of civil rights cases (for example, busing), and others, the Court, like other institutions, has overpromised with negative results. Since the court is not responsible for implementation of its decisions, its actions have compounded the problems of executive and legislative institutions, particularly the former, which are expected to deliver but cannot for reasons beyond their control.[29]

The precise function of U.S. Supreme Court decisions within the theory of federalism underlying the American system is a matter that has provoked debate in the past and could still benefit from systematic investigation. There are those, perhaps including members of the Court, who see the federal Supreme Court in hierarchical terms, at the apex not only of the federal judiciary but of the entire American legal system, and therefore as legitimately entitled to set judicial standards that must be accepted without question by all lower courts, federal and state. Others, who see the American system as a matrix of larger and smaller arenas and the governments that serve them, see the federal Supreme Court as a critical framing institution for the matrix as a whole and, as such, legitimately entitled to determine the character of the frame but not empowered to shape every detail within it as would be the case in a hierarchical system.

These contrasting approaches are particularly manifest in the question of compliance by other courts with U.S. Supreme Court decisions, which has been studied periodically at least since the 1950s. One conclusion that can be reached from those studies is that to the extent that the American system has shifted operationally from a matrix to a hierarchy over the past generation, this shift has been reflected in the patterns of compliance.[30]

This situation is less pronounced in other federal systems, perhaps excepting the Australian, because the courts do not play the same key role. On the other hand, particularly in Third World federal systems, where constitutional courts exist and were supposed to be more active in protecting the constitutional and federal rights of constituent polities, they have been unable to act as expected. Thus their publics also adjudge them to be failures.[31]

If institutional failure has been endemic to contemporary political systems, federal systems have done better in dealing with this problem because of their built-in fail-safe mechanisms. When institutions in one arena are unable to work, institutions in another often are able to pick up the slack and, indeed, in many cases they have. In some cases new institutions have been devised, taking advantage of the flexibility of federalism. If the Canadian and Australian parliaments have been weakened by the general tendency in parliamentary systems to transfer power to the cabinet, the emergence of first ministers' conferences has provided alternative mechanisms for decision making of a federalist character. If federal courts do not act appropriately, state courts have been known to step in to fill the gap. Although federal chief executives cannot control their bureaucracies, most state and local bureaucracies remain amenable to control by elected officials and publics.

Martin Landau and Vincent Ostrom have written extensively about the virtues of redundancy in political and administrative systems and how federalism is the way that redundancy is introduced and protected through constitutional means.[32] Increasingly, publics have come to understand that position even if they are unaware of its scientific basis. This has tended to strengthen decentralizing tendencies in federal systems.

Parties and Party Systems

Without elaborating on questions of cause and effect, the problem of institutional overreach and failure seems to be intimately connected with the contemporary problem of political parties in federal and other polities. These problems are different for centralized and noncentralized parties and party systems, but both are in difficulty.

Centralized parties are faced with a twofold problem. First, the rise of ethnic and localistic sentiments threatens the parties' ability to control the regime. Simultaneously, the decline of ideology, which served in the past as the only check on the rampant pursuit of private interest on the part of many party members, threatens the parties' ability to control themselves. This problem is particularly important in federal systems with centralized parties because for the most part the centralized character of federalism in those systems is the direct result of the role of the centralized parties. Thus the transformation of the party into what is essentially a monopolistic holding company for individual or group advancement and enrichment opens the possibility for weakening public willingness to accept its rule and increases the necessity for it to rely upon time-honored methods of control, namely secret police and violence. When this occurs in a multiethnic federation and is coupled with rising ethnic demands, the situation is likely to become even more difficult.[33]

Noncentralized parties are suffering from a different set of problems, which stem from many of the same sources. The demise of at least a minimal common programmatic dimension, which served to hold the various elements in the noncentralized framework together, coupled with the demise of strong party organizations in the constituent units or their subdivisions, has had the effect of diffusing power within the party system beyond anything heretofore experienced, leading to challenges to party control even in spheres in which such control is normally expected, such as the selection of candidates, the organization of campaigns, the turning out of the vote, and even the organization of governing conditions after the elections. In federal polities with noncentralized party systems, the tendency has been in this direction to a greater or lesser extent.[34]

The United States and India offer two prime examples of this trend. In the 1970s, India witnessed the fall from power of the Congress party, which was once all-powerful in the federal arena (although it had serious competitors in several states after 1947), and its fragmentation; the rise of a new national coalition built around the Janata party; and the collapse of that coalition in turn. National politics has moved in the direction of the pattern of personal and clique coalitions that became prevalent earlier in those states without powerful ruling party organizations. Consequently, party control has become a virtual fiction, with each politician working his own "deals" as he perceives his own best interests and those of his supporters.[35]

In the United States, shortly after World War II the American Political Science Association, in a rare public policy stance, issued a report entitled "Toward a More Responsible Two-Party System," in which it followed the then prevalent conventional wisdom among political scientists to the effect that two centralized British-style parties were more appropriate for exercising democratic control and for creating a proper politics of issues than the noncentralized, diffuse American system of two loose confederations of state parties, each of which in turn needed strong local roots in order to function.[36] The report and all that went with it—including the teaching of that position to two generations of students on campuses throughout the United States—stimulated a generation of efforts at political party reform in the United States. These efforts persisted long after the majority of political scientists had abandoned the idea that somehow the British party system was more virtuous than the American and many had come to realize the close functional relationship between noncentralized parties and noncentralized government.

The Democrats made an abortive effort to create a strong national party in the late 1950s under the leadership of national chairman Paul Butler. The Republicans made a short-lived attempt with a similar result when Barry Goldwater was their presidential candidate in 1964. Then the Democrats tried it again on a more massive scale after the confrontations surrounding the 1968 Democratic National Convention. For a while, it seemed that the last effort would succeed because the Democratic party did introduce a federal structure in place of its previous confederal one. Associated with the change, however, was a policy reform that did not set well with many party activists and certainly did not square with the sentiment in the country, which was to weaken party organization in every arena. As a result, the Democratic party may have emerged more highly structured on paper, but this did not lead to the sought-after presidential victories at the polls. Quite the contrary. At the grass roots, both the Democratic and the Republican parties have almost fallen apart as effective organizations, assisted in that direction, on one hand, by United States Supreme Court decisions weakening the effect of state laws that limited party control over the nominating process and, on the other, by voter apathy and openness to candidates whose appeal is highly personal.[37] In response, the Republican National Committee made its centralizing move in exactly the opposite way, by intervening locally to provide technical assistance and funding to develop strong local candidates. It has had greater success but as it succeeds, it must withdraw from the local arena, hence noncentralization is preserved.

In the Federal Republic of Germany, where the Social Democratic party was centralized and the Christian Democratic party noncentralized, the noncentralized character of the federal system has combined with the decline of socialism as an ideological force to weaken the central mechanisms of the SDP.[38] Today the *land* SDP organizations have emerged as the effective sources of the party's electoral strength. In Australia, where the Labour party tried to behave in an ideological fashion, it was roundly defeated at the polls, in what has to be considered a victory for federalism as well as whatever other issues were involved in the campaign.[39] The subsequent Labour party victory came only after it had returned to traditional state-based politics. In Nigeria, the breakdown of party politics altogether in a manner that has become all too familiar in the African setting led to a military takeover and a civil war in the late 1960s. The country returned to civilian rule in 1979 after a thorough reorganization of its federal system, only to suffer another breakdown and military coup in 1984.[40]

By and large, the party situation has also strengthened the tendency toward decentralization after functioning for a long time in the opposite direction. The major problem in all these cases is that although centralized parties are counterproductive, noncentralized parties are necessary for the proper functioning of federal government. They play a major role in assuring that federal systems do not follow the "iron law of oligarchy" and move too far in the direction of centralization, or in some cases, the "iron law of secession" and move in the other direction. The absence of appropriate party organization seems likely to open the gates to sporadic tendencies in either direction, depending on some combination of what politicians do to catch the public's eye and the balance of pressures of numerous interest groups. Indeed, the emergence of single-issue groups has been a major phenomenon of American politics and that of other Western countries since the 1970s and has generated a relatively high level of electoral instability.

In the case of parties as in the case of other institutions, what is happening in federal systems is comparable to what is happening in contemporary political systems generally. But whereas federal institutional frameworks serve to provide fail-safe mechanisms through redundancy that may temper the problems of institutional failure, it is not clear whether the same is true with regard to party failure.

Interim Conclusions

Had this book been written in the early 1970s, it would still have emphasized the centralizing tendencies in contemporary federal systems, although qualifying that emphasis with the caveats regarding noncentralization and the matrix model presented above. For the moment, the tendency seems to be in the other direction. This chapter has tried to suggest in broad outline why this is so. At the same time, the same caveats apply. Noncentralization means that seemingly contradictory tendencies not only exist within federal systems but are well-nigh inevitable.

Two decades ago, the late Morton Grodzins suggested that the press for decentralization that characterized the Eisenhower years in the United States would come to naught because in the American federal system the federal government was not sufficiently centralized to decentralize anything.[41] What Grodzins correctly claimed was true of the American system is equally true of other functioning federal systems. First, it is necessary to centralize drastically before decentralization can be undertaken, and as we know from experience in any number of cases, if the powers that be are able to achieve the necessary centralization, they are unlikely to be willing to decentralize afterward. Thus a mixture of centralizing and decentralizing trends is likely to continue as long as federalism exists.

7

Will the Postmodern Epoch Be an Era of Federalism?

Whither the Modern Nation-State?

The modern epoch lasted from the middle of the seventeenth until the middle of the twentieth centuries. It was during those three centuries that the civilization which has now become well-nigh universal on this planet, and of which we are all at least in some respects a part, was created.

For more than three hundred years—at least since the beginning of the modern epoch—almost the entire effort of European civilization, as well as that of those peoples and countries that were influenced by European civilization, has been directed to building reified, centralized, sovereign states that force the peoples in their respective territories into the procrustean bed of a single government. In other words, their goal has been one people, one government, and one territory.

In all too many cases, the centralized sovereign state became the procrustean state at the very least. Among democracies, France, the classic example of this form, is also the classic example of its excesses. Because all possible powers are centralized in Paris, the submerged ethnic, national, and religious groups of the periphery cannot maintain their languages or even name their children as they please. So the extremists among them must resort to dropping bombs in mailboxes or blowing up power lines to gain attention.

The very term that was invented to describe this new creature, "nation-state," was an ideal projection or a sleight

223

of hand. We now are far enough removed from the process to recognize that, though in a few cases there was a felicitous overlapping of nation and state, more often no nation preceded the creation of a given state embracing a given territory, a state whose limits were often established by violent means. The creation of the nation came afterward, subduing all the dissident elements within the territory to make the self-defined nation-state a reality. In the course of its development, the nation-state often became a citizen-state, wherein each person was individually a citizen but was not entitled to maintain any substantial group identity. So, too, many nations were too scattered or intertwined to acquire states of their own.[1]

The results of this situation have been challenged in the postmodern era, principally because the homogeneous polity with so close a linkage between people, government, and territory in every respect has not come to pass, even in countries where it seemed to be farthest along the road. One major characteristic of the postmodern era is the ethnic revival, the reemergence of the sense of primordial ties as central to individual identity. This development is reflected politically in the worldwide movement from class-based to ethnic-based politics.[2]

One consequence of this new ethnicity is the linkage of peoples across state borders, whether through interregional arrangements such as those in the Upper Rhine Valley, where people of Allemanian background living in the three nation-states, France, Germany and Switzerland, a number of Swiss cantons, and the German *land* of Baden-Württemberg are linked together in a variety of arrangements; through state-diaspora arrangements like those characteristic of the Jewish people; or through the interstate relations characteristic of the Arab world, which perceives itself to be one Arab nation divided into a number of states but with transstate linkages.[3]

The development of new governmental arrangements— at least new to the modern era (some have classic antecedents)—to accommodate postmodern trends has been treated in some detail in the previous chapters. These new governmental arrangements have moved in two directions simultaneously, to create both larger and smaller political units for different purposes, to gain economic or strategic advantage while at the same time maintaining an indigenous community, better to accommodate ethnic diversity. All embody the idea of more than one government exercising powers over the same territory. That idea, which was at the heart of the American invention of federalism, was anathema to the European fathers of the modern nation-state.

The existence of more than one government over the same territory is becoming an increasingly common phenomenon. This development, in turn, reflects the growing twentieth-century reality of limitations on state sovereignty. No state today is as sovereign as any state thought it was a century ago, if only because even the great powers recognize their limits in a nuclear age when it comes to making sovereign decisions about war and peace. Many states are accepting these increased limitations and trading them off, as it were, for advantages. The European Common Market is only one example of how the acceptance of limitations on sovereignty in certain spheres can be traded off for greater benefits.

Finally, in the intellectual sphere, the center-periphery model of statehood is being challenged by the champions of a new model, which views the polity as a matrix of overlapping, interlocking units, powers, and relationships. The efforts to come to grips intellectually with all of these phenomena have been much slower than the movement in the real world. The accepted intellectual models have tended to lag behind actual developments but, even so, are now beginning to change. The more than 3,000 ethnic or tribal groups in the world conscious of their respective identities are divided among nearly 150 multiethnic states—over 90 percent of the politically "sovereign" states now in existence. The single-nation state has become even more rare as the Third World has been decolonized. There are today more than one hundred functioning examples of institutional political arrangements that modify or transcend the classic nation-state model, ranging from classic federation to various cultural rights. They are to be found in fifty-six different "sovereign" states, more than one-third of the recognized states in the world today.[4]

The variety of arrangements includes the following:

- Federations.
- Confederations such as the European community.
- Unions in which there is regional and functional autonomy such as the United Kingdom.
- Feudal arrangements transformed (for example, Jersey, Guernsey, the Isle of Man, Monaco, and San Marino).
- Federacies, or associated state relationships such as those between the United States and Puerto Rico or Switzerland and Liechtenstein.
- Home rule of which there are at least two forms—that which is unilaterally granted with local consent, as in former colonial situations; or constitutional home rule, generally municipal, usually embodied in a constitutional charter, as in the American states.
- Cultural home rule, designed to preserve a minority language or religion, as in Belgium.
- Autonomous provinces or national districts (which the Communist world has developed extensively but which also exist in countries like Nigeria).
- Regional arrangements, both intranational, where there is regional decentralization as in Italy and Spain,

or transnational, such as the regional functional arrangements in the Upper Rhine Valley.

* Customs unions, an old-fashioned device that has taken on new meaning, particularly in southern Africa.
* Leagues based on common national or cultural ties, such as the Beneleux, the Nordic Union, or the Arab League.
* State-diaspora ties, such as those that link the Jewish people the world over or those in India that link the union's constituent states and their diaspora communities in other parts of the country.
* Extraterritorial arrangements or enclaves—Egypt and the Sudan have a fairly elaborate system of enclaves along their mutual border.
* Condominium, of which Andorra is the oldest functioning example in the world today.
* Special central government arrangements for specific regions or groups; even Greece, which stays faithfully with the old model of the centralized state, has a minister for Macedonian affairs located in Salonika.
* State structures imposed upon autonomous tribes; Afghanistan had such a two-tier system. When the Communist-oriented party captured the state structure, it was not able to impose its authority on the autonomous tribes, hence the civil war and the Soviet intervention.
* Consociational arrangements of two forms: equal pillars as in the Netherlands or ethnoreligious communities in rank order, one of which is dominant and others subordinate, as in South Africa.

Not all of these are federal solutions by any means. If we return to the model presented at the beginning of this book, we can use it to distinguish between federal and nonfederal forms of accommodation of demands for autonomy. In hierarchical systems, autonomy is possible through feudalism, that is, the impositon of a contractual framework on the power pyramid. This imposition can occur when those lower in the hierarchy are able to acquire sufficient power to compel those higher up to acknowledge their right to autonomy through appropriate contractual arrangements that preserve the illusion of hierarchy, and perhaps some measure of its reality, while accommodating the real division of power. Since the hierarchical system remains intact, conceptually as well as structurally, such arrangements can remain intact only as long as the empirical realities of the power distribution enable those lower down in the hierarchy to enforce the contracts made. A variant of this system emerged in Latin America after independence. Today, the state structures that encompass but do not rule autonomous tribes represent this form of accommodation.

In organic polities built on the center-periphery model, accommodation is achieved through the central authorities providing autonomy to peripheral regions or minority rights for peripheral groups. In such systems, the center must remain intact by virtue of the very nature of the polity. Hence it can extend itself only in a way that preserves its integrity, leaving the peripheral regions or groups virtually at the mercy of central decision making even if the arrangements are constitutionalized.

In fact, it is easier to establish autonomy on both a constitutionalized and a real basis in hierarchical systems through feudal or quasi-feudal mechanisms than in organic systems with their strong centers. This result is visible in the spread of federalism in the German-speaking countries of Europe, where hierarchical feudalism was most pronounced in medieval times, and in the inability of polities like France to decentralize. The latter can accommodate local demands for more power only by introducing local representatives into the central institutions of the state, which is one of the reasons why so many members of the French National Assembly are also mayors of their home municipalities. A mayor who sits in an official position in Paris can deliver the goods for his community in a way he cannot simply as mayor.

The special central government arrangements for specific regions in Greece or Iraq are contemporary examples of the grudging application of decentralization in the center-periphery model. Denmark and its two island federacies are happier expressions of the same. Some polities, notably Italy and the Sudan, have tried to use the necessity to accommodate peripheral regions to transform their polities entirely from a center-periphery to a matrix model, but the inherent strength of the center has generally prevented realization of those efforts.

Finally, there is the federal model, which, as a matrix, is almost indefinitely expandable both in scope and in character of the relationships. That is why where such arrangements have successfully taken root, they usually exist in multiples. The United States is not only a federation of fifty states but has established federacy arrangements with Puerto Rico and the Northern Marianas and is completing the establishment of associated state relationships with the three new states of Micronesia, one of which is itself a federation and the other two constitutionally decentralized polities. The fundamental sovereignty of the native American (American Indian) tribes has been reaffirmed by the American judiciary and, increasingly, in legislation; both have implicitly endorsed a federacy relationship between those tribes and the United States.

The United Kingdom represents the most successful combination of feudal and organic institutions, which its conservative commitment to tradition has encouraged it to maintain and thereby enabled it to also maintain a multiplicity of quasi-federal arrangements. Each of those relationships is unique: union with Scotland, with the maintenance of separate Scottish legal, religious, and administrative structures; special representation of Wales in the central government with a measure of cultural home rule in addition; quasi-federal home rule for Ulster; federacy arrangements with the Isle of Man, Jersey, Guernsey, and Sark, based on old feudal ties; and constitutional home rule for various overseas possessions. All of these together offer a felicitous combination of the center-periphery model characteristic of England proper with feudal and quasi-feudal arrangements that protect a greater or lesser degree of autonomy for the non-English segments of the United Kingdom.

It seems that when there is a turn away from the reified state the problem of dealing with diversity is essentially political rather than legal. In much of the discussion of these issues, there is a tendency to emphasize the legal aspects. But what counts are the political solutions; the law can be adapted to fit virtually every situation. There are forms of federalism to parallel virtually every form of rule, except authoritarian and totalitarian rule, which can be masked by federal systems and even influenced by their federal structures, but which are, in the last analysis, something else. The foregoing discussion suggests—properly—that the federal idea and its applications offer a comprehensive alternative to the idea of the reified sovereign state and its applications.

The domestic and international implications of the state sovereignty system should be clear. In the international arena, every sovereign state must preserve maximum separateness, joining with others only out of necessity and then in the most limited ways, with minimal concession of powers and control. Domestically, with one central government, all other governing bodies are merely authorities, deriving their powers from the central government as a matter of grace or utility rather than right, and continuing to possess those powers only as long as the central government wills.

The federalist alternative insists that no governments or states are sovereign as such—that political sovereignty resides in the people who delegate powers through constitutional devices on a limited basis to different governments as they see fit. Thus issues of sovereignty are subordinated to issues of constitutionality, utility, and propriety, and no state can exist for itself. In an increasingly complex and interdependent world, where the first principle of state sovereignty, namely that every sovereign state has the right and power to be the sole determinant of its own destiny, is clearly untenable, even in the case of superpowers, not to speak of ministates, it is not surprising that federal devices are spreading in number and variety in an effort to replace, ease, or counterbalance the existing system.

Federal Accommodation of Peoples and Publics

Popular sovereignty means, inter alia, that government with the consent of the governed is the only legitimate basis of political organization. Obtaining and maintaining such consent in modern and postmodern societies is a complex matter, involving various levels of initiative and response by the parties involved or their representatives. The degree of success or failure in the application of federal principles and arrangements to those ends depends not simply on the erection of federal structures but on the creation of appropriate publics as well. On that point federalism most clearly becomes a matter of structuring relationships and not simply institutions.

It has been emphasized throughout this volume that

federalism is republican by its very nature and that a republic is a *res publica,* a public entity or a commonwealth
belonging to its citizens. But for a *res publica* to exist, it must
rest on a public, not merely on a congeries of individuals (or
families) all pursuing their private interests exclusively. The
failure of republican institutions in many countries can be
attributed to the lack of appropriate publics to support
them.[5] That is why the Whigs, the founders of modern
republicanism, emphasized the necessity for republican virtue to sustain republican government, an understanding
that echoes the great political philosophers.[6]

Federal arrangements are often introduced to reconcile
the interests of different peoples within a common political
framework. It is in this connection that the distinction between peoples and publics becomes crucial. A people—*eth-
nos* in Greek, hence ethnic group—may be defined as a
multigenerational collectivity based upon kinship, consent,
or some combination of the two, whose existence has acquired a cultural character and which retains its identity and
character whether or not it possesses the means for civic life
and political expression. A public is a community that may
or may not be multigenerational but is inevitably characterized by its civic character and political expression. Not
every polity serves a separate people, but to survive every
one must have a public. Conversely, not every public is a
people. Indeed, a people may be divided into several publics, as in the case of the Arab states, or a public may embrace several peoples or parts of peoples, as in the case of
Yugoslavia.[7]

Cultural cleavages most frequently reflect the existence of
separate peoples, each of which is clamoring for its place in
the political sun. Under certain circumstances, federalism
offers the possibility of creating publics that transcend the
divisions among peoples and thereby make possible the
establishment of civil society and political order. Here is
where federalism transcends pluralism. Pluralism involves

the recognition of legitimate differences; federalism the structuring of relationships that permit the groups bearing those differences to function together within the same political system.

Federalism is additionally useful in this regard because, properly used, it not only allows several peoples and publics to combine self-rule and shared rule but to do so within the context of limited rule. Limited rule is a concomitant of federalism because sharing on a federalistic basis necessarily involves limits—to preserve liberty writ large for all and the specific liberties of the constituents. The successful application of federal principles and mechanisms must involve their constitutionalization in ways that are appropriate for maintaining limited rule as determined by the constituting elements. These ways are not a matter of pious constitutional pronouncements, which, even when necessary, are not sufficient, but rather ways and means in the most operational sense, beginning with the rule of law in place of the rule of an external sovereign. That, too, is dependent upon the existence of publics actively committed to the rule of law rather than merely restrained by the rule of a sovereign.

The polity-formation and maintenance function of federalism is well known. Indeed, the study of federalism in its various forms has focused on that function almost to the exclusion of all others. The function of public formation and maintenance has not been recognized as yet but is of first importance. A proper study of the degree of success or failure of federalism must focus on this public-building and maintenance function.

The revival of ethnic and regional identities runs parallel to the decline of state exclusivism. It goes to the heart of the question as to what constitutes peoples and publics. Since that question, too, is virtually insoluble except on an operational basis, federal arrangements become particularly valuable as operational devices for doing just that.

Federal accommodation of peoples and publics has taken

Table 7.1. Species of Federalism and Form of Accommodation

	Polities Crosscut Cleavages	Polities Used to Express Cleavages
Federation	Argentina Australia Austria Brazil Comoro Islands German Federal Republic Malaysia Mexico Pakistan United States Venezuela	Canada Cyprus[a] Czechoslovakia India Nigeria Papua/New Guinea Switzerland United Arab Emirates USSR
Confederation	Senegambia	European Community West Indies Yugoslavia
Federacy	Denmark–Faroe Islands German Federal Republic–Berlin U.S.–Channel Islands	Denmark–Greenland Finland–Aaland Islands New Zealand–Cook Islands U.K.–Isle of Man U.S.–Northern Marianas

Associated State	France–Monaco Italy–San Marino Netherlands–Curacao Switzerland–Liechtenstein	U.S.–Puerto Rico India–Bhutan South Africa–independent homelands U.K.–[various Caribbean associated states]
Regional/National Union (including the use of federal mechanisms)	Colombia Portugal-Azores	Belgium Burma China Italy Netherlands Philippines Republic of South Africa Solomon Islands Spain Sudan Tanzania United Kingdom
Condominium		Andorra
Consociation	Israel	Lebanon Namibia South Africa

[a]Cyprus is formally committed to a federal solution that has yet to be implemented.

235

two forms: either the structuring of the polity to cut across ethnic cleavages and thereby dilute them through the creation of a crosscutting public or structuring the comprehensive polity to give each people a primary means of expression through one or more of its constituent polities. These two dimensions are parallel to the two faces of territorial democracy.

Examples of the two forms of accommodation can be found among each of the several species of federalism, as Table 7.1 reveals. The assignment of each federal polity is based on its predominant tendency since, of necessity, both must be present to some degree.

In this connection, the following problem areas are worthy of special consideration as ones in which efforts to apply federal solutions to problems of ethnic cleavage are on the agenda. The list is by no means exhaustive.

- *Belgium:* implementing protofederal arrangements to accommodate Flemings and Walloons as separate peoples so that they will remain a public for common purposes.

- *Canada:* maintaining Canadian unity in light of separatist tendencies in Quebec, where the Quebecois think of themselves as a separate people, and western Canada with its separate provincial publics.

- *China:* applying federal mechanisms in a highly centralized totalitarian state with strong ethnic and tribal minorities in its peripheral regions.

- *Cyprus:* implementing the mutual agreement in principle to a federal solution to accommodate the interests of Greek and Turkish Cypriots, two ethnic fragments that must form a common public because of geographic realities.

- *Fiji:* accommodating a bipolar cleavage between the indigenous Fijian population and the descendants of

Indian settlers, who now form the majority in the islands.

- *European Community:* balancing a Europe of states with a Europe of ethnic groups which overlap state boundaries.
- *France:* regional decentralization to encourage local publics versus the revival of ethnic aspirations in the peripheral regions.
- *India:* perennial problems of federalism and cultural home rule for linguistic and religious publics.
- *Iraq:* accommodating the Kurds, a separate people, and Moslem sectarian publics.
- *Iran:* the Iranians as an ethnic majority united as a religious public as well versus Kurds, Arabs, and other ethnic minorities.
- *Israel and the Palestinians:* possible application of federal principles to resolve the conflict between the Jewish people and the Palestinian Arab public, focusing on the problem of governing the disputed territories.
- *Italy:* regionalism as a protofederal arrangement designed to build publics in a country that has suffered from political alienation on the part of individuals and families.
- *Lebanon:* the restoration of Lebanese unity on a consociational basis in a war-torn multicommand society.
- *Malaysia:* maintenance of a federal system crosscutting a deep ethnic cleavage separating Malays and Chinese.
- *Nigeria:* accommodating 3 major and 250 small ethnic groups through federalism.
- *Northern Ireland:* the struggle between Protestants and Catholics as two ethnoreligious communities and its effect on the links between Ulster, Eire, and the United Kingdom.
- *Pakistan:* accommodating internal communal and tribal divisions and the maintenance of political unity.

- *Southern Africa:* accommodating whites and nonwhites as separate tribes in a multiracial, multinational society.
- *Spain:* autonomy for national minorities and Spanish unity.
- *Switzerland and the Jura:* an apparently successful accommodation of a linguistic public through federalism.
- *USSR:* federalism as a means of maintaining Russian and Communist imperial rule over non-Russian peoples.
- *United Kingdom:* devolution of administrative powers and national rights to constituent countries inhabited by separate peoples.
- *United States and its peripheral territories and aggregations:* federal arrangements for Puerto Rico, the Northern Marianas, and Micronesia as extensions of the federal principle in new directions; finding a federal modus vivendi with the Indian tribes.
- *Yugoslavia:* maintaining a Yugoslav public compounded of separate peoples through federalism.

Federalism in the Third World

The prospects and problems of using federal principles and arrangements to deal with these and other situations is nowhere better illustrated than in the experiences of the newly independent states of the Third World. Why has federalism in its various forms been attractive to so many Third World peoples and polities? Why has it so often failed? Under what circumstances has it been successful? What benefits and costs has federalism brought in its wake? What uses can federal arrangements have in the context of Third World political life and what prospects are there for their future use?

Virtually all of the ninety-two new states created since

World War II are considered part of the Third World. Federal arrangements have or had a role to play in forty-six, or precisely half of them. Eleven were ordained by their colonial rulers to be federations or parts of a larger federation, and their struggle for independence was related to their rejection of a federal arrangement. Twenty came into existence as federal polities. Fifteen were involved in federal or confederal linkages with other states, ranging from full federation to common market arrangements. In three, their original political systems were subsequently reconstituted on a quasi-federal basis to accommodate particular needs. (Since a few of the new states were involved in more than one of the foregoing, the total is more than forty-six.)

At this writing, six states have remained federal systems, fourteen continue to be involved in more or less meaningful federal arrangements, and five are involved in arrangements that continue to exist on paper but have become essentially meaningless. The federations alone contain a population of some 750 million, or a quarter of the total Third World population of some 3 billion. It is evident that federalism, in one or another of its forms, has been widely tried in the Third World. Although the results have been mixed, federalism remains a reality for many people in Asia and Africa. Moreover, when all the varieties of federal arrangements are taken into consideration, the impact of federalism is seen to be far greater than is usually perceived.

By and large, federal arrangements for the internal structuring of the new states have reflected the felt need to accommodate ethnic, religious, or linguistic diversity, or some combination thereof, while efforts to create transstate or multistate linkages have been directed toward the achievement of economics of scale or, in the case of the Arab world, to implement a vision of national unity. Nowhere is there greater undiluted ethnic heterogeneity than in the Third World, where religious, tribal, and ethnic divisions exist in almost a pristine state, unmodified by overlays of modernization or new national identities tied to the newly emergent state system. With very few exceptions, these ethnic divisions are basic and enduring while the newly formed states are still struggling to acquire the loyalties and attachments of the people within their boundaries. Thus all questions of federalism, like all questions of state-building, modernization, development, and the like in the Third World, are dealt with, of necessity, within the context of the realities of ethnic diversity and heterogeneity.

Why Federations Failed

Every failed federation is a case study in and of itself, but some commonalities stand out clearly, seven of which are striking.

The federal arrangement was imposed from outside without ever having any serious internal support. Thus the Cameroun federation was brought into existence as the only acceptable way to unify a country that had been divided into British and French colonies. Federation was a device developed by the two colonialist powers, principally to allow the French to claim that French Cameroun would preserve its Gallic personality (to the extent that one had been established there). Despite the anticipated support for federation, in neither of the constituent units was there strong popular support for maintaining federalism. Thus when a strong centralizer came to power, he was able to eliminate the federal system without difficulty.[8]

In Ghana and Uganda the colonialist power attempted to impose a federal solution to accommodate very real ethnic claims which it perceived to be important, but those solutions were rejected by the time of independence or immediately thereafter. Ghana's Kwame Nkrumah wanted to concentrate power in his own hands, not disperse it. Since his fall, Ghana's rulers have experimented with quasi-federal arrangements from time to time, combining regional decentralization on a tribal basis with the inclusion of the traditional tribal leadership in the institutions of the state.[9] Uganda's rulers, on the other hand, have regularly turned to genocide to deal with that country's problems of diversity.

The ascendancy of a strong man has been a major factor in terminating federal structures. In the very nature of things, a strong man seeking to impose dictatorial rule is not interested in fostering the dispersion of power, even in a nominal way. Since federal arrangements rest upon the constitutional dispersion of power, they must necessarily conflict with strong-man rule. If the strong man survives, the federation is likely to be terminated. The strength of Kwame Nkrumah was undoubtedly a factor in aborting the proposed federal structure for Ghana before independence. In Libya, King Idris gutted that country's federal institutions as he grew in strength; with his overthrow, the junta put the formal finishing touches on their dismantling.[10] In Nigeria, however, where federalism has shown itself to be integral to the polity, the effort of a strong man to eliminate that country's federal system led to his downfall, a lesson learned by subsequent military rulers, who have fostered federalism, at least in some respectable way, rather than attempting to confront it at great political risk.[11]

In some cases, attempts to link newly independent states into larger federations have failed because of the competing interests of strong men in each. Thus the East African Community, which began as a common market and joint service entity that went beyond the kind of economic confederation represented by the European Economic Community, has since collapsed, in no small measure because of the competition between Jomo Kenyatta of Kenya, Julius Nyerere of Tanzania, and Idi Amin of Uganda.[12]

Ethnic conflict has been another cause of the breakup of

federal systems. It has had this effect when the conflict was too intense to be managed by the federal structures and arrangements. In some cases, the conflict may not be objectively more intense than it is in other circumstances where federalism has survived, but it is so structured that it falls along the basic cleavages around which the system is built. Thus the Central African Federation collapsed because of the white-black conflict and the ability of the blacks of two of the three constituent units to force the dissolution because they were in power in those units. In the third unit, Southern Rhodesia (now Zimbabwe), the white minority was so dominant that its blacks had to resort to other means in their struggle for self-determination, a struggle easily won by Malawi and Zambia on the basis of the breakup of the federation.[13]

In Burma, the overwhelming Burmese majority soon put to rest the quasi-federal institutions left by the British to guarantee the rights of ethnic minorities in that country. Significantly, although the institutions no longer survive, the conflict does, and Burma suffers from a perpetual, if low-key, interethnic civil war, the result of which has been the establishment of several de facto ethnic states within Burma.[14]

A fourth factor is lack of resources. In one sense, this is a minor consideration that bears only indirectly on the proximate reasons for the failure of federal arrangements in the Third World. That is, it is not at all clear that even Third World countries per se lack either the human or the monetary resources to maintain federal systems. If they had to maintain full-blown welfare states on the Western model and also support the redundancies inherent in federalism, perhaps this argument would be more significant. But considering the limited government that actually prevails in such countries, it is entirely conceivable that if local elites were mobilized to handle tasks of governance, those countries would be fully capable of fielding as complete a set of

governors at an affordable cost as was the case in late eighteenth-century United States or preindustrial Switzerland
or nineteenth-century Latin America.

Given the orientation against such local involvement in
political life, it is possible to speak of a lack of resources, not
in budget or manpower in the statistical sense, but in psy-
chospiritual resources. Contrast India with any of the failed
federations. Certainly in material resources India is in no
better a position than they and, indeed, is poorer than many
of them. Nor is India's manpower ratio much superior.
India's larger number of university graduates results not in
greater efficiency but in larger bureaucracies. Yet federalism
has been maintained in India in a workable condition because India has the orientation required for mobilizing
human resources to maintain diffused governmental institutions, power sharing, and the like.[15]

A fifth factor is the absence of a federally inclined political
culture. This dimension is one that has been explored least,
although perhaps written about most, by analysts of
federalism. Increasingly, those analysts have come to the
conclusion that the successful federal polities are those that
have a political culture that is either federalist in orientation
or open to the absorption of federal principles. Conversely,
the analysts agree, absence of a federal political culture, or
one open to it, makes the maintenance of federal arrangements very problematic indeed.

Lack of sufficient common interests is a sixth factor that
has contributed to the failure of federations, particularly
efforts at linking established states to one another. The Mali
Federation was founded on the basis of putative shared economic interests that proved to be insufficient. The secession
of Bangladesh from Pakistan and Singapore from Malaysia
reflected the lack of sufficient common interests within established federations. Conflicting interests led to the gut-
ting of the East African Community.

Unbalanced federal arrangements also rarely succeed.

Two-unit federations are particularly vulnerable because they do not offer sufficient opportunities for tension-reducing coalitions. Nor are federal arrangements likely to work where one entity is clearly dominant. The Ethiopian-Eritrean federation suffered from both of these defects, although other factors, such as the absolutism of Haile Selassie and his lack of interest in power sharing, were more immediately important.

Why Federations Succeeded

What, then, of the successful uses of federal principles or arrangements in the Third World? How are they to be explained? In most respects, by the very obverse of the reasons for the failures.

Federal systems have worked where they have served to manage ethnic or intercommunal conflict. In India, the commitment to managing ethnic conflict through federal arrangements—that is, constitutionally protected diversity on a federal basis—led the Indian government, however reluctantly, to change state boundaries and even to create new states to accommodate linguistic (and in one case, religious) diversity when it became apparent that this was the greatest desire of the Indian public. By making these changes, Indian federalism managed to defuse conflicts that had already reached the violent stage, demonstrating the effectiveness of federalism in the management of such conflicts and reinforcing its importance in the minds of the people who benefited from the changes.

Nigeria has also used federalism as a successful device for ethnic conflict management, although the issue there was briefly in doubt during the Biafra war. It has already been suggested that the one effort to abolish federalism in Nigeria led to the overthrow of the strong man who initiated it. Beyond that, once Biafran resistance ended, the Nigerian government used federal principles to restore amity, restoring to the Ibo their state government, even if in a smaller state than before the war (the victorious Yoruba and Hausa also had their states carved up in the expansion of the number of states) and allowing them to resume positions of influence through the federal structure.

Moreover, the Nigerian government has undertaken two reorganizations of the federal structure, both increasing the number of states in the Nigerian federation so as better to accommodate the country's great ethnic diversity. (Nigeria has more than one hundred different tribal or ethnic groups, more than all of Europe.) Beyond that, Nigeria has applied federal principles in the local arena as well, by encouraging the organization of the internal polities of the states in such a way as to accommodate tribal and ethnic groups too small to acquire states of their own. Thus many of the Nigerian local authorities, more or less equivalent to American counties, are so structured as to provide smaller tribes and ethnic groups with what are, in effect, autonomous regional governments.

The Sudanese constitutional reorganization to put an end to its civil war by granting regional autonomy to the southern part of the country and its inhabitants represents another, if more limited, application of federal principles to manage interethnic conflict, which also seems to be having a measure of success. The Sudan government has followed up that success with an effort to reconstitute the entire country on a regional basis through a major devolution of powers and functions.[16]

A second element leading to the successful adaptation of federal principles and arrangements is the substitution of government by an elite in place of government by a single strong man. It has been suggested that strong-man government, by its nature, is inimical to federalism. Although elite government may not be as fully democratic as some would like, a properly structured elite does make possible the application of federal principles.

In successful federal systems, the existence of such a properly structured elite is almost a sine qua non. Malaysia, for example, has been successful as a federation because of the existence of the sultans of its states, who find federalism a useful way for sharing power among more or less equals.[17] The one successful federal experiment in the Arab world to date, the United Arab Emirates (UAE), is based on a similar principle. The emirs of the Persian Gulf sheikhdoms that have federated together form an elite that is able to share power.[18]

In Nigeria, the elite is less oligarchical and formally structured. Nevertheless, military rule there is clearly rule by a group rather than by a single strong man, a group that includes representatives of the major ethnic groups and their states. India, the most democratic of the Third World countries, has a far more amorphous elite, one spread more fully among the country's total population and perhaps more closely approximating the elites found in the West in the sense that it is more representative. All this is reflected in the strength of Indian federalism.

Similarly, the availability of resources, both human and material, is an important dimension in the successful application of federal principles and arrangements in the Third World. Both India and Nigeria have large populations, and India especially has a substantial educated group available to run the machinery of government—although matters are not so simple because it is that same educated group seeking sinecures that leads to the multiplication of bureaucracy beyond any necessary proportions. More important than the numbers of people available is the cultural predisposition of people to work within shared power systems, a condition that not all Third World countries share. That

India is not rich yet is successfully federal and that many countries richer than the federal ones in the Third World have been unable to use federal mechanisms even when they have tried reinforce the view that it is not economic so much as human resources that are important here.

This brings us back to the question of political culture once again. What seems to be characteristic of successful federal systems in the Third World as elsewhere is the existence of a political culture that is at least predisposed toward federalism, if not federalist in orientation—a political culture that rests upon some basic commitment to power sharing, some notion of political self-restraint, and some orientation toward the involvement of larger numbers of people in the governing process.

Successful federal arrangements have not been imposed from the outside but have developed indigenously in ways that suit the entities involved. The Moslem world's tendency to federate rulers rather than populations is reflected in the more successful Malaysian and UAE experiences, as contrasted with the less successful Pakistani effort.[19] The still-working autonomy agreement in the Sudan was developed indigenously, whereas the three-unit Libyan federation that failed was imposed by the United Nations.

The existence of common interests, especially economic and security interests, is a necessary if not sufficient factor reinforcing successful federal efforts, although taken alone they can serve to encourage consolidation as well.

Multiunit federal arrangements have a far better chance of success than those of only a few units. India, Nigeria, and Malaysia have more than ten states each; the UAE has seven; Pakistan has only four.

Overall, Asia has proved to be more hospitable to federalism than Africa, apparently for political-cultural reasons. Although neither continent is known for fostering the liberality that is a prerequisite for federalism to flourish,

Africa has even fewer brakes on the centralization of power in the hands of strong men. Asia, on the other hand, tends to foster rule by elites, which is less incompatible with federal arrangements. Also, Asia has long since developed institutionalized modes of accommodating communal differences that are more compatible with the demands of modern statehood.

Accommodating Diversity

From the foregoing discussion, it should be possible to draw some conclusions about the uses of federalism in the Third World countries. Most immediately, federalism has proved useful in accommodating diversity. Indeed, once there is a commitment to the accommodation of diversity, federal solutions are likely to follow as a matter of course. Most of the resistance to federal solutions has come precisely from those who do not wish to accommodate diversity but to eliminate it. Perhaps enough has been said about this theme already, but it should be recalled that it has more than one dimension. That is, it is not only a question of particular rulers opposing diversity but of particular tribal, ethnic, or religious communities within the polity opposing it as well—some of whom are victims of discrimination and persecution because they are minorities but who would not behave differently if they were to acquire power.

Thus it is hard to say that Zaïre, which abandoned a proposed federal, or at least quasi-federal, arrangement upon achieving independence from Belgium—and which, as a result, was plagued by periodic efforts on the part of Katanga, now Shaba, to secede—would have become more federal had the Katangese won. When Moïse Tshombe, the original leader of the Katangese secession movement, briefly became president of all of Zaïre, he was no more friendly to diversity than were those who opposed him and ultimately had him assassinated. In short, the peoples of Zaïre, whatever their tribal, ethnic, or regional background, seem to be interested in promoting the exclusive rule of their particular group, not in finding a modus vivendi through power sharing.[20]

In Nigeria, constant efforts are required on the part of the other two major partners in the Nigerian federation plus the many minor ones to accommodate the demands of the centralistically oriented Hausa, which are not only substantively great but structurally difficult as well. The rule of the Nigerian military junta during the 1970s, whatever its other drawbacks, was, for its time, the most reasonable way of preventing Hausa dominance or secession, thereby preserving the federal structure as a means of accommodating diversity. Before returning power to the civil authorities, the junta succeeded in dividing the Hausa Northern State into a number of smaller ones as part of a general redivision of Nigeria's territory into nineteen states.

In situations in which federalism rests upon a structured elite, as in Malaysia or the United Arab Emirates, the elite has a strong commitment to maintaining the diversity it represents. Since the elites are dominant in both cases, it is difficult to analyze what would happen without them, although in both cases such diversity as exists among the population is not strictly along the lines of the federal territorial divisions. Malays representing the major force, if not the majority of all the states of Malaysia, have antipathy toward the Chinese, who form a minority everywhere. Only in Singapore do the Chinese represent a majority, which is one of the reasons why Singapore seceded from Malaysia—and was, indeed, allowed and even encouraged to do so by the other members of the federation. In the UAE, some tribal groupings cross emirate boundaries, others do not; but apparently there is not an intense problem of diversity among the population.

Pakistan, on the other hand, is a country founded ostensibly on the principle of unity—in this case, Islamic unity—
that did not give appropriate recognition to ethnic differences within the Islamic whole. Consequently, each suc-
cessive ruler of Pakistan has attempted to centralize power
in strong-man fashion, while at the same time the population insists on the diffusion of power to accommodate the
country's ethnic diversity. Federalism survives in Pakistan
on paper and, to a greater or lesser extent, diffusion of
power survives in practice, principally because of the weakness of the central government vis-à-vis the provincial and
subprovincial groups rather than out of any desire on the
part of the former to make federalism work.

The essentially abortive Philippine effort to grant some
measure of autonomy to the Moros of Mindanao and other
southern Philippine islands has failed to date because, despite a certain lip service to the accommodation of diversity,
neither side was particularly interested in such an accommodation. President Ferdinand Marcos enjoyed a sufficient
monopoly of power in the center to prevent implementation from that side, while the Moros possess sufficient
power to maintain the guerrilla war they are conducting on
behalf of their revolution. The result is a stalemate actively
reflected in continuing military operations rather than a
quasi-federal accommodation. Since it seems clear that neither side can achieve its exclusive goals, violent stalemate is
likely to continue indefinitely unless an agreement along
federal or quasi-federal lines is reached.

Diversity is not likely to disappear in the Third World,
any more than it has in the first or second, even, in some
cases, after centuries of concerted effort at national integration through homogenization. Only massacre or expulsion
of minorities can change that situation. In most of the Third
World countries, the number and diffusion of tribal, ethnic,
religious, or linguistic groups is such that even those ugly

options are not likely to bring about the desired homogeneity. Consequently, federal arrangements may be the only useful way to deal with diversity.

Strengthening Liberty

In the Third World, as elsewhere, federalism is a means for strengthening liberty. This, too, is one of the reasons that failures are more numerous than successes in that segment of the world. Very few of the Third World regimes are interested in strengthening liberty. Their commitment to independence and nation-building does not necessarily include a commitment to freedom for the people involved. Often, to the contrary, every argument is used to justify the restriction of freedom and even the elimination of those traditional liberties that do exist, such as tribal and customary liberties, in the name of national independence and national development. In such cases, federalism—which is, almost by its very nature, a constant goad in the direction of the maintenance of liberty and a certain reminder of its importance in a polity striving toward democracy—is at best an embarrassment and at worst a real hindrance. Again, the successful examples all testify to the importance of federalism for strengthening liberty, whether in the case of India, which has clear democratic aspirations, or in the cases of Malaysia and the UAE, which at least wish to preserve the liberties of the constituent rulers.

Spreading Economic Development

The importance of federalism in spreading economic development and its benefits has been almost entirely overlooked. By and large, what has passed for national development in the Third World is not national at all, but rather concentrated in a single metropolitan area, usually that of the capital. This area not only has monopolized the infusion of new resources to the country but has managed to drain the countryside of a major share of such resources as existed there prior to independence. The resultant impoverishment of the countryside without appreciable progress in the metropolis has become a feature of Third World national economies which reflects a vicious circle. As the countryside becomes impoverished, its people migrate to the metropolis in search of opportunity or, in most cases, sheer survival. In their masses, they overwhelm the metropolis and transform it into what has come to be known as the Calcutta syndrome. The metropolis absorbs all wealth-generating capacity; people rush to the center, so that the new capacity is lost in the magnitude of the problems created. The only ones to benefit are the ruling class, whose members are able to siphon off a substantial share of the development funds for their own personal use or for their Swiss bank accounts.

Development in federal countries suffers from some of these Third World problems. But because of the existence of federalism, the new resources are inevitably spread over a number of centers. At the very least, the capital of every federated state has some claim on the national resources, and together they work to prevent the single metropolis syndrome. This means that more people have a chance to benefit from development efforts. At least, it means that some of the worst excesses of resource concentration are eliminated, and a basis for truly national development begins to emerge.

India and Nigeria are prime examples. Although Calcutta and, of late, Bombay and Lagos suffer from the worst aspects of the rural-urban migration, in both countries one does not have to live in Calcutta, Bombay, or Lagos to gain benefit from economic development. Rather, development efforts have been spread throughout the country, if not uniformly, at least in significant ways. Many people who have stayed home or migrated to less prominent centers have managed to improve their lot, if not sufficiently, at least more than their peers in more centralized states. This phenomenon deserves to be studied in detail.

It is clear that, as always, politics influences economics as well as vice versa, particularly in the contemporary world, where state intervention is once again crucial in the economic realm. The way in which politics is structured affects the economic future of every inhabitant of any particular polity. Thus although economic measures that do not differentiate between segments of the polity may suggest equality, the realities of economic resource use and development may be quite different. The politics of federalism offers a means for extending economic benefits more widely than has otherwise been the case in the Third World.

The Future of Federalism in the Third World

At first glance, the future of federalism in the Third World would seem limited indeed. Although presently existing federal systems do not seem likely to lose their formally federal character, changes in regime could move them away from the realities of federal power sharing, even if the forms are preserved. At the same time, there is no evidence that nonfederal polities are likely to embrace federal principles, much less transform themselves into federal systems, even if objective conditions might recommend such solutions to their problems. So much for the short run. In the long run, however, federalism should not be written off as a means of coming to grips with Third World problems. In the first place—with one possible exception—it is unlikely that the problems of diversity that have stimulated and suggested federal solutions will significantly diminish in most

Third World countries. Thus some means of accommodating diversity will have to be found, and it is unlikely that any better means will emerge. Moreover, since there are many possible ways to implement federal principles through numerous different federal arrangements, some possibility should exist for almost every situation, although the will to implement them may not.

The use of federal principles in building new interstate arrangements may be hardly more promising. Nevertheless, at least one example of an incipient regional confederation has emerged suddenly and even unexpectedly. The Association of Southeast Asian Nations, which combines the Philippines, Malaysia, Indonesia, Singapore, and Thailand to create a regional community of more than 200 million people, has moved from a paper body to a league that is presently trying to build a common sense of political unity, a common economic policy, and even a common market. Four of the five states involved are highly centralized internally, but all seem to have a very strong commitment to building ASEAN as a joint enterprise, even emphasizing the political dimension above all.[21] On a smaller scale, the confederation of Senegal and Gambia as Senegambia offers similar promise.[22] These regional arrangements offer another opportunity to use federal principles for mutual advantage.

Urbanization and the Future of Federalism

The rapid spread of urbanization in all three worlds is indicative of another revolution which is coming to fruition in the postmodern epoch. Having engulfed and transformed all three, it will be a crucial factor in the future role of federalism.

The impact of federalism in shaping urbanization has already been noted. The converse is also true. Several examples come to mind. Most contemporary federal systems developed at a time when their polities were basically rural in character with cities small and subordinated to the purposes of an agricultural society or agriculturally based commerce. Thus the original bases for federal arrangements were rural territorial units that gave the system as a whole a particular character. Subsequent urbanization of those polities has led to varying degrees of dislocation as a result of the concentration of population in urban areas and the forging of new lines of communication and interaction between those areas and new hinterlands.

For example, apportionment of representation in legislative bodies was often based originally on strictly territorial principles because a rural population was spread over a particular territory more or less uniformly. The rise of cities led to great imbalances in the density of population in particular territories, necessitating new bases for apportionment in order to maintain the principles of equitable, if not equal, representation fundamental to democratic federal systems. Similarly, loyalty patterns originally based on the initial constituent units of government have sometimes undergone erosion where large new cities have developed to dominate the attachments of their residents. The development of urbanized regions often crossing the boundaries of the constituent polities has led to problems arising from political boundaries that bear little relation to the patterns of regional economic interaction. Although all of these problems tend to be exaggerated in contemporary discussion and the changes are often given more importance than they deserve, there is a certain reality to them which must be considered in any examination of contemporary federal systems.

In general, urbanization has tended to heighten or exaggerate the tensions that may already be present in federal systems but are more easily controlled where population is spread less densely and a rural culture prevails. For example, ethnic and racial tensions, manageable in the slower-paced rural setting where social arrangements are more clearly fixed and contact among diverse groups less frequent or intense, may well be exacerbated in the hurly-burly of the urban setting, thus leading to additional strains on the political system. Since migration seems to be a strong concomitant of urbanization, it contributes to these tensions by limiting the degree to which social stability can be achieved in any locality.

Urbanization also places greater demands upon government to provide services or undertake activities that could previously be left to private auspices. Moreover, to the extent that publics and interest groups are dissatisfied with the services they receive, they tend to blame the governments closest at hand, namely the local and state governments. In part this is because they are close at hand and in part because the dissatisfaction is usually with domestic programs that fall within their jurisdiction. This conflict in turn may lead to greater demands for general government intervention and a consequent tendency to centralize power and weaken the role of state and local government. It is important in this connection that federalism serves to retard the growth of reliance upon the general government, in part because of the constitutional framework which it imposes upon urbanization and in part because of its cultural impact. This is an area deserving of special consideration.

On the other hand, it may well be that federal systems provide their own antidotes for many of these urban-generated problems, perhaps even in ways that are impossible for more centralized political systems, and would serve to limit the adverse effects of urbanization upon the drive for self-government. The research of the Workshop in American Federalism under the late Morton Grodzins has suggested as much, and the work of Vincent and Elinor Ostrom and their colleagues certainly points in that direction.[23] Milton Kotler has argued to this effect on the basis of his experience.[24]

Although most of the interest in federalism has focused on nation-states, similar varieties of federal arrangements have existed for some time on the local plane and are growing in number. Federal arrangements involving local communities are a particular phenomenon of urbanization in its metropolitan dimension since they more often than not involve the linking of cities within metropolitan regions that are closely integrated internally for economic (and certain social) purposes but are divided governmentally. The Canadian experiments, particularly in Ontario (whose metropolitan Toronto is the best-known example), are recent examples of the use of federal principles and arrangements on that scale. The United States has tried somewhat different arrangements based on federal principles in metropolitan Miami (Dade County) and in the Twin Cities metropolitan region of Minnesota. In fact, however, federalism as a solution to the problems of governance in metropolitan regions has reached its highest development in such European cities as Paris and London—examples that have not been properly examined from this perspective by students of urbanization. The federated government of metropolitan regions is a subdivision of the study of federalism, worthy of consideration in and of itself.[25]

Up to this point, we have been talking about federalism strictly in a governmental context. The federal principle has also been used as the basis for nongovernmental associations, both public and private, that have become characteristic of an urban world. Labor unions in many countries are frequently organized along federal principles, certainly in regard to the connections that form the basis for the great national labor confederations. So, too, are business and industrial associations, chambers of commerce, and health

and welfare federations. All of these are public nongovernmental bodies. When they use federal arrangements, they
frequently do so in such a way that the constituent units are
not territorial but functional in character, thus adding another dimension to the use of federal principles.

The modern corporation has its roots to some degree in
one variant of the same compact idea that lies at the basis of
modern federalism.[26] Pragmatically, as corporations have
grown in size, they frequently have had to resort to the use
of federal arrangements, if not to fully federal forms of
organization, for many of the same reasons that have led
polities in that direction—to manage very complex enterprises more effectively.[27]

In recent years, conglomerates have carried this use of
federal principles farther than ever. Federal principles and
arrangements have become so widespread precisely because
they suit the modern temper. As basically contractual arrangements, they fit into a civilization governed by contracts more than by status (one in which even status is a
matter of contractual arrangement, not usually transmitted
by inheritance). Moreover, because, as contractual relationships, they place a premium on negotiation and bargaining, they are eminently suited to a civilization that seeks
to maximize individual liberty and equality among the parties to the social contract.

If this observer reads the signs correctly, we stand on the
threshold of a convergence of the two revolutions of urbanization and federalism. All around us we can see examples of
the widening of the use of federal solutions to current problems of government and organization, public and private.
These examples can be found at both the micro and macro
ends of the continuum. Use of federal principles to link
cities in metropolitan areas and countries across continental
expanses so as to gain the advantages of scale without sacri-
ficing their internal integrity as bodies politic is becoming

widespread and increasingly attractive in diverse places. The possibilities at both ends are enormous and, as yet, substantially unexplored.

Toward a New State System

The system of politically sovereign states reorganized under international law as part of the modern state system now embraces more than 160 polities. In addition, there are more than 300 federated states which form a parallel state system worldwide. Stated differently, there are some 500 polities in the world which are governed by general as distinct from municipal governments. Approximately 100, or one-fifth of them, are politically sovereign unitary states, in other words, classic examples of the modern state system. More than 400, or four-fifths, are either federal polities or their functional equivalent, or constituent states within federal systems or their functional equivalent. This distinction could be simply a technical point were it not that the two state systems are becoming increasingly intertwined, with the constituent states increasingly involved in foreign relations, once considered the exclusive province of federal governments.

In the United States, for example, the distinction was once thought to be absolute. If there was one thing that was clear about American federalism, it was that the general government had exclusive responsibility for foreign affairs while the states had exclusive responsibility in various domestic fields. Just as the latter is no longer the case, neither is the former. American states are increasingly involved in foreign affairs in many ways. Perhaps their biggest involvement is in foreign economic relations, in the promotion of foreign trade, and in the stimulation of foreign investment. In the economic realm, the states collectively are spending as much annually as the federal government and, since the Kennedy administration, have had the blessing of the federal government to undertake initiatives in the economic field. Beyond that, American border states have developed a wide range of relationships with their counterparts in Canada and Mexico and even have played a role in shaping U.S. policy toward the Canadian and Mexican governments, particularly in connection with Great Lakes and Columbia River Basin water matters and Mexican immigration to the United States.[28]

In a sense, the American case is the hardest because the United States federal Constitution makes foreign affairs so exclusively a federal responsibility. In a number of federal systems, the constituent states are constitutionally empowered to negotiate with their neighbors on matters affecting them provided that they do not contravene federal law. This is true with regard to the Swiss cantons and the Yugoslav republics.[29] It is theoretically true with regard to the Soviet republics as well, two of which, the Ukraine and Byelorussia, are even represented in the United Nations. Although their presence in the UN reflects a deal between the Great Powers at the time of that organization's founding to provide the USSR with more votes than it would otherwise have been entitled to in a body then overwhelmingly anti-Communist, the framework for the deal was based upon recognized principles of Soviet constitutional law which, of course, have no meaning in practice.[30]

Canada's constitution is vague on such matters, but in fact the Canadian provinces have come to represent one of the foremost examples of the new involvement of constituent states in foreign affairs. Quebec's cultural relationships with the francophone world and its efforts to gain special status in the international community even while it remains a full-fledged member of the Canadian confederation are only the most visible manifestations of this trend. Other

Canadian provinces, particularly Alberta and British Columbia, are also very active in foreign affairs, so much so that since the mid-1960s the Canadian Foreign Ministry has taken official cognizance of the provincial role, maintaining an office to serve provincial interests and to facilitate provincial involvement in foreign relations. Since most of the provinces' interest in foreign affairs relates to the United States, the Canadian Embassy in Washington has a foreign service officer permanently assigned to working with the provinces. Similarly, every Canadian embassy has standing instructions on how to help visiting provincial officials who have come to the countries in which they are located on provincial business.[31]

The new role of these federated states in foreign affairs reflects and symbolizes the growing breakdown of the distinction between sovereign and constituent systems on the world scene. Only a few years ago, it seemed that movement would be in the other direction—that the constituent states in mature federal systems would be reduced to municipal status as the federal governments acquired more power. Were federal systems to exist in a vacuum, that might indeed have been the case, but in an increasingly complex world, international trends have worked to strengthen the role of those states, as representatives of particular peoples or publics, as more efficient mobilizers of resources than the larger polities of which they are a part, or as articulators of particular interests that seek expression in the new environment.

In truth, the constituent states are pulled in both directions. If the federalist revolution continues, state sovereignty is further reduced in an interdependent world, and their involvements continue to grow, they are likely to move toward even greater equality with the conventionally sovereign states.

The Postmodern Epoch and the Federalist Revolution

The emergence of the federalist revolution rests on three basic phenomena of modern political life. First is the emergence of the modern nation-state encompassing, of necessity, relatively large territories and populations in order to maintain itself under modern conditions in the world of power politics and the resultant problems of the internal distribution of power within those newly enlarged polities.[32] Second, modernism brought with it the breakdown of the premodern community with its "organic" lines of authority based upon essentially fixed social relationships. With it came the concomitant need for the creation of new forms of local attachment and self-government. Finally, modernism led to the breakdown of the old aristocratic principles in favor of a new commitment to equality with its concomitant demand for the creation of a more democratic social and political order.

The federalist revolution emerged in response to all three of these phenomena and the problems to which they gave rise, suggesting itself as an antidote to them that is in keeping with the modern temper. Federalism has been used to enable nation-states to concentrate power and authority in large, energetic general governments while at the same time diffusing the exercise of powers so as to give most if not all segments of civil society a constitutionally guaranteed share in their governance. Federal ideas have made possible the development of new forms of community with new instruments for local self-government by making it possible to build new societies through contractual relationships rather than relying upon kinship or other traditional ties. Finally, the federalist revolution has been directed toward serving the cause of equality by creating better instrumentalities for citizen involvement in public affairs through the development of governmental arenas of differing size and scope, ranging from the immediately local to the most general. The great analyst of modernization, Alexis de Tocqueville, was the first to recognize the importance and utility of federalism in connection with all three phenomena mentioned above. His works remain important starting points for investigating and understanding the role of the federalist revolution in the development of modern political life.[33]

Beyond that, as more decisions need to be made in the international arena, the more need there is for creating the proper political mechanisms to make the decisions. This is not a simplistic argument for world federalism—far from it, since simplistic approaches to such problems are more likely to add paving stones on the road to hell. Just to take one example, many environmentalists are very opposed to anything like a federal distribution of power; they would like to see the United Nations strong enough to make environmental decisions. The first question to be asked, however, is why should they expect the United Nations to make the kinds of decisions that they want? Everything we know about the UN should lead us to expect just the reverse. With its Third World orientation toward development at any cost, it would ignore everything they advocate.

The reality principle suggests that the more humanity deals on an international plane—with regard to multinationals, or a United Nations–dominated by the Third World, or cartels, or whatever, the more we need precisely those dimensions which federalism offers best. These include the principle that there are no simple majorities and simple minorities, but that all majorities are compounded of congeries of groups, and the principle of minority rights, which not only protects the possibility for minorities to preserve themselves but the possibility for majorities to be compound and not simple ones artificially stimulated by those people who can push levers of power. This may ultimately lead to reshaping the matrix, to having an international dimension that would be more institutionalized than anything we have seen up until now. The world may have to address that issue someday soon, although the international system that presently exists is probably as much as the world can bear, given all the problematics of group, national, regional, and ideological differences that presently exist.

A greater immediate problem is the bureaucratic revolution that has engulfed us all. We have now reached a point at which bureaucracies are not simply instruments of service to other elements in the society but have become self-generating. They generate their own tasks. They create their own crises, which they are then called upon to solve. If people are wise enough, we can use federalism as a political-constitutional device to try to deal with this problem. If we use our political structures to prevent the coalescence of bureaucracy, we may have a fighting chance. The movement away from understanding federalism as a political-constitutional device to looking at it as an administrative device—as a matter of intergovernmental relations—makes it easier for bureaucracies to manage the polity rather than vice versa. Classically, in the United States, federalism provided the constitutional relationships and framework for managing the bureaucracies. When Americans needed to build bureaucracies to provide for the new social service or welfare state, they jettisoned the constitutional dimension. Then when the presidency acquired the individual power it had in the late 1960s and early 1970s, they abandoned the political dimension as well. We have all seen the results. In sum, the question is whether they rule us or we rule them. That is the struggle that is before us. Federalism has much to say about the question.

Today we are in the first decade of the second generation of a postmodern era whose future form or shape is not precisely clear to any of us. It does seem certain, however, that the new era will be based upon some extension of the principles of modernism, particularly the principles of equality and liberty as manifested in the well-nigh universal commitment to the ideal of popular government—however that ideal is understood. The virtual completion of the task of modernization in certain Western countries has given us a glimpse of the direction we may be heading. In those countries there has been distilled out of the three central political phenomena of the modern era a dual political interest in (1) creating more viable units of government (however understood) to undertake vast new responsibilities while (2) enhancing citizen participation in government to foster democracy (however understood). The federalist revolution is precisely addressed to these twin interests, which is why experimentation with federal arrangements is on the increase in a variety of new settings and ways. Increasingly, it is accompanied by a turn away from state centralism, which is part and parcel of the conception of exclusive sovereignty which has accompanied that view of the state since the sixteenth century. In short, there is a turning from the reified state—exclusive sovereignty—centralism syndrome toward one of partnership, negotiation, and sharing.

Notes

Chapter 1

1. For a detailed discussion of this transition, see John Kincaid and Daniel J. Elazar, eds., *The Covenant Connection: Federal Theology and the Origins of Modern Politics* (Durham, N.C.: Carolina Academic Press, 1985).

2. See Henri Frankfort, *Before Philosophy: The Intellectual Adventure of Ancient Man, an Essay on Speculative Thought in the Ancient Near East* (Baltimore: Penguin Books, 1967).

3. See, for example, Ernest Barker, trans. and ed., *The Politics of Aristotle* (New York: Oxford University Press, 1962); J. M. Moore, trans. with introduction and commentary, *Aristotle and Xenophon on Democracy and Oligarchy* (Berkeley and Los Angeles: University of California Press, 1975).

4. John F. A. Taylor, "Questions of Path and Questions of Covenant," *Publius* 10, no. 4 (1980): 59–70.

5. Thomas Hobbes, *Leviathan* (Indianapolis: Bobbs-Merrill, 1958); see also Vincent Ostrom, "Hobbes, Covenant, and Constitution," *Publius* 10, no. 4 (1980): 83–101.

6. See Delbert Hillers, *Covenant: The History of the Biblical Idea* (Baltimore: Johns Hopkins University Press, 1969); George E. Mendenhall, *Law and Covenant in Israel and the Ancient Near East* (Pittsburgh: University of Pittsburgh Press, 1955); and Moshe Weinfeld, "Covenant," in *Encyclopedia Judaica* (Jerusalem: Keter Books, 1973), 5:1012–22.

7. See, for example, G. H. Dodge, *The Political Theory of the Huguenots of Dispersion* (New York: Octagon Books, 1947); E. J. Shirley, *Richard Hooker and Contemporary Political Ideas* (Naperville, Ill.: Allenson, 1949); R. H. Murray, *The Political Consequences of the Reformation* (New York: Russell and Russell, 1960);

and Christopher Hill, *Intellectual Origins of the English Revolution* (New York: Oxford University Press, 1965).

8. "Peace" in *Encyclopedia Judaica,* 13:194–99; Daniel J. Elazar, *The Vocabulary of Covenant* (Philadelphia: Center for the Study of Federalism, 1983).

9. See Daniel J. Elazar, ed., *Federalism and Political Integration* (Ramat Gan, Israel: Turtledove Publishing, 1979), *Self-Rule/ Shared Rule* (Ramat Gan, Israel: Turtledove Publishing, 1979), and *Handbook of Federal and Autonomy Arrangements* (Jerusalem: Jerusalem Center for Public Affairs, forthcoming). What follows is a summary of the varieties of federal arrangements. The following chapters deal with them more elaborately.

10. Ivo D. Duchacek elaborates on this theme in "Antagonistic Cooperation: Territorial and Ethnic Communities," *Publius* 7, no. 4 (1977): 3–31.

11. Martin O. Heisler, ed., *Politics in Europe* (New York: David McKay, 1974); Leon N. Lindberg and Stuart A. Scheingold, *Europe's Would-Be Polity: Patterns of Change in the European Community* (Englewood Cliffs, N.J.: Prentice-Hall, 1970); Guy Heraud, *L'Europe des ethnics* (Nice: Presses de Europe, 1963).

12. See Benjamin Akzin, *States and Nations* (Garden City, N. Y.: Doubleday, Anchor Books, 1966); Cynthia Enloe, "Internal Colonialism, Federalism and Alternative State Development Strategies," *Publius* 7, no. 4 (1977): 145–61; and "The Neglected Strata: States in the City-Federal Politics of Malaysia," *Publius* 5, no. 2 (1975): 151–71; and Ivo D. Duchacek, ed., *Federalism and Ethnicity,* a special issue of *Publius* 7, no. 4 (1977).

13. Myron Weiner, "Matching Peoples, Territories and States: Post Ottoman Irredentism in the Balkans and in the Middle East," in Daniel J. Elazar, ed., *Governing Peoples and Territories* (Philadelphia: Institute for the Study of Human Issues, 1983), pp. 101–46.

14. See Filippo Sabetti and Harold M. Waller, eds., *Crisis and Continuity in Canadian Federalism,* special issue of *Publius* 14, no. 1 (1984); Murray Friedman, "Religion and Politics in an Age of Pluralism, 1945–1976: An Ethnocultural View," *Publius* 10, no. 3 (1980): 45–77; Russell L. Barsh and James Y. Henderson, *The Road: Indian Tribes and Political Liberty* (Berkeley and Los Angeles:

University of California Press, 1980); and Wilcomb E. Washburn, *Red Man's Law and White Man's Law: A Study of the Past and Present Status of the American Indian* (New York: Charles Scribner's Sons, 1971).

15. See Howard Penniman, ed., *Venezuela at the Polls: The National Elections of 1978* (Washington, D.C.: American Enterprise Institute for Public Policy Research, 1980).

16. Deil S. Wright traces the popularization of the term "intergovernmental relations" to William Anderson, W. Brooke Graves, and Clyde F. Snider in the 1930s. See his *Understanding Intergovernmental Relations* (North Scituate, Mass.: Duxbury Press, 1978), p. 6.

17. William Anderson, *Intergovernmental Relations in Review* (Minneapolis: University of Minnesota Press, 1960), p. 3, as quoted in Wright, *Understanding Intergovernmental Relations,* p. 5.

18. See, for example, the articles in W. Brooke Graves, ed., *Intergovernmental Relations in the United States, Annals* 207 (January 1940).

19. The term "federalism" emerged in theological and theopolitical usage in the sixteenth century and was first used as a strictly political term in the eighteenth century. The general outlines of its development can be found in the *Oxford English Dictionary*. It, in turn, rests on the Latin *foedus* used by the Romans to describe the relationships between Rome and other parts of the Roman Empire and then in medieval times to describe the various leagues that developed in central Europe. Rufus Davis briefly tours this ground in *The Federal Principle: A Journey through Time in Quest of a Meaning* (Berkeley and Los Angeles: University of California Press, 1978).

20. Max Kadushin, *Organic Thinking* (New York: Jewish Theological Seminary, 1938).

21. On self-rule/shared rule as a thumbnail definition of federalism, see Elazar, ed., *Self-Rule/Shared Rule,* particularly the editor's introduction.

22. See Daniel J. Elazar, "Federalism vs. Decentralization: The Drift from Authenticity," in Jeffrey L. Mayer, ed., *Dialogues on Decentralization, Publius* 6, no. 4 (1976): 9–19.

23. For examples of the usage in international relations see

Robert O. Keohane and Joseph S. Nye, Jr., eds., *Transnational Relations and World Politics* (Cambridge, Mass.: Harvard University Press, 1971), esp. Introduction and Conclusion. See also James N. Rosenau, *Linkage Politics: Essays on the Convergence of National and International Systems* (New York: Free Press, 1969); and Arnold Wolfers, *Discord and Collaboration: Essays on International Politics* (Baltimore: Johns Hopkins Press, 1962).

24. Arend Lijphart, "Consociation and Federation: Conceptual and Empirical Links," *Canadian Journal of Political Science* 12 (September 1979): 499–515, and Daniel J. Elazar, "Federalism," in David M. Sills, ed., *International Encyclopedia of the Social Sciences* (New York: Macmillan, 1968), 6:169–74.

25. Lijphart, "Consociation and Federation," and "Federal, Confederal, and Consociational Options for the South African Plural Society," in Robert I. Rotbarg and John Barrett, eds., *Conflictal Compromise in South Africa* (Lexington, Mass.: Lexington Books, 1980), pp. 51–75; and Daniel J. Elazar, "The Role of Federalism in Political Integration," in Elazar, ed., *Federalism and Political Integration,* pp. 13–57.

26. In addition to the citations in notes 24 and 25, see Ivo Duchacek, *Comparative Federalism: The Territorial Dimension of Politics* (New York: Holt, Rinehart and Winston, 1970).

27. For a theory of federalism emphasizing its structural character, see K. C. Wheare, *Federal Government,* 4th ed. (New York: Oxford University Press, 1964).

28. Heisler, ed., *Politics in Europe.*

29. Arend Lijphart, "Non-Majoritarian Democracy: A Comparison of Federal and Consociational Themes," *Publius* (forthcoming).

30. Ibid.

31. Ibid.

32. See Daniel J. Elazar, *Israel: From Territorial to Ideological Democracy* (New York: General Learning Press, 1970), and Howard Penniman, ed., *Israel at the Polls, 1977* (Washington, D.C.: American Enterprise Institute for Public Policy Research, 1979).

33. Leonard Binder, *Politics in Lebanon* (New York: Wiley,

1966); Yosef Olmert, "Wasted Time in Lebanon," *Jerusalem Post Magazine*, May 20, 1983.

34. *Keesing's Contemporary Archives, 1982*, vol. 28 (1982), s.v. "Cyprus," pp. 31601b–31602.

35. Ibid., s.v. "Surinam," pp. 31610a–31611.

36. Aristide R. Zolberg, "Splitting the Difference: Federalization without Federalism in Belgium," in Milton J. Esman, ed., *Ethnic Conflict in the Western World* (Ithaca: Cornell University Press, 1977), pp. 103–42.

37. Daniel J. Elazar, "The Generational Rhythm of American Politics," *American Politics Quarterly* 6 (January 1978): 55–94.

38. Jurg Steiner, *Amicable Agreement versus Majority Rule: Conflict Resolution in Switzerland* (Chapel Hill: University of North Carolina Press, 1974).

39. Binder, *Politics in Lebanon*, pp. 318–19.

40. Albert P. Blaustein and Gisbert H. Flanz, eds., *Constitutions of the Countries of the World* (Dobbs Ferry, N.Y.: Oceana Publications, 1984), vol. 14.

41. See Davis, *Federal Principle;* Davis, "Cooperative Federalism in Retrospect," *Historical Studies* 5 (Melbourne) (November 1952): 212–34.

42. William H. Stewart, "Metaphors, Models, and the Development of Federal Theory," *Publius* 12, no. 2 (1982): 5-24, and *Concepts of Federalism* (Lanham, Md.: University Press of America, 1984).

43. See Vincent Ostrom, *The Political Theory of the Compound Republic* (Blacksburg, Va.: Virginia Polytechnic Institute, Center for the Study of Public Choice, 1971); Martin Landau, "Federalism Redundancy and System Reliability," *Publius* 3, no. 2 (1973): 172–96; and Vincent Ostrom, "Can Federalism Make a Difference?" *Publius* 3, no. 2 (1973): 197–238.

Chapter 2

1. This chapter is an expansion and reworking of material presented in previous articles by the author, particularly "The Ends of Federalism," in Max Frenkel, ed., *Foedralismus als Partnerschaft* (Bern: Peter Lang, 1977), and "Urbanism and Fed-

eralism: Twin Revolutions of the Modern Era," *Publius* 5, no. 2 (1975): 15–40.

2. Most of the principal recent works dealing with federalism are cited below. Others of general interest include the articles "Federalism" and "Federation" in David M. Sills, ed., *International Encyclopedia of the Social Sciences* (New York: Macmillan, 1968), 6:169–78; *The Federal Polity,* special issue of *Publius* 3, no. 2 (1973); Arthur Maas, ed., *Area and Power: A Theory of Local Government* (Glencoe, Ill.: Free Press, 1959); Arthur Macmahon, ed., *Federalism: Mature and Emergent* (New York: Columbia University Press, 1955); and Stephen L. Schechter, ed., *Federalism and Community,* special issue of *Publius* 5, no. 2 (1975), especially the articles by Schechter, Duchacek, Djordevic, and Elazar.

3. In some cases, this noncentralization is written into the federal constitution itself. Articles 116–19 of the Yugoslav constitution of 1974, for example, delegate to the communes "the functions of power and management of social affairs, with the exception of those which under the constitution are exercised in the broader socio-political communities [the Federation and republics]." See *Constitution of the Socialist Federal Republic of Yugoslavia,* trans. Marko Pavicic for the Secretariat of the Federal Assembly Information Service (Belgrade, 1974). In others, it has become part of the constitutional tradition. See Morton Grodzins, *The American System: A New View of Government in the United States,* ed. Daniel J. Elazar (Chicago: Rand McNally, 1966).

4. Vincent Ostrom discusses this problem at length in *The Intellectual Crisis of American Public Administration* (University, Ala.: University of Alabama Press, 1973).

5. Martin Diamond discusses this transformation in "What the Framers Meant by Federalism," in Robert A. Goldwin, ed., *A Nation of States,* 2d ed. (Chicago: Rand McNally, 1974).

6. Jean Bodin is accepted as the first great exponent of this understanding of sovereignty (*De Republica Libri Six,* 2nd Latin ed., 1591). See the translation by M. J. Tooley, *The Six Books of the Commonwealth* (New York: Barnes and Noble, 1967). His views were echoed and used as the basis of a critique of federalism by Samuel Pufendorf in the eighteenth century. See *De jure naturae et gentium libri octo,* trans. W. A. Oldfather (Oxford: Clarendon

Press, 1934). Contrast the views of Johannes Althusius in *Politica Methodice Digesta* (1603), ed. Carl Friedrich (Cambridge, Mass.: Harvard University Press, 1935); Ludolf Hugo, *Dissertatio de statu regionum Germanice et regimine principum summae Imperii rei publicae aemulo* (1661) (Helmstadt: Sumptibus Hammianis, 1708); and G. W. Leibniz, who understood the federalist attack on this theory of sovereignty. See Leibniz, *Entretien de Philarete et d'Eugene* (1677) in *Oeuvres de Leibniz*, ed. A. Foucher de Careil (Paris: Firmin Didot frères, 1865), 6:347; Patrick Riley, *The Political Writings of Leibniz* (Cambridge: Cambridge University Press, 1972). See Carl J. Friedrich's Introduction to *Politica Methodice Digesta*, and Patrick Riley, "Three Seventeenth-Century Theorists of Federalism: Althusius, Hugo and Leibniz," *Publius* 6, no. 3 (1976): 7–42.

7. Martin Landau expands on this theme in "Federalism, Redundancy and System Reliability," *Publius* 3, no. 2 (1973): 173–96.

8. See Martin O. Heisler, ed., *Politics in Europe* (New York: David McKay, 1974), esp. chap. 5; see also Heisler, "Ethnic Division in Belgium," in Daniel J. Elazar, ed., *Self-Rule/Shared Rule* (Ramat Gan: Turtledove Publishing, 1979), pp. 138–48.

9. See Alain Greilsammer, *Les mouvements federalistes en France* (Nice: Presses d'Europe, 1975), and Heisler, ed., *Politics in Europe*.

10. Richard Rose and his colleagues at the University of Strathclyde have been working on an appropriate theory of the United Kingdom in this vein. See Center for the Study of Public Policy publications, which can be obtained by writing the center at the university, McCance Building, 16 Richmond Street, Glasgow G1 1XQ, Scotland; also see Richard Rose and Peter Madgwick, *The Territorial Dimension in United Kingdom Politics* (London: Macmillan, 1982).

11. See the notes of James Fratto on the post–Napoleonic Netherlands in the Archives of the Center for the Study of Federalism. See also James W. Skillen, "From Covenant of Grace to Tolerant Public Pluralism: The Dutch Calvinist Contribution" (paper presented at the Center for the Study of Federalism, Workshop on Covenant and Politics, Philadelphia, February 27–29, 1980).

12. Heisler, ed., *Politics in Europe*, chap. 5.

13. Arend Lijphart, "Consociational Democracy," *World Pol-*

itics 21 (1968–69): 205–25; Ivo Duchacek, "Consociations of Fatherlands: The Revival of Confederal Principles and Practices," *Publius* 12, no. 4 (1982): 129–77.

14. See Edward A. Freeman, *A History of Federal Government in Greece and Italy,* 2 vols. (London: Macmillan, 1893); Heinz H. F Eulau, "Theories of Federalism under the Holy Roman Empire," *American Political Science Review* 25 (August 1941): 643–64; Patrick Riley, "Historical Development of the Theory of Federalism" (Ph.D. dissertation, Harvard University, 1968); and Michael Curtis, *Western European Integration* (New York: Harper & Row, 1965). See also Christopher Hughes, *Confederacies* (Leicester: Leicester University Press, 1963).

15. Curtis, *Western European Integration.*

16. R. Michael Stevens, "Asymmetrical Federalism: The Federal Principle and the Survival of the Small Republic," *Publius* 7, no. 4 (1977): 177–204.

17. For the New Hebrides, see Patrick Cox, "Wun niu fela Kuntri: A Different Kind of Liberation Movement Emerges in the New Hebrides," *Reason* 12 (Spring 1982): 24–37; "Vanuato," *Courrier African-Caribbean-Pacific-European Community* (November–December 1982): 11–22. For the Sudan, see P. M. Holt and M. W. Daly, *The History of Sudan: From the Coming of Islam to the Present Day,* 3d ed. (London: Weidenfeld and Nicolson, 1979).

18. Ivo D. Duchacek, "Consociations of Fatherlands: The Revival of Confederal Principles and Practices," *Publius* 12, no. 4 (1982): 129–77.

19. Cesar Enrique Diaz Lopez, "The State of the Autonomic Process in Spain," *Publius* 11, nos. 3–4 (1981): 193–216.

20. See Daniel J. Elazar, "The Compound Structure of Public Service Delivery Systems in Israel," in Vincent Ostrom and Francine Pennell Bish, eds., *Comparing Urban Service Delivery Systems* (Beverly Hills: Sage Publications, 1977), pp. 47–82.

21. Stefan Dupre, *Regional Government* (Toronto: Institute of Public Administration of Canada, 1968). Dupre provides a thorough discussion of the possibilities of metropolitan federalism in light of the Toronto experience. See also Joseph Zimmerman, *The Federated City: Community Control in Large Cities* (New York: St. Martin's Press, 1972).

22. See, for example, Andrew C. McLaughlin, *The Founda-*

tions of American Constitutionalism (Greenwich, Conn.: Fawcett, 1961), and Peter F. Drucker, *The Concept of the Corporation*, rev. ed. (New York: Day, 1972).

23. The articles in Valerie Earle, ed., *Federalism: Infinite Variety in Theory and Practice* (Itasca, Ill.: F. E. Peacock, 1969), and Aaron Wildavsky, ed., *American Federalism in Perspective* (Boston: Little, Brown, 1967), emphasize various dimensions of federalism as a unifying force and as a means to maintain diversity. In connection with the former, see also William H. Riker, *Federalism: Origin, Operations, Significance* (Boston: Little, Brown, 1964), and with the latter, Ivo D. Duchacek, *Comparative Federalism: The Territorial Dimension of Politics* (New York: Holt, Rinehart and Winston, 1970).

24. For a further discussion of noncentralization versus decentralization, see Daniel J. Elazar, *American Federalism: A View from the States*, 3d ed. (New York: Harper & Row, 1984).

25. Denis de Rougemont has frequently made the contrast. See, for example, *La Suisse, ou l'histoire d'un peuple heureux* (Lausanne: Le Livre du Mois, 1965).

26. See, for example, Riker, *Federalism,* and Duchacek, *Comparative Federalism.*

27. For a theory of federalism emphasizing its structural character, see K. C. Wheare, *Federal Government,* 4th ed. (New York: Oxford University Press, 1964).

28. See, for example, Walter Kolarz, *Russia and Her Colonies* (New York: Praeger, 1953); Robert J. Osborn, *The Evolution of Soviet Politics* (Homewood, Ill.: Dorsey Press, 1974); and Frank Sherwood, *Institutionalizing the Grass Roots in Brazil: A Study in Comparative Local Government* (San Francisco: Chandler, 1961).

29. See, for example, Pierre-Joseph Proudhon, *Du principe federatif* (Paris, 1863); Yves Simon, "A Note on Proudhon's Federalism," trans. Vukan Kuic, *Publius* 3, no. 1 (1973): 19–30; Alexandre Marc and Robert Aron, *Principes du federalisme* (Paris: Le Portulan, 1948). See also *Le federalisme et Alexandre Marc* (Lausanne: Centre de Recherches Duropeennes, 1974), for a recent restatement of this perspective.

30. See Lijphart, "Consociational Democracy."

31. Ibid.

32. Several Indian scholars have suggested to me that such Third World nations as India and those of the Arab world should be considered federal nations—peoples who sense themselves to be united as a single nation but are internally divided into several states or subnational groupings that are fully articulated in their own right through significant linguistic, religious, or sociocultural differences. This distinction could represent a third dimension of federalism as a social phenomenon in the sense suggested here.

33. See, for example, Benjamin Barber, *The Death of Communal Liberty: A History of Freedom in a Swiss Mountain Canton* (Princeton: Princeton University Press, 1974); George Codding, Jr., *Governing the Commune of Veyrier: Politics in Swiss Local Government* (Boulder: Bureau of Government Research, University of Colorado, 1967).

34. Arend Lijphart, *The Politics of Accommodation: Pluralism and Democracy in the Netherlands* (Berkeley and Los Angeles: University of California Press, 1969).

35. Daniel J. Elazar, "Field Notes—Nigeria" (July 1974).

Chapter 3

1. Most American federalists fall into this category. See, for example, the works of John C. Calhoun or Woodrow Wilson.

2. See, for example, the works of Proudhon, Marc, and de Rougement. Martin Buber treats federalism as means and end in *Paths in Utopia* (Boston: Beacon Press, 1958), and *Kingship of God* (New York: Harper & Row, 1956).

3. Jean-Jacques Rousseau, *The Social Contract and Discourse on the Origin of Inequality* (New York: Washington Square Press, 1967). See also Patrick Riley, "Rousseau as a Theorist of National and International Federalism," *Publius* 3, no. 1 (1973): 5–18.

4. See, for example, Pierre-Joseph Proudhon, *Du principe federatif* (Paris, 1863).

5. E.g., Buber, *Paths* and *Kingship*.

6. E.g., James Madison in Alexander Hamilton, James Madison, and John Jay, *The Federalist* (1789), ed. with introduction by Clinton Rossiter (New York: Mentor Books, 1961).

7. E.g., Woodrow Wilson, *Congressional Government* (Boston: Houghton-Mifflin, 1885).

8. See, for example, S. Rufus Davis, *The Federal Principle: A Journey through Time in Quest of a Meaning* (Berkeley and Los Angeles: University of California Press, 1978); David B. Walker, *Towards a Functioning Federalism* (Cambridge, Mass.: Winthrop, 1981); and Deil S. Wright, *Understanding Intergovernmental Relations* (North Scituate, Mass.: Duxbury Press, 1978).

9. I have elaborated on the relationship between power and justice and its manifestations in the American polity in *American Federalism: A View from the States,* 3d ed. (New York: Harper & Row, 1984). See also Daniel J. Elazar and John Kincaid, *Federal Democracy* (forthcoming), chap. 1.

10. *The Federalist* 51.

11. See Martin Diamond, *Notes on the Political Theory of the Founding Fathers* (Philadelphia: Center for the Study of Federalism, 1973); Vincent Ostrom, *The Political Theory of the Compound Republic* (Blacksburg, Va.: Virginia Polytechnic Institute, Center for the Study of Public Choice, 1971); and the articles by Ostrom and Martin Landau in *The Federal Polity,* a special issue of *Publius* 3, no. 2 (1973).

12. Robert Dahl is perhaps the foremost American political scientist to have emphasized pluralism without acknowledging the role of federalism in its maintenance. His most comprehensive statement of the pluralist view can be found in *A Preface to Democratic Theory* (Chicago: University of Chicago Press, 1956), and his textbook on American government originally titled *Pluralist Democracy in America* (Chicago: Rand McNally, 1968). (Perhaps significantly the second edition of the textbook was retitled to drop the word "pluralist.") Harold Laski and Franz Neumann were earlier proponents of the view, the former from the perspective of the British tradition and the latter from a continental European perspective. See, for example, Laski's "The Obsolescence of Federalism," *New Republic,* May 3, 1939, pp. 367–69.

13. By pluralism, I mean the existence of multiple or plural ways of human expression built into the universe itself, whose existence is thereby legitimate and even necessary for the world to function, as distinct from being an ephemeral phenomenon re-

sulting from human deficiency, to be at best tolerated out of generosity or necessity until the day comes when some form of monism will prevail. This definition follows that of William James, the great American philosopher of pluralism, who gave intellectual form and substance to American reality. See his *A Pluralistic Universe* (Cambridge, Mass.: Harvard University Press, 1977). James also made the connection between federalism and pluralism. See Henry S. Levinson, "William James and the Federal Republican Principle," *Publius* 9, no. 4 (1979): 65–86.

14. For a discussion of territorial democracy, see Daniel J. Elazar, *The American System as a Federal Democracy* (Lincoln: University of Nebraska Press, forthcoming), and "The Cities of the Prairie and the American Partnership," in Daniel J. Elazar, *Cities of the Prairie: the Metropolitan Frontier and American Politics* (New York: Basic Books, 1970), pp. 367–419.

15. Frederick B. Tolles, *Meeting House and Counting House: The Quaker Merchants of Colonial Philadelphia, 1682–1763* (Chapel Hill: University of North Carolina Press, 1948); Carl Bridenbaugh and Jessica Bridenbaugh, *Rebels and Gentlemen: Philadelphia in the Age of Franklin* (New York: Reynal & Hitchcock, 1942); E. Digby Baltzell, *Philadelphia Gentlemen: The Making of an Upper Class* (Glencoe, Ill.: Free Press, 1958); Sam Bass Warner, *The Private City: Philadelphia in Three Periods of Its Growth* (Philadelphia: University of Pennsylvania Press, 1968); Russell J. Ferguson, *Early Western Pennsylvania Politics* (Pittsburgh: University of Pittsburgh Press, 1938); Howard M. Jenkins, ed., *Pennsylvania, Colonial and Federal: A History, 1608–1903* (Philadelphia: Pennsylvania Historical Publishing Association, 1903); John P. Selsam, *The Pennsylvania Constitution of 1776: A Study of Revolutionary Democracy* (Philadelphia: University of Pennsylvania Press, 1936); Thomas J. Condon, *New York Beginnings: The Commercial Origins of New Netherlands* (New York: New York University Press, 1968); and Louis B. Wright, *The Atlantic Frontier: Colonial American Civilization* (New York: Knopf, 1947).

16. See Edmund S. Morgan, *The Puritan Dilemma*, ed. Oscar Handlin (Boston: Little, Brown, 1958); and Perry Miller, *The New England Mind: The Seventeenth Century*, vol. 2: *From Colony to Province* (Cambridge, Mass.: Harvard University Press, 1953).

17. See, for example, Lewis Atherton, *Main Street on the Middle Border* (Bloomington: Indiana University Press, 1984); and Page Smith, *As a City upon a Hill: The Town in American History* (New York: Knopf, 1966).

18. Barbara Haskell, ed., *Southern California: Attitudes 1972* (Berkeley: D. L. Hennessey, 1972); and Lance Jenicks, *The Wisdom of Southern California* (Irvine, Calif.: Lindenhof Press, 1982).

19. See Daniel J. Elazar, "Confederation and Federal Liberty," *Publius* 12, no. 4 (1982): 1–14.

20. Ibid.

21. John David Unruh, *The Plains Across: The Overland Emigrants and the Trans-Mississippi West, 1840–60* (Urbana: University of Illinois Press, 1979).

22. See Martin Diamond, "On the Relationship of Federalism and Decentralization," in Daniel J. Elazar et al., eds., *Cooperation and Conflict: Readings in American Federalism* (Itasca, Ill.: F E. Peacock, 1969), pp. 72–81; and Morton Grodzins, "The Future of American Federalism," in ibid., pp. 61–71.

23. Harold J. Laski, *The American Democracy: A Commentary and an Interpretation* (New York: Viking Press, 1948); and Laski, "The Obsolescence of Federalism."

24. Morton Grodzins, *The American System: A New View of Government in the United States,* ed. Daniel J. Elazar (Chicago: Rand McNally, 1966).

25. Ibid., pp. 274–76.

26. Leon N. Lindberg and Stuart A. Scheingold, *Europe's Would-Be Polity: Patterns of Change in the European Community* (Englewood Cliffs, N.J.: Prentice-Hall, 1970).

27. Martin Diamond discusses the distinction between this and the former end in connection with the American situation in "On the Relationship of Federalism and Decentralization." Diamond suggests that the distinction is between modern and premodern federalism, a position I do not share.

28. Alexis de Tocqueville makes this argument in *Democracy in America,* trans. Lawrence Mayer (Garden City, N.Y.: Doubleday, 1969). See John C. Koritansky, "Decentralization and Civic Virtue in Tocqueville's 'New' Science of Politics," *Publius* 5, no. 3 (1975): 63–82.

29. *The Federalist* is ambiguous on this point, but James Madison at least seems to have moved in that direction. See also Walter H. Bennett, *American Theories of Federalism* (University, Ala.: University of Alabama Press, 1966).

30. See, for example, William Stokes, "The Centralized Federal Republics of Latin America," in *Essays in Federalism* (Claremont, Calif.: Claremont Men's College Institute for Studies in Federalism, 1963); Herman G. James, *The Constitutional System of Brazil* (Washington, D.C.: Carnegie Institution, 1921); and L. S. Rowe, *The Federal System in the Argentine Republic* (Washington, D.C.: Carnegie Institution, 1921).

31. See Alain Greilsammer, *Les mouvements federalistes en France* (Nice: Presses d'Europe, 1975); and Ralph Nelson, "The Federal Idea in French Political Thought," *Publius* 5, no. 3 (1975): 7–62.

32. See Buber, *Paths in Utopia*.

33. Carl J. Friedrich, Introduction to Johannes Althusius, *The Politica Methodice Digesta* (Cambridge, Mass.: Harvard University Press, 1935); and Diamond, "On the Relationship of Federalism and Decentralization."

34. See Ivo Duchacek, *Comparative Federalism: The Territorial Dimension of Politics* (New York: Holt, Rinehart and Winston, 1970).

35. Alexis de Tocqueville has given us the classic discussion of this process and its political implications in *Democracy in America* and *L'ancien regime* (Oxford: Blackwell, 1949).

Chapter 4

1. See Delbert Hillers, *Covenant: The History of the Biblical Idea* (Baltimore: Johns Hopkins University Press, 1969); and Perry Miller, *The New England Mind: The Seventeenth Century* (New York: Macmillan, 1939).

2. Thomas Hobbes, *Leviathan* (Indianapolis: Bobbs-Merrill, 1958), and John Locke, *First and Second Treatises on Government,* ed. Peter Laslett (New York: Mentor Books, 1965). See also Vincent Ostrom, "Hobbes, Covenant, and Constitution," *Publius* 10, no. 4 (1980): 83–100.

3. Charles de Secondat, Baron Montesquieu, *The Spirit of the Laws* (1748), trans. T. Nugent (London, 1878); and Alexander

Hamilton, John Jay, and James Madison, *The Federalist,* ed. with introduction by Clinton Rossiter (New York: Mentor Books, 1961).

4. See, for example, Daniel J. Elazar, "Federalism," in David M. Sills, ed., *International Encyclopedia of the Social Sciences* (New York: Macmillan, 1968), 6:169–78; Sobei Mogi, *The Problem of Federalism,* 2 vols. (London: George Allen & Unwin, 1931), a compendius historical survey of the various theories of federalism.

5. The book of Joshua may have been designed to set forth the Prophetic conception of the ideal commonwealth based on federal principles. See Exodus and Deuteronomy for a further description of the Israelite political system and Judges, Samuel, and Kings for a discussion of its problems. See also, Daniel J. Elazar, *The Book of Joshua as a Political Classic* (Jerusalem: Center for Jewish Community Studies, 1980), and *The Covenant Idea and the Jewish Political Tradition* (Ramat Gan: Bar Ilan University Department of Political Studies and Center for Jewish Community Studies, 1983), esp. chap. 2; and Yehezel Kaufman, *The Religion of Israel,* trans. Moshe Greenberg (Chicago: University of Chicago Press, 1960), with important discussions of the origins of covenant theory in the Bible.

6. Hillers, *Covenant;* Moshe Weinfeld, "Covenant," in *Encyclopedia Judaica* (Jerusalem: Keter Books, 1973), 5:1012–22; and John Bright, *A History of Israel* (Philadelphia: Westminister Press, 1946).

7. See the *Federalism as Grand Design* issue of *Publius* 9, no. 4 (1979), for an examination of each of the aforementioned points.

8. Edward A. Freeman, *A History of Federal Government in Greece and Italy,* 2d ed. (London: Macmillan, 1893), is a classic attempt to trace the origins of federalism in the classic world.

9. Fustel des Coulanges, *The Ancient City* (Garden City, N.Y.: Doubleday, 1956). See also Harry V. Jaffe, "Aristotle," in Leo Strauss and Joseph Cropsey, *A History of Political Thought* (Chicago: Rand McNally, 1963).

10. Freeman, *History of Federal Government;* and Howard S. Levie, *The Status of Gibraltar* (Boulder, Colo.: Westview Press, 1893).

11. Freeman, *History of Federal Government;* L. LeFurand P.

Posener, *Bundesstaat und Staatendund in geschichtlicher Entwicklung* (Breslau, 1902), pp. 75–89; and Heinz Eulau, "Theories of Federalism under the Holy Roman Empire," *American Political Science Review* 25 (1941): 643–64.

12. Field Notes, Workshop on Covenant Idea and the Jewish Political Tradition of the Jerusalem Center for Public Affairs. See also Gordon Freeman, *The Heavenly Kingdom* (Lanham, Md.: University Press of America and Jerusalem Center for Public Affairs, 1985).

13. James Bryce, *The Holy Roman Empire* (New York: Macmillan, 1895); Giorgio Falco, *The Holy Roman Republic: A Historical Profile of the Middle Ages,* trans. from Italian by K. V. Kent (Westport, Conn.: Greenwood Press, 1972); and Herbert A. Fisher, *Medieval Empire,* 2 vols. (1898; rpt. New York: AMS Press, n.d.).

14. Otto Gierke, *Political Theories of the Middle Ages* (Cambridge: Cambridge University Press, 1938), and Gierke, *The Development of Political Theory* (New York: Norton, 1939).

15. Irving Agus, *Rabbi Meir of Rothenburg* (Philadelphia: Dropsie College for Hebrew and Cognate Learning, 1947); Agus, *Urban Civilization in Pre-Crusade Europe* (New York: Yeshiva University, 1967); Menachem Elon, "On Power and Authority: Halachic Stance of the Traditional Community and Its Contemporary Implications," in Daniel J. Elazar, ed., *Kinship and Consent: The Jewish Political Tradition and Its Contemporary Manifestations* (Washington, D.C.: University Press of America, 1982); and Daniel J. Elazar and Stuart A. Cohen, *The Jewish Polity: Jewish Political Organization from Biblical Times to the Present* (Bloomington: Indiana University Press, 1985), chap. 11.

16. Denis de Rougemont, *La Suisse, ou l'histoire d'un pueple heureux* (Lausanne: Le Livre de Mois, 1965), and de Rougemont, *Vingt-huit siècle d'Europe: La conscience europenne a travers les textes, d'Hesiode a nos jours* (Paris: Payot, 1961).

17. Cesar Enrique Diaz Lopez, "The State of Autonomic Process in Spain," *Publius* 11, nos. 3–4 (1981): 193–216. J. H. Elliott, *Imperial Spain, 1469–1716* (New York: St. Martin's Press, 1964), provides a historical description of Spanish protofederal systems and their decline.

18. Arend Lijphart, *The Politics of Accommodation: Pluralism and*

Democracy in the Netherlands (Berkeley and Los Angeles: University of California Press, 1969); Hinn Pirenne, *Early Democracies in the Low Countries: Urban Society and Political Conflict in the Middle Ages and the Renaissance* (New York: Harper & Row, 1963); and Herbert H. Rowen, ed., *The Low Countries in Early Modern Times: A Documentary History* (New York: Harper & Row, 1972).

19. De Rougemont, *La Suisse.*

20. J. Wayne Baker, *Heinrich J. Bullinger and the Covenant* (Athens: University of Ohio Press, 1981); G. H. Dodge, *The Political Theory of the Huguenots of the Dispersion* (New York: Octagon Books, 1947); John Kincaid and Daniel J. Elazar, eds., *The Covenant Connection: The Federal Theology Bridge, 1500–1800* (forthcoming); and Gierke, *Development of Political Theory.*

21. Johannes Althusius, *Politica Methodice Digesta,* ed. Carl J. Friedrich (Cambridge, Mass.: Harvard University Press, 1935). The text in Latin, published by Friedrich, is based on the 1603 edition and has a comprehensive English introduction. For an abridged English version, see the translation by Frederick Carney, trans., *Johannes Althusius, Politics* (Boston: Beacon Press, 1964). See also Thomas Hueglin, "Johannes Althusius: Medieval Constitutionalist or Modern Federalist?" *Publius* 9, no. 4 (1979): 9–42. For a different view of Althusius, see Patrick Riley, "Three Seventeenth-Century German Theorists of Federalism: Althusius, Hugo and Leibniz," *Publius* 6, no. 3 (1976): 7–42.

22. See, for example, Samuel H. Beer and Adam B. Ulam, eds., *Patterns of Government: The Major Political Systems of Europe* (New York: Random House, 1962); Gwendolyn M. Carter and John H. Herz, *Major Foreign Powers: The Governments of Great Britain, France, Germany and the Soviet Union* (New York: Harcourt Brace Jovanovich, 1972); Alex N. Dragnich, *Major European Governments* (Homewood, Ill.: Dorsey Press, 1970); and Robert G. Neumann, *European Government* (New York: McGraw-Hill, 1968).

23. Neumann, *European Government.*

24. Hueglin, "Johannes Althusius."

25. See, for example, Walter Kolarz, *Russia and Her Colonies* (New York: Praeger, 1953); Robert J. Osborn, *The Evolution of Soviet Politics* (Homewood, Ill.: Dorsey Press, 1974); and Vernon

V. Aspaturian, "The Theory and Practice of Soviet Federalism," *Journal of Politics* 12 (1950): 20–51.

26. See Andrew C. McLaughlin, *The Foundations of American Constitutionalism*, intro. by Henry Steele Commager (1932; rpr. Gloucester, Mass.: Peter Smith, 1972).

27. Martin Diamond, "What the Framers Meant by Federalism," in Robert A. Goldwin, ed., *A Nation of States*, 2d ed. (Chicago: Rand McNally, 1974). See also Bernard Bailyn, *The Origins of American Politics* (New York: Knopf, 1968), and Bailyn, *The Ideological Origins of the American Revolution* (Cambridge, Mass.: Belknap Press of Harvard University Press, 1967); and Gordon S. Wood, *The Creation of the American Republic, 1776–1787* (Chapel Hill: University of North Carolina Press for the Institute of Early American History and Culture, 1969).

28. See Daniel J. Elazar, "How Federal Is the Constitution? Thoroughly!" in Robert Goldwin, ed., *How Federal Is the Constitution?* (Washington, D.C.: American Enterprise Institute for Public Policy Research, forthcoming).

29. Robert I. Vexler, *Scandinavia: Denmark, Norway, Sweden* (Dobbs Ferry, N.Y.: Oceana Publications, 1977); Ewan Butler, *The Horizon Concise History of Scandinavia* (New York: American Publishing Co., 1973); and Thomas Kingston Derry, *A History of Scandinavia* (Minneapolis: University of Minnesota Press, 1979).

30. Ernest Heinrich Kossmann, *The Low Countries, 1780–1940* (New York: Clarendon Press, 1978); and Georges Henri Dumont, *Histoire de la Belgique* (Paris: Hachette, 1977).

31. Henry Arthur Kamen, *A Concise History of Spain* (London: Thames and Hudson, 1973); Harold Victor Livermore, *A History of Spain* (London: Allen & Unwin, 1966); and Livermore, *A New History of Portugal* (Cambridge: Cambridge University Press, 1976).

32. Halil Inalcik, *The Ottoman Empire: The Classical Age, 1300–1600*, trans. Norman Itzkowitz and Calin Imber (New York: Praeger, 1973); Peter Mansfield, *The Ottoman Empire and Its Successors* (New York: St. Martin's Press, 1973); and William Miller, *Ottoman Empire and Its Successors, 1801–1927* (New York: Octagon Books, 1966).

33. Thomas O. Hüglin, "The Idea of Empire: Conditions for

Integration and Disintegration in Europe," *Publius* 12, no. 3 (1982): 11–42.

34. James W. Skillen and Stanley W. Carlison, "Religion and Political Development in Nineteenth Century Holland," *Publius* 12, no. 4 (1982): 43–64; and Arend Lijphart, "Consociational Democracy," *World Politics* 21 (1968–69): 205–25.

35. Filippo Sabetti, "The Making of Italy as an Experiment in Constitutional Choice," *Publius* 12, no. 4 (1982): 65–84.

36. Donald V. Smiley, "The Canadian Federation and the Challenge of Quebec Independence," *Publius* 8, no. 1 (1978): 199–224.

37. See Anthony G. Careless and Donald W. Stevenson, "Canada: Constitutional Reform as a Policy-Making Instrument," *Publius* 12, no. 4 (1982): 85–98.

38. William Anderson, *The Nation and the States: Rivals or Partners?* (Minneapolis: University of Minnesota Press, 1955); Daniel J. Elazar, *The American Partnership: Intergovernmental Cooperation in the Nineteenth-Century United States* (Chicago: University of Chicago Press, 1962); Elazar, *American Federalism: A View from the States,* 3d ed. (New York: Harper & Row, 1984); Elazar, ed., *The Federal Polity, Publius* 3, no. 2 (1973); Elazar, "The Evolving Federal System," in Richard M. Pious, ed., *The Power to Govern, Proceedings of the Academy of Political Science* 34, no. 2 (New York: Academy of Political Science, 1981); William Brooke Graves, *American Intergovernmental Relations: Their Origins, Historical Development, and Current Status* (New York: Charles Scribner's Sons, 1964); Morton Grodzins, *The American System: A New View of Government in the United States,* ed. Daniel J. Elazar (Chicago: Rand McNally, 1966); Robert B. Hawkins, Jr., ed., *American Federalism: Toward a New Partnership* (San Francisco: Institute for Contemporary Studies, 1982); and Michael Reagan and John S. Sanzone, *The New Federalism* (New York: Oxford University Press, 1981).

39. William Stokes, "The Centralized Federal Republic of Latin America," in *Essays in Federalism* (Claremont, Calif.: Claremont Men's College Institute for Studies in Federalism, 1963); Herman G. James, *The Constitutional System of Brazil* (Washington, D.C.: Carnegie Institution, 1921); and L. S. Rowe, *The Federal System in the Argentine Republic* (Washington, D.C.: Carnegie Institution, 1921).

40. Ronald L. Watts, *New Federations: Experiments in the Commonwealth* (Oxford: Clarendon Press, 1966); and Amitai Etzioni, *Political Unification* (New York: Holt, Rinehart, 1965).

41. For an analysis of Kant's federalist thought, see Patrick Riley, "Federalism in Kant's Political Philosophy," *Publius* 9, no. 4 (1979): 43–64.

42. See, for example, Riley, "Three Seventeenth-Century German Theorists."

43. Zacharias P. Thundyl, *Covenant in Anglo-Saxon Thought* (Madras: Macmillan Company of India, 1972); and Carl Joachim Friedrich, *The Philosophy of Law in Historical Perspective* (Chicago: University of Chicago Press, 1965).

44. Thomas Hobbes, *Leviathan* (Indianapolis: Bobbs-Merrill, 1958); John Locke, *First and Second Treatises of Government,* ed. Peter Laslett (New York: Mentor Books, 1965).

45. James Harrington, *Political Writings: Representative Selections,* ed. with intro. by Charles Blitzer (New York: Liberal Arts Press, 1955).

46. Daniel J. Elazar and John Kincaid, eds., *Covenant, Polity, and Constitutionalism,* special issue of *Publius* 10, no. 4 (1980).

47. Charles S. Hyneman and Donald S. Lutz, *American Political Writings during the Founding Era, 1769–1805* (Indianapolis: Liberty Press, 1983).

48. Adam Smith, *An Inquiry into the Nature and Causes of the Wealth of Nations,* ed. Edwin Cannon, intro. John Chamberlain (New Rochelle, N.Y.: Arlington House, 1966).

49. Edmund Burke, *A Vindication of Natural Society* (1757), ed. Frank N. Pagano (Indianapolis: Liberty Classics, 1983). See also Louis I. Brevold and Ralph E. Ross, eds., *The Philosophy of Edmund Burke: A Selection from His Speeches and Writings* (Ann Arbor: University of Michigan Press, 1970), pp. 147–48.

50. Jeremy Bentham, *The Works of Jeremy Bentham,* ed. John Bowring (New York: Russell and Russell, 1962).

51. Cf. McLaughlin, *Foundations;* Carl L. Becker, *The Declaration of Independence* (New York: Vintage Books, 1958).

52. Cf. Martin Diamond, "The Federalist," in Leo Strauss and Joseph Cropsey, eds., *History of Political Philosophy* (Chicago: Rand McNally, 1963), pp. 573–93; and Marvin Meyers, *The Mind of the Founder* (Indianapolis: Bobbs-Merrill, 1973).

53. Herbert Storing and Murray Dry, *The Complete Anti-Federalist* (Chicago: University of Chicago Press, 1981).

54. Donald Lutz, "The Relative Influence of European Writers on Late Eighteenth Century American Political Thought," *American Political Science Review* 78 (1984): 189–97.

55. Ralph Henry Gabriel, *The Course of American Democratic Thought*, 2d ed. (New York: Ronald Press, 1956); Morton Frisch and Richard J. Stevens, *The Political Thought of American Statesmen* (Itasca, Ill.: F. E. Peacock, 1973); Stevens and Frisch, *American Political Thought: The Philosophic Dimension of American Statesmanship* (Dubuque, Iowa: Kendall/Hunt Publishing Co., 1973); Rozann Rothman, "Political Method in the Federal System: Albert Gallatin's Contribution," *Publius* 1, no. 2 (1971): 123–40; Daniel J. Elazar, "The Constitution, the Union and the Liberties of the People," *Publius* 8, no. 3 (1978): 141–76.

56. Walter Lippmann, *Public Philosophy* (Boston: Little, Brown, 1955).

57. Alexis de Tocqueville, *Democracy in America*, trans. Lawrence Mayer (Garden City, N.Y.: Doubleday, 1969), and *L'ancien regime* (Oxford: Blackwell, 1949); Pierre-Joseph Proudhon, *Du principe federatif* (Paris, 1863); John C. Koritansky, "Alexander Hamilton's Philosophy of Government and Administration," *Publius* 9, no. 2 (1979): 99–122; and Delba Winthrop, "Tocqueville on Federalism," *Publius* 6, no. 3 (1976): 93–117.

58. Otto Gierke, *Natural Law and the Theory of Society*, trans. Ernest Barker (Cambridge: Cambridge University Press, 1934).

59. Cf. Alexandre Marc, "New and Old Federalism: Faithful to the Origins," *Publius* 9, no. 4 (1979): 117–30; and Ferdinand Kinsky, "Personality and Federalism," *Publius* 9, no. 4 (1979): 131–56.

60. On Tocqueville, see his works and Koritansky, "Hamilton's Philosophy," and Winthrop, "Tocqueville." On Bryce, see James Bryce, *The American Commonwealth*, rev. ed. (New York: Macmillan, 1914), vol. 1.

61. Johann Kasper Bluntschli, *The Theory of the State* (Oxford: Clarendon Press, 1892).

62. Freeman, *History of Federal Government*.

63. For discussion of the Imperial Federation League, see

Ronald Hyam and Ged Martin, *Reappraisals in British Imperial History* (Toronto: Macmillan Company of Canada, 1975), chap. 6.

64. Richard Simeon, *Federal-Provincial Diplomacy: The Making of Recent Policy in Canada* (Toronto: University of Toronto Press, 1972).

65. Bryce, *American Commonwealth;* Albert V. Dicey, *Introduction to the Study of the Law of the Constitution,* 10th ed. (New York: St. Martin's Press, 1962); Henry Sidgwick, *The Elements of Politics* (London: Macmillan, 1919).

66. K. C. Wheare, *Federal Government,* 4th ed. (New York: Oxford University Press, 1964).

67. On Latin American federalism, see, for example, William Stokes, "The Centralized Federal Republics of Latin America," in *Essays on Federalism* (Claremont, Calif.: Claremont Men's Institute for Studies in Federalism, 1963).

68. See, for example, R. Michael Stevens, "Asymmetrical Federalism: The Federal Principle and the Survival of the Small Republic," *Publius* 7, no. 4 (1977): 177–204.

69. See, for example, Ronald L. Watts, *New Federations: Experiments in the Commonwealth* (Oxford: Clarendon Press, 1966).

70. See, for example, Ivo Duchacek, "Consociations of Fatherlands: The Revival of Confederal Principles and Practices," *Publius* 12, no. 4 (1982): 129–77.

Chapter 5

1. K. C. Wheare, *Federal Government,* 4th ed. (New York: Oxford University Press, 1964). For a direct challenge to the Wheare thesis using the Canadian example, see Milton J. Esman, "Federalism and Modernization: Canada and the United States," *Publius* 14, no. 1 (1984): 21–38.

2. See Richard Simeon, *Federal-Provincial Diplomacy: The Making of Recent Policy in Canada* (Toronto: University of Toronto Press, 1972).

3. See, for example, Richard Reich, "Notes on the Local and Cantonal Influence in Swiss Federal Consultation Process," *Publius* 5, no. 2 (1975): 117–26.

4. See Cesar Enrique Diaz Lopez, "The State of the Autonomic Process in Spain," *Publius* 11, nos. 3–4 (1981): 193–216.

5. Arthur Macmahon, ed., *Federalism: Mature and Emergent* (New York: Columbia University Press, 1955), confronts this issue with emphasis on the United States and Europe; Francis L. Petre, *The Republic of Columbia: An Account of the Country, Its People, Its Institutions and Its Resources* (New York: Gordon Press Publishers, 1976).

6. For a complete discussion, see a special issue of *Publius* devoted to this theme, *State Constitutional Design in Federal Systems, Publius* 12, no. 1 (1982), which includes Daniel J. Elazar, "The Principles and Traditions Underlying American State Constitutions," pp. 11–26; and Donald S. Lutz, "The Purposes of American State Constitutions," pp. 27–44.

7. From the vast literature on the U.S. Constitution, see, for example, E. S. Corwin, *The Constitution of the United States of America: Analysis and Interpretation* (Washington, D.C.: U.S. Government Printing Office, 1953); Arthur E. Sutherland, *Constitutionalism in America: Origin and Evolution of Its Fundamental Ideas* (New York: Blaisdell, 1965); and Donald S. Lutz, "The Purposes of American State Constitutions," *Publius* 12, no. 1 (1982): 27–44.

8. For the relationship and distinction between covenant and compact, see Daniel J. Elazar, "The Political Theory of Covenant: Biblical Origins and Modern Developments," *Publius* 10, no. 4 (1980): 3–30.

9. Ibid., p. 25.

10. Blaustein and Flanz, *Constitutions,* vol. 14.

11. Ibid., vol. 16.

12. Vincent Ostrom, *The Political Theory of the Compound Republic: A Reconstruction of the Logical Foundations of American Democracy as Presented in the Federalist* (Blacksburg, Va.: Virginia Polytechnic Institute, Center for the Study of Public Choice, 1971), and "The Political Architecture of American Federalism: An Inquiry into Federalism as Means to Ends," in Max Frenkel, ed., *Partnership in Federalism* (Bern: Peter Lang, 1977), pp. 87–128. I am greatly indebted to Professor Ostrom for teaching me how to understand constitutional choice.

13. Alexander Hamilton, John Jay, and James Madison, *The*

Federalist 2, in *The Federalist Papers,* ed. with intro. by Jacob E. Cooke (Cleveland: World, 1961).

14. P. A. Allum and G. Amyet discuss this issue in "Regionalism in Italy: Old Wine in New Bottles," *Parliamentary Affairs* 24 (Winter 1970–71): 53–78. See also Peter Gourevitch, "Reforming the Napoleonic State: The Creation of Regional Governments in France and Italy," in Sidney Tarrow, Peter J. Katzenstein, and Luigi Graziano, eds., *Territorial Politics in Industrial Nations* (New York: Praeger, 1978), pp. 28–63.

15. Diaz Lopez, "The State of Autonomic Process."

16. See Arthur Maas, ed., *Area and Power: A Theory of Local Government* (Glencoe, Ill.: Free Press, 1959); and Russell Kirk, "The Prospects for Territorial Democracy in the United States," in Robert A. Goldwin, ed., *A Nation of States,* 2d ed. (Chicago: Rand McNally, 1974), pp. 42–64.

17. See Ivo D. Duchacek, *Comparative Federalism: The Territorial Dimension of Politics* (New York: Holt, Rinehart and Winston, 1970).

18. Ibid.; Wheare, *Federal Government;* William H. Riker, *Federalism: Origin, Operation, Significance* (Boston: Little, Brown, 1964).

19. Ramash Dutta Dikshit, *The Political Geography of Federalism* (New York: Halsted Press, 1975); and Carl J. Friedrich, *Trends of Federalism in Theory and Practice* (New York: Praeger, 1968).

20. Ivo Duchacek, "Antagonistic Cooperation: Territorial and Ethnic Communities," *Publius* 7, no. 4 (1977): 3–31; Duchacek, *Comparative Federalism.*

21. Duchacek, *Comparative Federalism;* Wheare, *Federal Government;* Valerie Earle, ed., *Federalism: Infinite Variety in Theory and Practice* (Itasca, Ill.: F. E. Peacock, 1968).

22. William S. Stokes, *Latin American Politics* (New York: Thomas Y. Crowell, 1959).

23. Ann Schulz, *Local Politics and Nation-States: Case Studies in Politics and Policy* (Santa Barbara, Calif.: Clio Press, 1979).

24. Duchacek, *Comparative Federalism;* and Christa Altenstetter, "Intergovernmental Profiles in the Federal Systems of Austria and Germany," *Publius* 5, no. 2 (1975): 89–116.

25. Anthony G. Careless and Donald W. Stevenson, "Canada:

Constitutional Reform as a Policy-Making Instrument," *Publius* 12, no. 3 (1982): 85–98.

26. Albert Sturm, "The Development of American State Constitutions," *Publius* 12, no. 1 (1982): 57–99.

27. Hans Peter Tschaeni, "Constitutional Change in Swiss Cantons: An Assessment of a Recent Phenomenon," *Publius* 12, no. 1 (1982): 113–31.

28. Steven L. Burg, "Republican and Provincial Constitution-Making in Yugoslavia Politics," *Publius* 12, no. 1 (1982): 131–55. See also Jovan Djordjevic, "Remarks on the Yugoslav Model of Federalism," *Publius* 5, no. 2 (1975): 77–88.

29. L. Adele Jinadu, "The Constitutional Situation of the Nigerian States," *Publius* 12, no. 1 (1982): 155–87; and John A. A. Ayoade, "Ethnic Management in the 1979 Nigerian Constitution," *Publius* (forthcoming).

30. Morton Grodzins, "Centralization and Decentralization in the American Federal System," in Goldwin, ed., *A Nation of States,* pp. 1–23; Austin Ranney and Wilmore Kendall, *Democracy and the American Party System* (New York: Harcourt, Brace, World, 1956).

31. Simeon, *Federal-Provincial Diplomacy.*

32. See Friedrich, *Trends of Federalism in Theory and Practice;* Duchacek, *Comparative Federalism.*

33. See, for example, S. A. H. Haggi, "Federalism, Single Dominant Party, and the Problem of Linguistic Autonomy in India" (paper presented at the Sixth World Congress of the International Political Science Association, Geneva, 1964); Haggi, ed., *Union-State Relations in India* (Meerut: Meenakshi Prakshan, 1967); and Myron Weiner, *India at the Polls* (Washington, D.C.: American Enterprise Institute for Public Policy Research, 1978).

34. Harry Kantor, "Latin American Federalism: Aspiration and Futility," in Earle, ed., *Federalism,* pp. 185–208; Robert Jackson Alexander, *Latin American Political Parties* (New York: Praeger, 1973); and Ronald H. McDonald, *Party Systems and Elections in Latin America* (Chicago: Markham, 1971).

35. Cynthia Enloe, *Ethnic Conflict and Political Development* (Boston: Little, Brown, 1973); and Richard Lawrence Sklar,

Nigerian Political Parties (Princeton: Princeton University Press, 1963).

36. John A. Armstrong, "Federalism in the USSR: Ethnic and Territorial Aspects," *Publius* 7, no. 4 (1977): 89–106; and Bogdan Denitch, "The Evolution of Yugoslav Politics," *Publius* 7, no. 4 (1977): 107–18.

37. Albert V. Dicey, *Introduction to the Study of the Law of the Constitution,* 10th ed. (New York: St. Martin's Press, 1962); Richard E. Johnston, *The Effect of Judicial Review on Federal-State Relations* (Baton Rouge: Louisiana State University Press, 1969); Henry Hart and Herbert Wechsler, *The Federal Courts and the Federal System,* 2d ed. (Brooklyn: Foundation Press, 1973); Zelman Cowan, *Federal Jurisdiction in Australia* (Melbourne: Oxford University Press, 1951); William S. Livingston, *Federalism and Constitutional Change* (Oxford: Clarendon Press, 1956); and Edward McWhinney, *Judicial Review in the English Speaking World,* 2d ed. (Toronto: University of Toronto Press, 1960).

38. See Arend Lijphart, *Democracies: Patterns of Majoritarian and Consensus Government in Twenty-One Countries* (New Haven: Yale University Press, 1984).

39. Daniel J. Elazar, "Field Notes—Brazil," July–August 1974; and Frank P. Sherwood, *Institutionalizing the Grass Roots in Brazil: A Study in Comparative Local Government* (San Francisco: Chandler, 1961).

40. See Altenstetter, "Intergovernmental Profiles in the Federal Systems of Austria and Germany"; Reich, "Notes on the Local and Cantonal Influence in Swiss Consultation Process"; Max Frenkel, *Föderalismus und Bundesstat, Band I: Föderalismus* (Bern: Verlag Peter Lang AG, 1984); and Fried Esterbauer, Guy Héraud, and Peter Pernthaleis, eds., *Föderalismus* (Vienna: Wilhelm Braumüller, 1977).

41. For a greater explanation, see chapter 2, note 3.

42. In recent years, a substantial literature has been developed documenting this thesis. Even earlier, Morton Grodzins articulated this understanding in depth in *The American System: A New View of Government in the United States,* ed. Daniel J. Elazar (Chicago: Rand McNally, 1966). See also Paul Ylvisaker, *Intergovern-*

mental Relations at the Grass Roots (Minneapolis: University of Minnesota Press, 1956).

43. See George Codding, Jr., *Governing the Commune of Veyrier: Politics in Swiss Local Government* (Boulder: Bureau of Government Research, University of Colorado, 1967).

44. I have discussed this point in depth in *The American Partnership: Intergovernmental Cooperation in the Nineteenth-Century United States* (Chicago: University of Chicago Press, 1962).

45. Stefan Dupre, *Regional Government* (Toronto: Institute of Public Administration of Canada, 1968); John C. Bollens and Henry J. Schmandt, *The Metropolis,* 2d. ed. (New York: Harper & Row, 1970), chap. 12; Harold Kaplan, Urban Political Systems: A Functional Analysis of Metro Toronto (New York: Columbia University Press, 1967); Frank Smallwood, *Metro Toronto: A Decade Later* (Toronto: Bureau of Municipal Research, 1963).

46. Duchacek, *Comparative Federalism,* chap. 10; Frenkel, *Föderalismus;* Freidrich, *Trends of Federalism;* and William S. Livingston, "Legal and Political Determinants of American Federalism," *Southwestern Social Science Quarterly* 34 (June 1953): 40–56.

47. J. F. Aubert, *Petite histoire constitutionelle de la Suisse* (Bern: Francke Editions, 1974); Denis de Rougemont, *La Suisse, ou l'histoire d'un peuple heureux* (Lausanne: Le Livre du Mois, 1965); and André Siegfried, *Switzerland,* trans. Edward Fitzgerald (New York: Duell, Sloan and Pearce, n.d.).

48. On U.S. political culture and federalism, see Daniel J. Elazar, *American Federalism: A View from the States,* 3d ed. (New York: Harper & Row, 1984), chaps. 5 and 6; John Kincaid, ed., *Political Culture, Public Policy, and the American States* (Philadelphia: Institute for the Study of Human Issues, 1983); and Alexis de Tocqueville, *Democracy in America,* trans. Lawrence Mayer (Garden City, N.Y.: Doubleday, 1969).

49. Ikenna Nzimiro, *Studies in Ibo Political Systems* (Berkeley and Los Angeles: University of California Press, 1972); John N. Paden, *Religion and Political Culture in Kano* (Berkeley and Los Angeles: University of California Press, 1973); Frederick A. O. Schwarz, Jr., *Nigeria: The Tribes, the Nation, or the Race* (Cambridge, Mass.: MIT Press, 1973).

50. Paul R. Brass, *Language, Religion and Politics in North India* (London: Cambridge University Press, 1974); Richard I. Cashman, *The Myth of the Lokamanya* (Berkeley and Los Angeles: University of California Press, 1975); Jyotirindra Das Gupta, *Language Conflict and National Development* (Berkeley and Los Angeles: University of California Press, 1970); Robert L. Hardgrove, Jr., *The Nadars of Tamiland* (Berkeley and Los Angeles: University of California Press, 1969); Rodney W. Jones, *Urban Politics in India* (Berkeley and Los Angeles: University of California Press, 1974); and Richard Sisson, *The Congress Party in Rajasthan* (Berkeley and Los Angeles: University of California Press, 1972).

51. See Filippo Sabetti, "Covenant Language in Canada: Continuity and Change" (paper presented at the Covenant Workshop on Language of Covenant held at the Center for the Study of Federalism, Philadelphia, December 17–18, 1980).

52. See Daniel J. Elazar, "Civil War and the Preservation of American Federalism," *Publius* 1, no. 1 (1971): 39–59; and Rozann Rothman, "The American Civil War and Reconstruction: A Crisis in Political Integration," in Daniel J. Elazar, ed., *Federalism and Political Integration* (Ramat Gan, Israel: Turtledove Publishing, 1979), pp. 89–105.

53. Daniel J. Elazar, "Field Notes—Nigeria, 1974," available through the Center for the Study of Federalism Archives, Temple University, Philadelphia, Pa.

54. Aubert, *Petite histoire;* de Rougemont, *La Suisse;* Siegfried, *Switzerland.*

Chapter 6

1. The first scholars to make this point were William Anderson and Morton Grodzins, the first in *The Nation and the States: Rivals or Partners?* (Minneapolis: University of Minnesota Press, 1955), and the second in *The American System: A New View of Government in the United States,* ed. Daniel J. Elazar (Chicago: Rand McNally, 1966).

2. Daniel J. Elazar, "Authentic Federalism for America," *National Civic Review* 61 (1973): 474–78.

3. Stephen L. Schechter, "The State of American Federalism: 1978," *Publius* 9, no. 1 (1979): 3–10.

4. See, for example, Ivo Duchacek, *Comparative Federalism: The Territorial Dimension of Politics* (New York: Holt, Rinehart and Winston, 1970), introduction; William H. Riker, *Federalism: Origin, Operation, Significance* (Boston: Little, Brown, 1964); Jeffrey L. Mayer, ed., *Dialogues on Decentralization*, special issue of *Publius* 6, no. 4 (1976); and Arend Lijphart, *Democracies: Patterns of Majoritarian and Consensus Government in Twenty-one Countries* (New Haven: Yale University Press, 1984).

5. Karl Deutsch, *Political Community and the North Atlantic Area: International Organization in the Light of Historical Experience* (Westport, Conn.: Greenwood Press, 1966); and Amitai Etzioni, *Political Unification* (New York: Holt, Rinehart and Winston, 1965).

6. See Daniel J. Elazar, "The Generational Rhythm of American Politics," *American Politics Quarterly* 6 (January 1978): 55–94. For a discussion of the transition to a new political question after 1976, see Elazar, "The 1980's: Entering the Citybelt-Cybernetic Frontier," *Publius* 10, no. 1 (1980): 13–26.

7. Donald V. Smiley, "The Canadian Federation and the Challenge of Quebec Independence," *Publius* 8, no. 1 (1978): 199–224; and Steven L. Burg, "Ethnic Conflict and the Federalization of Socialist Yugoslavia," *Publius* 7, no. 4 (1977): 119–44.

8. Mayer, ed., *Dialogues on Decentralization;* Fried Esterbauer, "The Austrian Experience," in Daniel J. Elazar, ed, *Self-Rule/Shared Rule* (Ramat Gan, Israel: Turtledove Publishing, 1979), pp. 133–37; Russell Mathews, ed., *Federalism in Australia: Current Trends*, special issue of *Publius* 7, no. 3 (1977); Graeme Starr, "Federalism as a Political Issue: Australia's Two 'New Federalisms,'" *Publius* 7, no. 1 (1977): 7–26; and Irene Fraser Rothenberg, "National Intervention and Urban Development in Colombia and Mexico," *Publius* 12, no. 2 (1982): 111–34.

9. These initiatives are regularly analyzed in the *Publius Annual Review of the State of American Federalism,* published annually since 1978.

10. Personal observation and interviews in India, January–February 1977.

11. Starr, "Federalism as a Political Issue."

12. Cf. Duchacek, *Comparative Federalism;* and K. C. Wheare, *Federal Government,* 4th ed. (New York: Oxford University Press, 1964).

13. Daniel J. Elazar, *The American Partnership: Intergovernmental Cooperation in the Nineteenth–Century United States* (Chicago: University of Chicago Press, 1962).

14. Edgar Gallant, "The Machinery of Federal–Provincial Relations, I," *Canadian Public Administration* 8 (1965): 515; R. M. Burns, "The Machinery of Federal–Provincial Relations, II," *Canadian Public Administration* 8 (1965): 527; Richard Simeon, *Federal–Provincial Diplomacy: The Making of Recent Policy in Canada* (Toronto: University of Toronto Press, 1972).

15. Stephen L. Burg, "Republican and Provincial Constitution–Making in Yugoslav Politics," *Publius* 12, no. 1 (1982): 113–21.

16. Gabriel Ben Dor, "Federalism in the Arab World," in Daniel J. Elazar, ed., *Federalism and Political Integration* (Ramat Gan, Israel: Turtledove Publishing, 1979), pp. 191–210; and Cynthia Enloe, "The Neglected Strata: States in the City–Federal Politics of Malaysia," *Publius* 5, no. 2 (1975): 151–70.

17. Max Frenkel, "Kooperative und andere Foederalisme," *Schweizer Monatschrifte* 54 (January 1975): 725–36.

18. See Christa Altenstetter, "Intergovernmental Profiles in the Federal Systems of Austria and Germany," *Publius* 5, no. 2 (1975): 89–116; William T. Bluhm, *Building an Austrian Nation* (New Haven: Yale University Press, 1973); Frenkel, "Kooperative and andere Foederalisme."

19. Frederick Thayer, *An End to Hierarchy, An End to Competition* (New York: New Viewpoints, 1973).

20. Anthony Barker, ed., *Quangos in Britain: Government and the Networks of Public Policy-Making* (London: Macmillan, 1982).

21. See Robert B. Hawkins, Jr., *Self-Government by District, Myth and Reality* (Stanford: Stanford University Press, 1973); and Grodzins, *American System,* esp. chaps. 1 and 6.

22. Leonard D. White, who was unhappy with those arrangements, provides the best description of the practice in *The Federalists* (New York: Macmillan, 1948); White, *The Jeffersonians*

(New York: Macmillan, 1951); White, *The Jacksonians* (New York: Macmillan, 1954); White, *The Republican Era* (New York: Macmillan, 1958). In the United States, this was even true of the military services. See Walter Millis, *Arms and Men* (New York: Mentor Books, 1956). See also, James Sterling Young, *The Washington Community, 1800–1828* (New York: Columbia University Press, 1966), for a systematic view of the situation.

23. The Prussian and French models are embodied in the theories of Weber and Michels, among others; see Max Weber, *The Theory of Social and Economic Organizations,* trans. A. M. Henderson and Talcott Parsons, ed. with intro. by Talcott Parsons (New York: Free Press of Glencoe, 1964); Robert Michels, *Political Parties: A Sociological Study of the Oligarchical Tendencies of Modern Democracy* (Gloucester, Mass.: Peter Smith, 1978). Woodrow Wilson brought them to the United States. See Wilson, *Congressional Government* (Boston: Houghton–Mifflin, 1885), and Wilson, "The Study of Administration," *Political Science Quarterly* 2 (June 1887): 197–222.

24. William S. Livingston, *Federalism and Constitutional Change* (Oxford: Clarendon Press, 1956); and Arthur Macmahon, *Administering Federalism in a Democracy* (New York: Oxford University Press, 1972).

25. *Federalism and Prefectorial Administration,* special issue of *Publius* 11, no. 2 (1981); Daniel J. Elazar, "Comparative Federalism: The State of the Art and the State of the Field," in Ellis Katz and Benjamin R. Schuster, eds., *Dialogue on Comparative Federalism* (Philadelphia: Center for the Study of Federalism, 1978); Elazar, "The Role of Federalism in Political Integration," in Elazar, ed., *Federalism and Political Integration,* pp. 13–57.

26. Thayer, *An End to Hierarchy;* Robert B. Hawkins, Jr., ed., *Federalism and Government Reorganization,* special issue of *Publius* 8, no. 2 (1978).

27. Arend Lijphart, *Democracies: Patterns of Majoritarian and Consensus Government in Twenty-one Countries* (New Haven: Yale University Press, 1984); Roy C. Macridis and Bernard E. Brown, *Comparative Politics,* 3d ed. (Homewood, Ill.: Dorsey Press, 1968); and Charles Press, "Second Thoughts on Strengthening State Legislatures," *Publius* 4, no. 2 (1974): 117–22.

28. See, for example, Gary McDowell, "Were the Anti-Federalists Right? Judicial Activism and the Problem of Consolidated Government," *Publius* 12, no. 3 (1982): 99–108; Neil D. Mcfeeley, "The Supreme Court and the Federal System: Federalism from Warren to Burger," *Publius* 8, no. 4 (1978): 5–36; Charles L. Cotrell and R. Michael Stevens, "The 1978 Voting Rights Acts and San Antonio, Texas: Toward a Federal Guarantee of a Republican Form of Local Government," *Publius* 8, no. 1 (1978): 79–100; Werner F. Grunbaum and Lettie M. Wenner, "Comparing Environmental Litigation in State and Federal Courts," *Publius* 10, no. 3 (1980): 129–42; Robert S. Hirschfield, *The Constitution and the Court* (New York: Random House, 1962); Samuel Krislov, *The Supreme Court in the Political Process* (New York: Macmillan, 1965); Alpheus Thomas Mason and William M. Beaney, *The Supreme Court in a Free Society* (New York: Norton, 1968); and Robert G. McCloskey, *The American Supreme Court* (Chicago: University of Chicago Press, 1960).

29. See, for example, G. Theodore Mitau, *Decade of Decision* (New York: Charles Scribner's Sons, 1967); Harold J. Spaeth, *The Warren Court* (San Francisco: Chandler, 1966); Debra W. Stewart and Charles V. Stewart, "Bakke and Beyond: Cooperation and Power Sharing in the Federal System," *Publius* 9, no. 1 (1979): 141–60; and Alfred R. Light, "Federalism, FERC v. Mississippi, and Product Liability Reform," *Publius* 13, no. 2 (1983): 85–96.

30. See Krislov, *Supreme Court;* John Gruhl, "Patterns of Compliance with U.S. Supreme Court Rulings: The Case of Libel in Federal Courts of Appeals and State Supreme Courts," *Publius* 12, no. 3 (1982): 109–26; Jeanne Bell Nicholson and Debra W. Stewart, "The Supreme Court, Abortion, and State Response," *Publius* 8, no. 1 (1978): 159–78; Mary Cornelia Porter, "State Supreme Courts and the Legacy of the Warren Court: Some Old Inquiries for a New Situation," *Publius* 8, no. 4 (1978): 55–74; Daniel C. Kramer and Robert Riga, "The New York Court of Appeals and the United States Supreme Court, 1960–76," *Publius* 8, no. 4 (1978): 75–112.

31. See, for example, G. Sawer, "Constitutional Issues in Australian Federalism," *Publius* 7, no. 3 (1977): 21–34; Wheare, *Federal Government,* pp. 93–208; Richard E. Johnston, *The Effect of*

Judicial Review on Federal State Relations in Australia, Canada and the United States (Baton Rouge: Louisiana State University Press, 1969); J. A. Corry, "Constitutional Trends and Federalism," in A. R. M. Lower, F. R. Scott, et al., *Evolving Canadian Federalism* (Durham, N.C.: Duke University Press, 1958); Elmer Plischke, *Contemporary Governments of Germany,* 2d ed. (Boston: Houghton Mifflin, 1969), chap. 7; and Donald V. Smiley, *Canada in Question: Federalism in the Eighties,* 3d ed. (Toronto: McGraw-Hill Ryerson, 1980); and Philip M. Blair, *Federalism and Judicial Review in West Germany* (Oxford: Clarendon Press, 1981).

32. See Martin Landau, "Federalism, Redundancy and System Reliability," *Publius* 3, no. 2 (1973): 173–96; and Vincent Ostrom, "Can Federalism Make a Difference?" ibid., pp. 197–238.

33. See, for example, John A. Armstrong, "Federalism in the USSR: Ethnic and Territorial Aspects," *Publius* 7, no. 4 (1977): 89–106; Robert C. Scott, *Mexican Government in Transition* (Urbana: University of Illinois Press, 1959); Aaron Wildavsky, "Party Discipline under Federalism: Implications of Australian Experience," *Social Research* 28 (Winter 1961): 437–58; Andrew Oxley, A. Pravda, and A. Richie, *Czechoslovakia: the Party and the People* (New York: St. Martin's Press, 1973); Bernard W. Eissenstat, ed., *The Soviet Union: the Seventies and Beyond* (Lexington, Mass.: Lexington Books, 1975); and Kurt Steiner, *Politics in Austria* (Boston: Little, Brown, 1972).

34. William Buchanan, "Politics and Federalism: Party or Anti-Party," *Annals of the American Academy* 259 (May 1965): 107–15; Grodzins, *American System,* chap. 10; and Smiley, *Canada in Question.*

35. M. F. Franda, "Federalizing India: Attitudes, Capacities and Constraints," *South Asian Review* 3 (1970): 199–213; and Myron Weiner, *India at the Polls* (Washington, D.C.: American Enterprise Institute for Public Policy Research, 1978).

36. "Toward a More Responsible Two-Party System," published as a supplement to *American Political Science Review* 44 (1950).

37. Jeffrey L. Mayer, ed., *Dialogues on Decentralization,* special issue of *Publius* 6, no. 4 (1976): 35–62; John F. Bibby, "Political Parties and Federalism: The Republican National Committee Involvement in Gubernatorial and Legislative Elections," *Publius* 9,

no. 1 (1979): 229–36; M. Margaret Conway, "Republican Political Party Nationalization, Campaign Activities, and Their Implications for the Party System," *Publius* 13, no. 1 (1983): 1–18; Steven E. Schier, "New Rules, New Games: National Party Guidelines and Democratic National Convention Delegate Selection in Iowa and Wisconsin, 1968–1976," *Publius* 10, no. 3 (1980): 101–28; and Robert A. Goldwin, *Political Parties in the Eighties* (Washington, D.C.: American Enterprise Institute for Public Policy Research, 1980).

38. Plischke, *Contemporary Governments of Germany,* chap. 8, p. xi; Altenstetter, "Intergovernment Profiles in the Federal Systems of Austria and Germany"; and Klaus von Beyne, "West Germany: Federalism," *International Political Science Review* 5 (1984): 381–96.

39. Starr, "Australia's Two 'New Federalisms'"; Wildavsky, "Party Discipline under Federalism"; and Jean Holmes, "The Australian Federalism System," *International Political Science Review* 5 (1984): 397–414.

40. Pauline H. Baker, *Urbanization and Political Change: The Politics of Lagos, 1917–1967* (Berkeley and Los Angeles: University of California Press, 1974); Bill Dudley, *Instability and Political Order: Politics and Crisis in Nigeria* (Ibadan: Ibadan University Press, 1973); William Gavin, *State and Society in Nigeria* (Idanre: Afrografika Publishers, 1980); "Nigeria: First Year in Office of President Shehu Shagari," *International Herald Tribune,* October 6, 1980, pp. 14–15; P. Mawhood, *Local Government in the Third World: the Experience of Tropical Africa* (New York: Wiley, 1983); Ronald L. Watts, *New Federations: Experiments in the Commonwealth* (Oxford: Clarendon Press, 1966); Frederick A. O. Schwarz, Jr., *Nigeria: The Tribes, the Nation, or the Race* (Cambridge, Mass.: MIT Press, 1965); and Howard Wolpe, *Urban Politics in Nigeria* (Berkeley and Los Angeles: University of California Press, 1974).

41. Grodzins, *American System,* chap. 12.

Chapter 7

1. This theme is treated more fully in *Publius* 12, no. 3 (1982), most of which is devoted to an exploration of the conflict between nationalism and federalism in European state-building.

2. For an overview of this shift, see Nathan Glazer, "From

Class-Based to Ethnic-Based Politics," in Daniel J. Elazar, ed., *Governing Peoples and Territories* (Philadelphia: Institute for the Study of Human Issues, 1983), pp. 47–56.

3. These phenomena have been the subjects of several special issues of *Publius,* including Stephen L. Schechter, ed., *Federalism and Community: A Comparative View* (5, no. 2 [1977]); Ivo D. Duchacek, ed., *Federalism and Ethnicity* (7, no. 4 [1977]); and Duchacek, ed., *Transborder Relations among Constituent States* (14, no. 4 [1984]).

4. For a complete list and description of these arrangements, see Daniel J. Elazar et al., *Handbook of Federal and Autonomy Arrangements* (Jerusalem: Jerusalem Center for Public Affairs, forthcoming).

5. Robert T. Bowie and Carl J. Friedrich, eds., *Studies in Federalism* (Boston: Little, Brown, 1954); Thomas Franck, ed., *Why Federations Fail: An Inquiry into the Requisites for a Successful Federation* (New York: New York University Press, 1968).

6. See Donald S. Lutz, *Popular Consent and Popular Control: Whig Political Theory in the Early State Constitutions* (Baton Rouge: Louisiana State University Press, 1980).

7. John Dewey's *The Public and Its Problems* (Chicago: Gateway Books, 1946) is the starting point for this discussion.

8. On the Cameroun federation, see Willard Johnson, *Cameroun Federation: Political Integration in a Fragmentary Society* (Princeton: Princeton University Press, 1970); and F. M. Stark, "Persuasion and Power in Cameroon," *Canadian Journal of African Studies* 14 (1980): 273–93.

9. David Apter, *The Political Kingdom of Uganda* (Princeton: Princeton University Press, 1967); and V. B. Thompson, *Africa and Unity: The Evolution of Pan Africanism* (London: Longman, 1969).

10. Harold D. Nelson, ed., *Libya: A Country Study* (Washington, D.C.: American University, 1979).

11. A. H. M. Kirk-Greene, *Crisis and Conflict in Nigeria: A Documentary Sourcebook,* vol. 2 (London: Oxford University Press, 1971); J. P. Mackintosh, *Nigerian Government and Politics* (Evanston: Northwestern University Press, 1966); Robert Melson, "A Failure of Federalism: The Nigerian Case," in Daniel

J. Elazar, ed., *Self-Rule/Shared Rule* (Ramat Gan, Israel: Tur-tledove Publishing, 1979), pp. 148–52; John A. A. Ayoade, "Secession Threat as a Redressive Mechanism in Nigerian Federalism," *Publius* 3, no. 1 (1973): 57–74; Daniel J. Elazar, "Federalism in Theory and Practice: Some French, American and Nigerian Examples," *Publius* 3, no. 1 (1973): 1–4; and L. Adele Jinadu, "The Constitutional Situation of the Nigerian States," *Publius* 12, no. 1 (1982): 155–86.

12. Donald Rothchild, *Politics of Integration: An East African Documentary* (Nairobi: East African Publishing House, 1968).

13. Gwendolyn M. Carter, ed., *National Unity and Regionalism in Eight African States* (Ithaca: Cornell University Press, 1966).

14. Frank N. Trager, *Building a Welfare State in Burma* (New York: Institute of Pacific Relations, 1958).

15. Paul Appleby, *Public Administration in India* (Delhi: Manager of Publication, 1953); V. P. Menon, *The Integration of the Indian States* (New York: Crowell-Collier-Macmillan, 1956); Selig S. Harrison, *India: The Most Dangerous Decade* (Princeton: Princeton University Press, 1960); and M. V. Pylee, *Constitutional Government in India* (Bombay: Asia Publishing House, 1961).

16. On post-1972 Sudan, see John Howell, "Politics in the Southern Sudan," *African Affairs* 72 (April 1973): 163–78; R. K. Badal, "The Rise and Fall of Separation in Southern Sudan," *African Affairs* 75 (1976): 463–74. At this writing (1984), the Sudanese situation has deteriorated as a result of President Nimeiry's efforts to impose Islamic law on all of Sudan, thereby nullifying crucial aspects of this devolution plan.

17. Willard Hanna, *The Formation of Malaysia: New Factor in World Politics* (New York: American Universities Field Staff, 1965); Hanna, *The Separation of Singapore from Malaysia* (New York: American Universities Field Staff, 1965); Lennox A. Mills, *Malaysia: A Political and Economic Appraisal* (Minneapolis: University of Minnesota Press, 1958).

18. See Gabriel Ben Dor, "Federalism in the Arab World," in Daniel J. Elazar, ed., *Federalism and Political Integration* (Ramat Gan, Israel: Turtledove Publishing, 1979), pp. 191–210.

19. Choudry Kaliquzzaman, *Pathway to Pakistan* (Lahore: Longmans Pakistan Branch, 1961); Sachin Sen, *The Birth of*

Pakistan (Calcutta: General Printers and Publishers, 1955); and Robert LaPorte, Jr., *Power and Privilege* (Berkeley and Los Angeles: University of California Press, 1975).

20. René Lemarchand et al., *Political Awakening in the Belgian Congo* (Westport, Conn.: Greenwood Press, 1982); E. Jefferson Murphy, *History of African Civilization* (New York: Crowell, 1972); and W. Arthur Lewis, *Politics in West Africa* (London: Allen & Unwin, 1965).

21. G. P. Bhattacharjee, *Southeast Asian Politics: Malaysia and Indonesia* (Columbia, Mo.: South Asia Books, 1977).

22. "The Confederation of Senegambia," *Background Brief* (London: Foreign and Commonwealth Office, 1983); and Robert Fraser, ed., *Keesing's Contemporary Archives, 1982* (London: Keesing's Publications, 1982), pp. 31548, 31834.

23. See Morton Grodzins, *The American System: A New View of Government in the United States,* ed. Daniel J. Elazar (Chicago: Rand McNally, 1966), and Elazar et al., *Cooperation and Conflict: Readings in American Federalism* (Itasca, Ill.: F. E. Peacock, 1969), for the best representations of the Chicago Workshop. The Ostroms' work includes Vincent Ostrom, "Can Federalism make a Difference?" in *The Federal Polity, Publius* 3, no. 2 (1973): 197–238; *The Political Theory of a Compound Republic: A Reconstruction of the Logical Foundations of American Democracy as Presented in the Federalist* (Blacksburg, Va.: Virginia Polytechnic Institute, Center for the Study of Public Choice, 1971); Vincent Ostrom, Charles Tiebout, and Robert Warren, "The Organization of Government in Metropolitan Areas: A Theoretical Inquiry," *American Political Science Review* 55 (1961): 831–42; and Vincent Ostrom and Elinor Ostrom, "A Behavioral Approach to the Study of Intergovernmental Relations," *Annals of the American Academy of Political and Social Sciences* 359 (May 1965): 137–46.

24. Milton Kotler, *Neighborhood Government: The Local Foundation of Political Life* (Indianapolis: Bobbs-Merrill, 1969). See also his remarks in the transcript of the third "Toward '76" Conference of the Center for the Study of Federalism, "Serving the Public in a Metropolitan Society," Philadelphia, August 25–27, 1974.

25. Joseph Zimmerman, *The Federated City: Community Control in Large Cities* (New York: St. Martin's Press, 1972); John C.

Bollens and Henry J. Schmandt, *The Metropolis,* 2d ed. (New York: Harper & Row, 1970); League of Women Voters Education Fund, *Super City/Hometown, U.S.A.: Prospects for Two-Tier Government* (New York: Praeger, 1974). Stefen Dupre, in *Regional Government* (Toronto: Institute of Public Administration, 1968), provides a thorough discussion of the possibilities of metropolitan federalism in light of the Toronto experience.

26. Andrew C. McLaughlin, *The Foundations of American Constitutionalism* (1932; rpr. Gloucester: Peter Smith, 1972).

27. Peter F. Drucker, *The Concept of the Corporation* (New York: Mentor Books, 1964).

28. Roger F. Swanson, *Intergovernmental Perspective on the Canada-U.S. Relationship* (New York: New York University Press, 1978); and Robert Jones Shafer and Donald Mabry, *Neighbors: Mexico and the United States* (Chicago: Nelson Hall, 1981).

29. Jean Rodolphe de Salis, *Switzerland and Europe: Essays and Reflections,* trans. from the German by Alexander Henderson and Elizabeth Henderson, intro. by Christopher Hughs (University, Ala.: University of Alabama Press, 1971); and Gabriel D. Raanan, *Yugoslavia after Tito: Scenarios and Implications* (Boulder, Colo.: Westview Press, 1977).

30. Bernard W. Eissenstat, ed., *The Soviet Union: The Seventies and Beyond* (Lexington, Mass.: Lexington Books, 1975); and Adam Bruno Ulam, *Dangerous Relations: The Soviet Union in World Politics, 1970–1982* (New York: Oxford University Press, 1983).

31. See special issue of *Publius* 14, no. 1 (1984), *Crisis and Continuity in Canadian Federalism,* ed. Filippo Sabetti and Harold M. Waller.

32. Ivo D. Duchacek discusses this in detail in *Comparative Federalism: The Territorial Dimension of Politics* (New York: Holt, Rinehart and Winston, 1970).

33. Alexis de Tocqueville has given us the classic discussion of this process and its political implications in *Democracy in America,* trans. Lawrence Mayer (Garden City, N.Y.: Doubleday, 1969).

Selected Bibliography

Books

Adams, Henry, ed. *Documents Relating to New England Federalism, 1800–1815*. Boston: Little, Brown, 1905.

Agus, Irving. *Rabbi Meir of Rothenburg*. Philadelphia: Dropsie College for Hebrew and Cognate Learning, 1947.

———. *Urban Civilization in Pre-Crusade Europe*. New York: Yeshiva University, 1967.

Ake, Claude. *A Theory of Political Integration*. Homewood, Ill.: Dorsey Press, 1967.

Alexander, Robert Jackson. *Latin American Political Parties*. New York: Praeger, 1973.

Althusius, Johannes. *Politica Methodice Digesta* (1603). Edited by Carl J. Friedrich. Cambridge, Mass.: Harvard University Press, 1935.

Anderson, William. *Intergovernmental Relations in Review*. Minneapolis: University of Minnesota Press, 1960.

Anderson, William, and Grodzins, Morton. *The Nation and the States: Rivals or Partners?* Minneapolis: University of Minnesota Press, 1955.

Appleby, Paul. *Public Administration in India*. Delphi: Manager of Publication, 1953.

Apter, David. *The Political Kingdom of Uganda*. Princeton: Princeton University Press, 1967.

Aron, Robert, and Marc, Alexandre. *Principes du Federalisme*. Paris: Le Portulan, 1948.

Atherton, Lewis. *Main Street on the Middle Border*. Bloomington: Indiana University Press, 1984.

Aubert, J. F. *Petit histoire constitutionelle de la Suisse*. Bern: Francke Editions, 1974.

Bailyn, Bernard. *The Ideological Origins of the American Revolution.* Cambridge, Mass.: Belknap Press of Harvard University Press, 1967.

————. *The Origins of American Politics.* New York: Knopf, 1968.

Baker, J. Wayne. *Heinrich J. Bullinger and the Covenant.* Athens: University of Ohio Press, 1981.

Baker, Pauline H. *Urbanization and Political Change: The Politics of Lagos, 1917–1967.* Berkeley and Los Angeles: University of California Press, 1974.

Baltzell, E. Digby. *Philadelphia Gentlemen: The Making of an Upper Class.* Glencoe, Ill.: Free Press, 1958.

Barber, Benjamin. *The Death of Communal Liberty: A History of Freedom in a Swiss Mountain Canton.* Princeton: Princeton University Press, 1974.

Baker, Anthony, ed. *Quangos in Britain: Government and the Networks of Public Policy Making.* London: Macmillan, 1982.

Barker, Ernest, trans. and ed. *The Politics of Aristotle.* New York: Oxford University Press, 1962.

Barsh, Russell L., and Henderson, James Y. *The Road: Indian Tribes and Political Liberty.* Berkeley and Los Angeles: University of California Press, 1980.

Becker, Carl L. *The Declaration of Independence.* New York: Vintage Books, 1958.

Beer, Samuel H., and Ulam, Adam B., eds. *Patterns of Government: The Major Political Systems of Europe.* New York: Random House, 1962.

Bennett, Walter H. *American Theories of Federalism.* University, Ala.: University of Alabama Press, 1966.

Bentham, Jeremy. *The Works of Jeremy Bentham.* Edited by John Bowring. New York: Russell and Russell, 1962.

Bhattacharjee, G. P. *Southeast Asian Politics: Malaysia and Indonesia.* Columbia, Mo.: South Asia Books, 1977.

Binder, Leonard. *Politics in Lebanon.* New York: Wiley, 1966.

Blair, Philip M. *Federalism and Judicial Review in West Germany.* Oxford: Clarendon Press, 1981.

Blaustein, Albert P., and Flanz, Gisbert H. *Constitutions of the Countries of the World.* Dobbs Ferry, N.Y.: Oceana Publications, 1984.

Bluhm, William T. *Building an Austrian Nation*. New Haven: Yale University Press, 1973.

Bluntschli, Johann. *The Theory of the State*. Oxford: Clarendon Press, 1892.

Bodin, Jean. *The Six Books of the Commonwealth*. Translated by M. J. Tooley. New York: Barnes & Noble, 1967.

Bollens, John C., and Schmandt, Henry J. *The Metropolis*. 2d ed. New York: Harper & Row, 1970.

Bowie, Robert T., and Friedrich, Carl J., eds. *Studies in Federalism*. Boston: Little, Brown, 1954.

Brass, Paul R. *Language, Religion and Politics in North India*. London: Cambridge University Press, 1974.

Bridenbaugh, Carl, and Bridenbaugh, Jessica. *Rebels and Gentlemen: Philadelphia in the Age of Franklin*. New York: Reynal & Hitchcock, 1942.

Bryce, James. *The American Commonwealth*. Rev. ed. New York: Macmillan, 1914.

————. *The Holy Roman Empire*. New York: Macmillan, 1895.

Buber, Martin. *Kingship of God*. New York: Harper & Row, 1956.

————. *Paths in Utopia*. Boston: Beacon Press, 1958.

Burke, Edmund. *A Vindication of Natural Society* (1757). Edited by Frank N. Pagano. Indianapolis: Liberty Classics, 1983.

Butler, Ewan. *The Horizon Concise History of Scandinavia*. New York: American Publishing Co., 1973.

Carney, Frederick, trans. *Johannes Althusius' Politics*. Boston: Beacon Press, 1964.

Carter, Gwendolyn M., ed. *National Unity and Regionalism in Eight African States*. Ithaca: Cornell University Press, 1966.

Cashman, Richard I. *The Myth of the Lokamanya*. Berkeley and Los Angeles: University of California Press, 1975.

Codding, George, Jr. *Governing the Commune of Veyrier: Politics in Swiss Local Government*. Boulder: Bureau of Government Research, University of Colorado, 1967.

Condon, Thomas J. *New York Beginnings: The Commercial Origins of New Netherlands*. New York: New York University Press, 1968.

Coswin, E. S. *The Constitution of the United States of America: Analysis and Interpretation*. Washington, D.C.: U.S. Government Printing Office, 1953.

Cowan, Zelman. *Federal Jurisdiction in Australia*. Melbourne: Oxford University Press, 1951.

Curtis, Michael. *Western European Integration*. New York: Harper & Row, 1965.

Dahl, Robert. *Pluralist Democracy in America*. Chicago: University of Chicago Press, 1968.

————. *A Preface to Democratic Theory*. Chicago: University of Chicago Press, 1956.

Davis, S. Rufus. *The Federal Principle: A Journey through Time in Quest of a Meaning*. Berkeley and Los Angeles: University of California Press, 1978.

Das Gupta, Jyotirindra. *Language Conflict and National Development*. Berkeley and Los Angeles: University of California Press, 1970.

de Rougemont, Denis. *La Suisse, ou l'histoïre d'un peuple heureux*. Lausanne: Le Livre du Mois, 1965.

————. *Vingt-huit siècle d'Europe: La conscience europenne a travers les textes, d'Hesiode a nos jours*. Paris: Payot, 1961.

Derry, Thomas K. *A History of Scandinavia*. Minneapolis: University of Minnesota Press, 1979.

de Salis, Jean Rodolphe. *Switzerland and Europe: Essays and Reflections*. Translated from the German by Alexander Henderson and Elizabeth Henderson, introduction by Christopher Hughes. University, Ala.: University of Alabama Press, 1971.

des Coulanges, Fustel. *The Ancient City*. Garden City, N.Y.: Doubleday, 1956.

Deutsch, Karl. *Political Community and the North Atlantic Area: International Organization in the Light of Historical Experience*. Westport, Conn.: Greenwood Press, 1960.

Dewey, John. *The Public and Its Problems*. Chicago: Gateway Books, 1946.

Dicey, Albert V. *Introduction to the Study of the Law of the Constitution*. 10th ed. New York: St. Martin's Press, 1962.

Dikshit, Ramash Dutta. *The Political Geography of Federalism*. New York: Halsted Press, 1975.

Dodge, G. H. *The Political Theory of the Huguenots of Dispersion*. New York: Octagon Books, 1947.

Dragnich, Alex N. *Major European Governments*. Homewood, Ill.: Dorsey Press, 1970.

Drucker, Peter F. *The Concept of the Corporation*. New York: Mentor Books, 1964.

Duchacek, Ivo D. *Comparative Federalism: The Territorial Dimension of Politics*. New York: Holt, Rinehart and Winston, 1970.

————, ed. *Federalism and Ethnicity*. A special issue of *Publius* 7, no. 4 (1977).

————, ed. *Transborder Relations among Constituent States*. A special issue of *Publius* 14, no. 4 (1984).

Dupre, Stefan. *Regional Government*. Toronto: Institute of Public Administration of Canada, 1968.

Earle, Valerie, ed. *Federalism: Infinite Variety in Theory and Practice*. Itasca, Ill.: F. E. Peacock, 1968.

Eissenstat, Bernard W., ed. *The Soviet Union: The Seventies and Beyond*. Lexington, Mass.: Lexington Books, 1975.

Elazar, Daniel J. *American Federalism: A View from the States*. 3d ed. New York: Harper & Row, 1984.

————. *The American Partnership: Intergovernmental Cooperation in the Nineteenth-Century United States*. Chicago: University of Chicago Press, 1962.

————. *The Book of Joshua as a Political Classic*. Jerusalem: Center for Jewish Community Studies, 1980.

————. *Cities of the Prairie: The Metropolitan Frontier and American Politics*. New York: Basic Books, 1970.

————. *Continuity and Change in American Federalism*. Philadelphia: Center for the Study of Federalism, n.d.

————. *The Covenant Idea and the Jewish Political Tradition*. Ramat Gan: Bar Ilan University, Department of Political Studies and Center for Jewish Community Studies, 1983.

————. *Israel: From Territorial to Ideological Democracy*. New York: General Learning Press, 1970.

————. *The Outlook for Creative Federalism*. Philadelphia: Center for the Study of Federalism, n.d.

————. *The Politics of Belleville: Profile of the Civil Community*. Philadelphia: Temple University Press, 1971.

————. *The Principles and Practices of Federalism: A Comparative Historical Approach*. Philadelphia: Center for the Study of Federalism, n.d.

————. *Some Preliminary Observations on the Vocabulary of Covenant*. Philadelphia: Center for the Study of Federalism, 1983.

————, and Stuart A. Cohen. *The Jewish Polity: Jewish Political Organization from Biblical Times to the Present.* Bloomington: Indiana University Press, 1985.

————, et al. *Handbook of Federal and Autonomy Arrangements.* Jerusalem: Jerusalem Center for Public Affairs, forthcoming.

————, ed. *Federalism and Political Integration.* Lanham, Md. and Jerusalem: University Press of America and Jerusalem Center for Public Affairs, 1984.

————, ed. *From Autonomy to Shared Rule: Options for Judea, Samaria and Gaza.* Jerusalem: Jerusalem Center for Public Affairs, 1983.

————, ed. *Governing Peoples and Territories.* Philadelphia: Institute for the Study of Human Issues, 1983.

————, ed. *Self-Rule/Shared Rule.* Ramat Gan: Turtledove Publishing, 1979.

————, ed. *State Constitutional Design in Federal Systems.* A special issue of *Publius* 12, no. 1 (1982).

————, et al., eds. *Cooperation and Conflict: Readings in American Federalism.* Itasca, Ill.: F. E. Peacock, 1969.

Elliott, J. H. *Imperial Spain, 1469–1716.* New York: St. Martin's Press, 1964.

Enloe, Cynthia. *Ethnic Conflict and Political Development.* Boston: Little, Brown, 1973.

Esman, Milton J. *Essays in Federalism.* Claremont, Calif.: Institute for Studies in Federalism, 1961.

————, ed. *Ethnic Conflict in the Western World.* Ithaca: Cornell University Press, 1977.

Esterbauer, Fried; Héraud, Guy; and Pernthalers, Peter, eds. *Föderalismus.* Vienna: Wilheim Braumüller, 1977.

Etzioni, Amitai. *Political Unification.* New York: Holt, Rinehart and Winston, 1965.

Ferguson, Russell. *Early Western Pennsylvania Politics.* Pittsburgh: University of Pittsburgh Press, 1938.

Franck, Thomas, ed. *Why Federations Fail: An Inquiry into the Requisites for a Successful Federation.* New York: New York University Press, 1966.

Frankfort, Henri. *Before Philosophy: The Intellectual Adventure of Ancient Man, an Essay on Speculative Thought in the Ancient Near East.* Baltimore: Penguin Books, 1967.

Fraser, Robert, ed. *Keesing's Contemporary Archives, 1982.* London: Keesing's Publications, 1982.

Freeman, Edward A. *A History of Federal Government in Greece and Italy.* 2d ed. London: Macmillan, 1893.

Freeman, Gordon. *The Heavenly Kingdom.* Lanham, Md.: University Press of America and Jerusalem Center for Public Affairs, 1985.

Frenkel, Max. *Föderalismus und Bundesstat, Band I: Föderalismus.* Bern: Verlag Peter Lang AG, 1984.

————, ed. *Partnership in Federalism.* Bern: Peter J. Lang, 1977.

Friedrich, Carl J. *Trends of Federalism in Theory and Practice.* New York: Praeger, 1968.

Friedrich, Joachim. *The Philosophy of Law in Historical Perspective.* Chicago: University of Chicago Press, 1965.

Frisch, Morton, and Stevens, Richard J. *The Political Thought of American Statesmen.* Itasca, Ill.: F. E. Peacock, 1973.

Gabriel, Ralph Henry. *The Course of American Democratic Thought.* 2d ed. New York: Ronald Press, 1956.

Gavin, William. *State and Society in Nigeria.* Idanre: Afrografika Publishers, 1980.

Gierke, Otto. *The Development of Political Theory.* New York: Norton, 1939.

————. *Natural Law and the Theory of Society.* Translated by Ernest Barker. Cambridge: Cambridge University Press, 1934.

————. *Political Theories of the Middle Ages.* Cambridge: Cambridge University Press, 1938.

Goldwin, Robert A., ed. *A Nation of States.* 2d ed. Chicago: Rand McNally, 1974.

————, ed. *Political Parties in the Eighties.* Washington, D.C.: American Enterprise Institute for Public Policy Research, 1980.

Graves, William Brooke. *American Intergovernmental Relations: Their Origins, Historical Development, and Current Status.* New York: Charles Scribner's Sons, 1964.

Greilsammer, Alain. *Les mouvements federalistas en France.* Nice: Presses d'Europe, 1975.

Grodzins, Morton. *The American System: A New View of Government in the United States.* Edited by Daniel J. Elazar. Chicago: Rand McNally, 1966.

Haggi, S. A. H., ed. *Union-State Relations in India.* Meerut: Meenakshi Prakshan, 1967.

Hamilton, Alexander; Madison, James; and Jay, John. *The Federalist.* Edited with introduction and notes by Jacob E. Cooke. Cleveland: World, 1961.

Hanna, Willard. *The Formation of Malaysia: New Factor in World Politics.* New York: American Universities Field Staff, 1965.

————. *The Separation of Singapore from Malaysia.* New York: American Universities Field Staff, 1965.

Hardgrove, Robert. *The Nadars of Tamiland.* Berkeley and Los Angeles: University of California Press, 1969.

Harrington, James. *Political Writings: Representative Selections.* Edited by Charles Blitzer. New York: Liberal Arts Press, 1955.

Harrison, Selig S. *India: The Most Dangerous Decade.* Princeton: Princeton University Press, 1960.

Hart, Henry, and Wechsler, Herbert. *The Federal Courts and the Federal System.* 2d ed. Brooklyn: Foundation Press, 1973.

Haskill, Barbara, ed. *Southern California: Attitudes 1972.* Berkeley: D. L. Hennessey, 1972.

Hawkins, Robert B., Jr. *Federalism and Government Reorganization.* A special issue of *Publius* 8, no. 2 (1978).

————, ed. *American Federalism: A New Partnership for the Republic.* San Francisco: Institute for Contemporary Studies, 1982.

————, ed. *Self-Government by District, Myth and Reality.* Stanford: Stanford University Press, 1973.

Heisler, Martin O., ed. *Politics in Europe.* New York: David McKay, 1974.

Hellbling, Ernest C.; Mayer-Maly, Theo; and Michsler, Herbert. *Theorie und Praxis des Bundesstaates.* Vienna: Universitätsverlag Anton Pustes, 1974.

Heraud, Guy. *L'Europe des ethnics.* Nice: Presses d'Europe, 1963.

Hill, Christopher. *Intellectual Origins of the English Revolution.* New York: Oxford University Press, 1965.

Hillers, Delbert. *Covenant: The History of the Biblical Idea.* Baltimore: Johns Hopkins University Press, 1969.

Hirschfield, Robert S. *The Constitution and the Court.* New York: Random House, 1962.

Hobbes, Thomas. *Leviathan.* Indianapolis: Bobbs-Merrill, 1958.

Holcombe, Arthur. *Our More Perfect Union.* Cambridge, Mass.: Harvard University Press, 1955.

Holt, P. M., and Daly, M. W. *The History of Sudan: From the Coming of Islam to the Present Day.* 3d ed. London: Weidenfeld and Nicolson, 1979.

Horowitz, Robert. *The Moral Foundations of the American Republic.* Charlottesville: University Press of Virginia, 1979.

Hughes, Christopher. *Confederacies.* Leicester: Leicester University Press, 1963.

Hyam, Ronald, and Martin, Ged. *Reappraisals in British Imperial History.* Toronto: Macmillan Company of Canada, 1975.

Hyneman, Charles S., and Lutz, Donald S. *American Political Writings during the Founding Era, 1769–1805.* Indianapolis: Liberty Press, 1983.

————. *A Bibliography of American Political Writings from the Founding Era.* Philadelphia: Center for the Study of Federalism, 1982.

James, Herman G. *The Constitutional System of Brazil.* Washington, D.C.: Carnegie Institution, 1921.

Jenkins, Howard M., ed. *Pennsylvania, Colonial and Federal: A History, 1608–1903.* Philadelphia: Pennsylvania Historical Publishing Association, 1903.

Johnson, Willard. *Cameroun Federation: Political Integration in a Fragmentary Society.* Princeton: Princeton University Press, 1970.

Johnston, Richard E. *The Effect of Judicial Review on Federal-State Relations in Australia, Canada and the United States.* Baton Rouge: Louisiana State University Press, 1969.

Jones, Rodney W. *Urban Politics in India.* Berkeley and Los Angeles: University of California Press, 1974.

Kadushin, Max. *Organic Thinking.* New York: Jewish Theological Seminary, 1938.

Kamen, Henry Arthur. *A Concise History of Spain.* London: Thames and Hudson, 1973.

Kaplan, Harold. *Urban Political Systems: A Functional Analysis of Metro Toronto.* New York: Columbia University Press, 1967.

Katz, Ellis, and Schuster, Benjamin R., eds. *Dialogue on Comparative Federalism.* Philadelphia: Center for the Study of Federalism, 1978.

Kaufman, Yehezel. *The Religion of Israel.* Translated by Moshe Greenberg. Chicago: University of Chicago Press, 1960.

Khaliquzzaman, Choudry. *Pathway to Pakistan.* Lahore: Longman Pakistan Branch, 1961.

Kincaid, John, ed. *Political Culture, Public Policy and the American States.* Philadelphia: Institute for the Study of Human Issues, 1983.

Kincaid, John, and Elazar, Daniel J., eds. *The Covenant Connection: Federal Theology and the Origins of Modern Politics.* Durham, N.C.: Carolina Academic Press, 1985.

King, Preston. *Federalism and Federation.* Baltimore: Johns Hopkins University Press, 1982.

Kirk-Greene, A. H. M. *Crisis and Conflict in Nigeria: A Documentary Sourcebook.* Vol. 2. London: Oxford University Press, 1971.

Koehane, Robert O., and Nye, Joseph S., Jr., eds. *Transnational Relations and World Politics.* Cambridge, Mass.: Harvard University Press, 1971.

Kolarz, Walter. *Russia and Her Colonies.* New York: Praeger, 1953.

Kotler, Milton. *Neighborhood Government: The Local Foundation of Political Life.* Indianapolis: Bobbs-Merrill, 1969.

Krislov, Samuel. *The Supreme Court in the Political Process.* New York: Macmillan, 1965.

LaPorte, Robert, Jr. *Power and Privilege.* Berkeley and Los Angeles: University of California Press, 1975.

Laski, Harold J. *The American Democracy: A Commentary and an Interpretation.* New York: Viking Press, 1948.

Leach, Richard. *American Federalism.* New York: Norton, 1970.

League of Women Voters Education Fund. *Super City/Hometown U.S.A.: Prospects for Two-Tier Government.* New York: Praeger, 1974.

Lewis, W. Arthur. *Politics in West Africa.* London: Allen & Unwin, 1965.

Lijphart, Arend. *Democracies: Patterns of Majoritarian and Consensus Government in Twenty-One Countries.* New Haven: Yale University Press, 1984.

———. *The Politics of Accommodation: Pluralism and Democracy in the Netherlands.* Berkeley and Los Angeles: University of California Press, 1969.

Lindberg, Leon N., and Scheingold, Stuart A. *Europe's Would-Be Polity: Patterns of Change in the European Community.* Englewood Cliffs, N.J.: Prentice-Hall, 1970.

Lippmann, Walter. *Public Philosophy.* Boston: Little, Brown, 1955.

Livingston, William S. *Federalism and Constitutional Change.* Oxford: Clarendon Press, 1956.

Locke, John. *First and Second Treatises of Government.* Edited by Peter Laslett. New York: Mentor Books, 1965.

Lower, A.R.M.; Scott, F. R.; et al. *Evolving Canadian Federalism.* Durham, N.C.: Duke University Press, 1958.

Lutz, Donald S. *Popular Consent and Popular Control: Whig Political Theory in the Early State Constitutions.* Baton Rouge: Louisiana State University Press, 1980.

Maas, Arthur, ed. *Area and Power: A Theory of Local Government.* Glencoe, Ill.: Free Press, 1959.

Macmahon, Arthur. *Administering Federalism in a Democracy.* New York: Oxford University Press, 1972.

———, ed. *Federalism: Mature and Emergent.* New York: Columbia University Press, 1955.

Mackintosh, J. P. *Nigerian Government and Politics.* Evanston: Northwestern University Press, 1966.

Mansfield, Peter. *The Ottoman Empire and Its Successors.* New York: St. Martin's Press, 1973.

Marc, Alexandre. *Europe terre decicive.* Paris: Editions de Vieux Columbier, 1959.

———. *A hauteur d'homme: La revolution federaliste.* Paris: Editions de sers, 1948.

———, and Aron, Robert. *Principles du federalisme.* Paris: Le Portulan, 1948.

———. *Dialectique du dechainement, fondements philosophiques du federalisme.* Paris: Editions du Vieux Columbier, 1961.

Mason, Alpheus Thomas, and Beaney, William M. *The Supreme Court in a Free Soceity.* New York: Norton, 1968.

Mathews, Russell, ed. *Federalism in Australia: Current Trends.* A special issue of *Publius* 7, no. 3 (1977).

Mawhood, P. *Local Government in the Third World: The Experience of Tropical Africa.* New York: Wiley, 1983.

Mayer, J. P. *Alexis de Tocqueville: A Bibliographical Study of Political Science.* Gloucester, Mass.: Peter Smith, 1966.

Mayer, Jeffrcy L., ed. *Dialogues on Decentralization*. A special issue of *Publius* 6, no. 4 (1976).

McCloskey, Robert G. *The American Supreme Court*. Chicago: University of Chicago Press, 1960.

McDonald, Ronald H. *Party Systems and Elections in Latin America*. Chicago: Markham, 1971.

McLaughlin, Andrew C. *The Foundations of American Constitutionalism*. Introduction by Henry Steele Commager. 1932. Reprint. Gloucester, Mass.: Peter Smith, 1972.

McWhinney, Edward. *Judicial Review in the English Speaking World*. 2d. ed. Toronto: University of Toronto Press, 1960.

Menden, George E. *Law and Covenant in Israel and the Ancient Near East*. Pittsburgh: University of Pittsburgh Press, 1955.

Menon, V. P. *The Integration of the Indian States*. New York: Crowell-Collier-Macmillan, 1956.

Michels, Robert. *Political Parties: A Sociological Study of the Oligarchical Tendencies of Modern Democracy*. Gloucester, Mass.: Peter Smith, 1979.

Miller, Perry. *The New England Mind: The Seventeenth Century*. Vol. 2, *From Colony to Province*. New York: Macmillan, 1939.

Millis, Walter. *Arms and Men*. New York: Mentor Books, 1956.

Mills, Lennox A. *Malaysia: A Political and Economic Appraisal*. Minneapolis: University of Minnesota Press, 1958.

Mitau, G. Theodore. *Decade of Decision*. New York: Charles Scribner's Sons, 1967.

Moore, J. M., trans. *Aristotle and Xenophon on Democracy and Oligarchy*. Berkeley and Los Angeles: University of California Press, 1975.

Morgan, Edmund S. *The Puritan Dilemma*. Edited by Oscar Handlin. Boston: Little, Brown, 1958.

Murphy, E. Jefferson. *History of African Civilization*. New York: Crowell, 1972.

Nelson, Harold D., ed. *Libya: A Country Study*. Washington, D.C.: American University, 1979.

Neumann, Robert G. *European Government*. New York: McGraw-Hill, 1968.

Nzimiro, Ikenna. *Studies in Ibo Political Systems*. Berkeley and Los Angeles: University of California, 1972.

Ostrom, Vincent. *The Intellectual Crisis of American Public Admin-

istration. University, Ala.: University of Alabama Press, 1973.

————. *The Political Theory of the Compound Republic: A Reconstruction of the Logical Foundations of American Democracy as Presented in the Federalist*. Blacksburg, Va.: Virginia Polytechnic Institute, Center for the Study of Public Choice, 1971.

Oxley, Andrew; Pravda, A.; and Richie, A. *Czechoslovakia: The Party and the People*. New York: St. Martin's Press, 1973.

Paden, John N. *Religion and Political Culture in Kano*. Berkeley and Los Angeles: University of California Press, 1973.

Penniman, Howard, ed. *Israel at the Polls, 1977*. Washington, D.C.: American Enterprise Institute for Public Policy Research, 1979.

————, ed. *Venezuela at the Polls: The National Elections of 1978*. Washington, D.C.: American Enterprise Institute for Public Policy Research, 1980.

Pirenne, Hinn. *Early Democracies in the Low Countries: Urban Society and Political Conflict in the Middle Ages and the Renaissance*. New York: Harper & Row, 1963.

Plischke, Elmer. *Contemporary Governments of Germany*. 2d. ed. Boston: Houghton Mifflin, 1969.

Proudhon, Pierre Joseph. *Du principe federatif*. Paris, 1863.

Pufendorf, Samuel. *De jure naturae et gentium libri octo*. Translated by W. A. Oldfather. Oxford: Clarendon Press, 1934.

Pylee, M. V. *Constitutional Government in India*. Bombay: Asia Publishing House, 1961.

Raanan, Gabriel D. *Yugoslavia after Tito: Scenarios and Implications*. Boulder, Col.: Westview Press, 1977.

Ranney, Austin, and Kendall, Wilmore. *Democracy and the American Party System*. New York: Harcourt, Brace, World, 1956.

Ratborg, Robert I., and Barrett, John, eds. *Conflict and Compromise in South Africa*. Lexington, Mass.: Lexington Books, 1980.

Riker, William H. *Federalism: Origin, Operation, Significance*. Boston: Little, Brown, 1964.

Riley, Patrick. *The Political Writings of Leibniz*. Cambridge: Cambridge University Press, 1972.

Ritter, Alan. *The Political Thought of Pierre Joseph Proudhon*. Princeton: Princeton University Press, 1969.

Rosenau, James N. *Linkage Politics: Essays on the Convergence of National and International Systems*. New York: Free Press, 1969.

Rothchild, Donald. *Politics of Integration: An East African Documentary*. Nairobi: East African Publishing House, 1968.

Rousseau, Jean-Jacques. *The Political Writings of Jean Jacques Rousseau*. Edited by C. Vaughan, Basil Blackwell. London: Oxford, 1962.

————. *The Social Contract and Discourse on the Origin of Inequality*. New York: Washington Square Press, 1967.

Rowe, L. S. *The Federal System in the Argentine Republic*. Washington, D.C.: Carnegie Institution, 1921.

Rowen, Herbert H., ed. *The Low Countries in Early Modern Times: A Documentary History*. New York: Random House, 1962.

Sabetti, Filippo, and Waller, Harold M., eds. *Crisis and Continuity in Canadian Federalism*. Special issue, *Publius*, 14, no. 1 (1984).

Schechter, Stephen L., ed. *Federalism and Community: A Comparative View*. A special issue of *Publius*, 5, no. 2 (1975).

————, ed. *The State of American Federalism, 1982. Publius*, 13, no. 2 (1983).

Schulz, Ann. *Local Politics and Nation-States: Case Studies in Politics and Policy*. Santa Barbara, Calif.: Clio Press, 1979.

Schwarz, Frederick A. O., Jr. *Nigeria: The Tribes, the Nation, or the Race*. Cambridge, Mass.: MIT Press, 1973.

Scott, Robert C. *Mexican Government in Transition*. Urbana: University of Illinois Press, 1959.

Selsman, John P. *The Pennsylvania Constitution of 1776: A Study of Revolutionary Democracy*. Philadelphia: University of Pennsylvania Press, 1936.

Sen, Sachin. *The Birth of Pakistan*. Calcutta: General Printers and Publishers, 1955.

Shafer, Robert Jones, and Mabry, Donald. *Neighbors: Mexico and the United States*. Chicago: Nelson Hall, 1981.

Sherwood, Frank P. *Institutionalizing the Grass Roots in Brazil: A Study in Comparative Local Government*. San Francisco: Chandler, 1967.

Shirley, E. J. *Richard Hooker and Contemporary Political Ideas*. Naperville, Ill.: Allenson, 1949.

Sidgewick, Henry. *The Elements of Politics*. London: Macmillan, 1919.

Siegfried, Andre. *Switzerland*. Translated by Edward Fitzgerald. New York: Duell, Sloan and Pearce, n.d.

Sills, David M., ed. *International Encyclopedia of the Social Sciences.* New York: Macmillan, 1968.

Simeon, Richard. *Federal-Provincial Diplomacy: The Making of Recent Policy in Canada.* Toronto: University of Toronto Press, 1972.

Sisson, Richard. *The Congress Party in Rajasthan.* Berkeley and Los Angeles: University of California Press, 1972.

Sklar, Richard Lawrence. *Nigerian Political Parties.* Princeton: Princeton University Press, 1963.

Smallwood, Frank. *Metro Toronto: A Decade Later.* Toronto: Bureau of Municipal Research, 1963.

Smiley, Donald V. *Canada in Question: Federalism in the Eighties.* 3d. ed. Toronto: McGraw-Hill Ryerson, 1980.

Smith, Adam. *An Inquiry into the Nature and Causes of the Wealth of Nations.* Edited by Edwin Cannon; introduction by John Chamberlain. New Rochelle, N.Y.: Arlington House, 1966.

Smith, Perceval. *A History of Modern Culture.* New York: Holt, Rinehart and Winston, 1934.

Spaeth, Harold J. *The Warren Court.* San Francisco: Chandler, 1966.

Steiner, Kurt. *Politics in Austria.* Boston: Little, Brown, 1972.

Stewart, William H. *Concepts of Federalism.* Lanham, Md.: University Press of America, 1984.

Stokes, William S. *Latin American Politics.* New York: Thomas Y. Crowell, 1959.

Storing, Herbert, and Dry, Murray. *The Complete Anti-Federalist.* Chicago: University of Chicago Press, 1981.

Strauss, Leo. *Natural Right and History.* Chicago: University of Chicago Press, 1953.

_____. *The Political Philosophy of Hobbes: Its Basis and Its Genesis.* Translated by Elsa M. Sinclair. Chicago: University of Chicago Press, 1952.

Strauss, Leo, and Cropsey, Joseph, eds. *History of Political Philosophy.* Chicago: Rand McNally, 1963.

Sutherland, Arthur E. *Constitutionalism in America: Origin and Evolution of Its Fundamental Ideas.* New York: Blaisdell, 1965.

Swanson, Roger F. *Intergovernmental Perspective on the Canada-U.S. Relationship.* New York: New York University Press, 1978.

Thayer, Frederick. *An End to Hierarchy, An End to Competition.* New York: New Viewpoints, 1973.

Thompson, V. B. *Africa and Unity: The Evolution of Pan Africanism.* London: Longman, 1969.

Thundyl, Zacharias P. *Covenant in Anglo–Saxon Thought.* Madras: Macmillan Company of India, 1972.

Tocqueville, Alexis de. *L'ancien regime.* Oxford: Blackwell, 1949.

————. *Democracy in America.* Translated by Lawrence Mayer. Garden City, N.Y.: Doubleday, 1969.

Tolles, Fredrick B. *Meeting House and Counting House: The Quaker Merchants of Colonial Philadelphia, 1682–1763.* Chapel Hill: University of North Carolina Press, 1948.

Trager, Frank N. *Building a Welfare State in Burma.* New York: Institute of Pacific Relations, 1958.

Ulam, Adam Bruno. *Dangerous Relations: The Soviet Union in World Politics, 1970–1982.* New York: Oxford University Press, 1983.

Unruh, John David. *The Plains Across: The Overland Emigrants and the Trans-Mississippi West, 1840–60.* Urbana: University of Illinois Press, 1979.

Vexler, Robert I. *Scandinavia: Denmark, Norway, Sweden.* Dobbs Ferry, N.Y.: Oceana Publications, 1977.

Walker, David B. *Towards a Functioning Federalism.* Cambridge, Mass.: Winthrop, 1981.

Warner, Sam Bass. *The Private City: Philadelphia in Three Periods of Its Growth.* Philadelphia: University of Pennsylvania Press, 1968.

Watts, Ronald L. *New Federations: Experiments in the Commonwealth.* Oxford: Clarendon Press, 1966.

Weber, Max. *The Theory of Social and Economic Organizations.* Translated by A. M. Henderson and Talcott Parsons; edited with introduction by Talcott Parsons. New York: Free Press of Glencoe, 1964.

Weiner, Myron. *India at the Polls.* Washington, D.C.: American Enterprise Institute for Public Policy Research, 1978.

Wheare, K. C. *Federal Government.* 4th ed. New York: Oxford University Press, 1964.

White, Leonard D. *The Federalists.* New York: Macmillan, 1948.

———. *The Jeffersonians.* New York: Macmillan, 1951.

———. *The Jacksonians.* New York: Macmillan, 1954.

———. *The Republican Era.* New York: Macmillan, 1958.

———. *The States and the Nation.* Baton Rouge: Louisiana State University Press, 1958.

Wildavsky, Aaron, ed. *American Federalism in Perspective.* Boston: Little, Brown, 1967.

Wilson, Woodrow. *Congressional Government.* Boston: Houghton-Mifflin, 1885.

Wolfers, Arnold. *Discord and Collaboration: Essays on International Politics.* Baltimore: Johns Hopkins University Press, 1962.

Wolpe, Howard. *Urban Politics in Nigeria.* Berkeley and Los Angeles: University of California Press, 1974.

Wood, Gordon S. *The Creation of the American Republic, 1776–1787.* Chapel Hill: University of North Carolina Press for the Institute of Early American History and Culture, 1969.

Woodcock, George. *Pierre Joseph Proudhon.* London: Routledge & Kegan Paul, 1956.

Wright, Deil S. *Understanding Intergovernmental Relations.* North Scituate, Mass.: Duxbury Press, 1978.

Wright, Louis B. *The Atlantic Frontier: Colonial American Civilization.* New York: Knopf, 1947.

Ylvisaker, Paul. *Intergovernmental Relations at the Grass Roots.* Minneapolis: University of Minnesota Press, 1956.

Young, James Sterling. *The Washington Community, 1800–1828.* New York: Columbia University Press, 1966.

Zimmerman, Joseph. *The Federated City: Community Control in Large Cities.* New York: St. Martin's Press, 1972.

Articles

Allum, P. A., and Amyet, G. "Regionalism in Italy: Old Wine in New Bottles." *Parliamentary Affairs* 24 (Winter 1970–71): 53–78.

Altenstetter, Christa. "Intergovernmental Profiles in the Federal Systems of Austria and Germany." *Publius* 5, no. 2 (1975): 89–116.

Armstrong, John A. "Federalism in the USSR: Ethnic and Territorial Aspects." *Publius* 7, no. 4 (1977): 89–106.

Ayoade, John A. A. "Ethnic Management in the 1979 Nigerian Constitution." *Publius* (forthcoming).

————. "Secession Threat as a Redressive Mechanism in Nigerian Federalism." *Publius* 2, no. 1 (1972): 57–74.

Badal, R. K. "The Rise and Fall of Separation in Southern Sudan." *African Affairs* 75 (1976): 463–74.

Buchanan, William. "Politics and Federalism: Party or Anti-Party." *Annals of the American Academy* 259 (May 1965): 107–15.

Burg, Steven L. "Ethnic Conflict and the Federalization of Socialist Yugoslavia." *Publius* 7, no. 4 (1977): 119–44.

Burns, R. M. "The Machinery of Federal-Provincial Relations, II." *Canadian Public Administration* 8 (1965): 527.

Careless, Anthony G., and Stevenson, Donald W. "Canada: Constitutional Reform as a Policy-Making Instrument." *Publius* 12, no. 3 (1982): 85–98.

"The Confederation of Senegambia." *Background Brief.* London: Foreign and Commonwealth Office (January 1983).

Conway, M. Margaret. "Republican Political Party Nationalization, Campaign Activities and Their Implications for the Party System." *Publius* 13, no. 1 (1983): 1–18.

Cotrell, Charles L., and Stevens, R. Michael. "The 1975 Voting Rights Acts and San Antonio, Texas: Toward a Federal Guarantee of a Republican Form of Local Government." *Publius* 8, no. 1 (1978): 79–100.

Cox, Patrick. "Wun niu fela Kuntri: A Different Kind of Liberation Movement Emerges in the New Hebrides." *Reason* 12 (Spring 1982): 24–37.

Diamond, Martin. "Notes on the Political Theory of the Founding Fathers." Center for the Study of Federalism, Working Paper No. 7, 1973.

————. "What the Framers Meant by Federalism." In Robert A. Goldwin, ed., *A Nation of States.* 2d. ed. Chicago: Rand McNally, 1974.

Diaz y Lopez, Cesar Enrique. "The State of the Autonomic Process in Spain." *Publius* 11, nos. 3–4 (1981): 193–216.

Duchacek, Ivo D. "Antagonistic Cooperation: Territorial and Ethnic Communities." *Publius* 7, no. 4 (1977): 3–31.

———. "Consociations of Fatherlands: The Revival of Confederal Principles and Practices." *Publius* 12, no. 4 (1982): 129–77.

Elazar, Daniel J. "Civil War and the Preservation of American Federalism." *Publius* 1, no. 1 (1971): 39–59.

———. "Federalism in Theory and Practice: Some French, American and Nigerian Examples." *Publius* 3, no. 1 (1973): 1–4.

———. "Federalism vs. Decentralization: The Drift from Authenticity." *Publius* 6, no. 4 (1976): 9–19.

———. "First Principles." In Daniel J. Elazar, ed. *The Federal Polity, Publius* 3, no. 2 (1973): 1–10.

———. "From the Editor of Publius: Federalism as Grand Design." *Publius* 9, no. 4 (1979): 1–8.

———. "The Generational Rhythm of American Politics." *American Politics Quarterly* 6 (January 1978): 55–94.

———. "Government in Biblical Israel." *Tradition* 13–14, no. 4–1 (1973): 105–23.

———. "Harmonizing Government Organization with the Political Tradition." *Publius* 8, no. 2 (1978): 49–58.

———. "Is Federalism Compatible with Prefectorial Administration?" *Publius* 11, no. 2 (1981): 3–22.

———. "The New Federalism: Can the States Be Trusted?" *Public Interest* (Spring 1974): 89–192.

———. "The 1980's: Entering the Citybelt-Cybernetic Frontier." *Publius* 10, no. 1 (1980): 13–26.

———. "Urbanism and Federalism: Twin Revolutions of the Modern Era." *Publius* 5, no. 2 (1975): 15–40.

Enloe, Cynthia. "Internal Colonialism, Federalism and Alternative State Development Strategies." *Publius* 7, no. 4 (1977): 145–61.

Esman, Milton J. "Federalism and Modernization: Canada and the United States." *Publius* 14, no. 1 (1984): 21–38.

Eulau, Heinz H. F. "Polarity in Representational Federalism: A Neglected Theme of Political Theory." *Publius* 3, no. 2 (1973): 153–72.

————. "Theories of Federalism under the Holy Roman Empire." *American Political Science Review* 25 (August 1941): 643–64.

Franda, M. F. "Federalizing India: Attitudes, Capacities and Constraints." *South Asian Review* 3 (1970): 199–213.

Frenkel, Max. "Kooperative und audere Foederalisme." *Schweizer Montaschrifte* 54 (January 1975): 725–36.

Friedman, Murray. "Religion and Politics in an Age of Pluralism, 1945–1976: An Ethnocultural View." *Publius* 10, no. 3 (1980): 45–77.

Gallant, Edgar. "The Machinery of Federal-Provincial Relations, I." *Canadian Public Administration* 8 (1965): 515–26.

Gruhl, John. "Patterns of Compliance with U.S. Supreme Court Rulings: The Case of Libel in Federal Courts of Appeals and State Supreme Courts." *Publius* 12, no. 3 (1982): 109–26.

Grunbaum, Werner F., and Wenner, Lettie M. "Comparing Environmental Litigation in State and Federal Courts." *Publius* 10, no. 3 (1980): 129–42.

Haggi, S. A. H. "Federalism, Single Dominant Party, and the Problem of Linguistic Autonomy in India." Paper presented at the Sixth World Congress of the International Political Science Association, Geneva, 1964.

Holmes, Jean. "The Australian Federalism System." *International Political Science Review* 5 (1984): 397–414.

Howell, John. "Politics in the Southern Sudan." *African Affairs* 72 (1973): 163–78.

Koritansky, John C. "Alexander Hamilton's Philosophy of Government Administration." *Publius* 9, no. 2 (1979): 99–122.

————. "Decentralization and Civic Virtue in Tocqueville's 'New' Science of Politics." *Publius* 5, no. 3 (1975): 63–82.

Kramer, Daniel C., and Riga, Robert. "The New York Court of Appeals and the United States Supreme Court, 1960–76." *Publius* 8, no. 4 (1978): 75–112.

Landau, Martin. "Federalism, Redundancy and System Reliability." *Publius* 3, no. 2 (1973): 173–96.

Laski, Harold J. "The Obsolescence of Federalism." *New Republic,* May 3, 1939, pp. 367–69.

Levinson, Henry S. "William James and the Federal Republican Principle." *Publius* 9, no. 4 (1979): 65–86.

Light, Alfred R. "Federalism, FERC v. Mississippi, and Product Liability Reform." *Publius* 13, no. 2 (1983): 85–96.

Lijphart, Arend. "Consociation and Federation: Conceptual and Empirical Links." *Canadian Journal of Political Science* 12 (September 1979): 499–515.

———. "Consociational Democracy." *World Politics* 21 (1968–69): 205–25.

———. "Non-Majoritarian Democracy: A Comparison of Federal and Consociational Themes." *Publius* (forthcoming).

Lutz, Donald S. "The Purposes of American State Constitutions." *Publius* 12, no. 1 (1982): 27–44.

McDowell, Gary. "Were the Anti-Federalists Right? Judicial Activism and the Problem of Consolidated Government." *Publius* 12, no. 3 (1982): 99–108.

McFeeley, Neil D. "The Supreme Court and the Federal System: Federalism from Warren to Burger." *Publius* 8, no. 4 (1978): 5–36.

Nelson, Ralph. "The Federal Idea in French Political Thought." *Publius* 5, no. 3 (1975): 7–62.

Nicholson, Jeanne Bell, and Stewart, Debra W. "The Supreme Court, Abortion, and State Response." *Publius* 8, no. 1 (1978): 159–78.

"Nigeria: First Year in Office of President Sheku Shagari." *International Herald Tribune,* October 6, 1980, pp. 14–15.

Olmert, Yosef. "Wasted Time in Lebanon." *Jerusalem Post Magazine,* May 20, 1983.

Ostrom, Elinor; Parks, Roger B.; and Whitaker, Gordon P. "Defining and Measuring Structural Variations in Interorganizational Arrangements." *Publius* 4, no. 4 (1974): 87–108.

———. "Size and Performance in a Federal System." *Publius* 6, no. 2 (1976): 33–74.

Ostrom, Vincent. "Can Federalism Make a Difference?" *Publius* 3, no. 2 (1973): 197–238.

———. "Hobbes, Covenant and the Constitution." *Publius* 10, no. 4 (1980): 83–100.

Ostrom, Vincent, and Ostrom, Elinor. "A Behavioral Approach

to the Study of Intergovernmental Relations." *Annals of the American Academy of Political and Social Sciences* 359 (May 1965): 137–46.

Ostrom, Vincent; Tiebout, Charles; and Warren, Robert. "The Organization of Government in Metropolitan Areas: A Theoretical Inquiry." *American Political Science Review* 55 (1961): 831–42.

Porter, Mary Cornelia. "State Supreme Courts and the Legacy of the Warren Court: Some Old Inquiries for a New Situation." *Publius* 8, no. 4 (1978): 55–74.

Press, Charles. "Second Thoughts on Strengthening State Legislatures." *Publius* 4, no. 2 (1974): 117–22.

Riley, Patrick. "Federalism in Kant's Political Philosophy." *Publius* 9, no. 4 (1979): 43–64.

———. "Rousseau as a Theorist of National and International Federalism." *Publius* 3, no. 1 (1973): 5–18.

———. "Three Seventeenth Century Theorists of Federalism: Althusius, Hugo, and Leibiz." *Publius* 6, no. 3 (1976): 7–42.

Rothenberg, Irene Fraser. "National Intervention and Urban Development in Colombia and Mexico." *Publius* 12, no. 2 (1982): 111–34.

Sabetti, Filippo. "Covenant Language in Canada: Continuity and Change." Paper presented at the Covenant Workshop on Language of Covenant held at the Center for the Study of Federalism, Philadelphia, December 17–18, 1980.

Sawer, G. "Constitutional Issues in Australian Federalism." *Publius* 7, no. 3 (1977): 21–34.

Schechter, Stephen L. "The State of American Federalism: 1978." *Publius* 9, no. 1 (1979): 3–10.

Schier, Steven E. "New Rules, New Games: National Party Guidelines and Democratic National Convention Delegate Selection in Iowa and Wisconsin, 1968–1976." *Publius* 10, no. 3 (1980): 101–28.

Simon, Yves. "A Note on Proudhon's Federalism." *Publius* 3, no. 1 (1973): 19–30.

Skillen, James W., and Carlison, Stanley W. "Religion and Political Development in Nineteenth Century Holland." *Publius* 12, no. 4 (1982): 43–64.

Smiley, Donald V. "The Canadian Federation and the Challenge of Quebec Independence." *Publius* 8, no. 1 (1978): 199–224.

Stark, F. M. "Persuasion and Power in Cameroon." *Canadian Journal of African Studies* 14 (1980): 273–93.

Starr, Graeme. "Federalism as a Political Issue: Australia's Two 'New Federalisms.'" *Publius* 7, no. 1 (1977): 7–26.

Stevens, R. Michael. "Asymmetrical Federalism: The Federal Principle and the Survival of the Small Republic." *Publius* 7, no. 4 (1977): 177–204.

Stewart, Debra W., and Stewart, Charles V. "Bakke and Beyond: Cooperation and Power Sharing in the Federal System." *Publius* 9, no. 1 (1979): 141–60.

Stewart, William H. "Metaphors, Models and the Development of Federal Theory." *Publius* 12, no. 2 (1982): 5–24.

"Toward a More Responsible Two-Party System." Supplement to *American Political Science Review* 44 (September 1950).

von Beyme, Klaus. "West Germany: Federalism." *International Political Science Review* 5, no. 4 (1984): 381–96.

Wildavsky, Aaron. "Party Discipline under Federalism: Implications of Australian Experience." *Social Research* 28 (Winter 1961): 437–58.

Wilson, Woodrow. "The Study of Administration." *Political Science Quarterly* 2 (June 1887): 197–222.

Winthrop, Delba. "Tocqueville on Federalism." *Publius* 9, no. 4 (1979): 131–56.

Index

327

About the Author

Daniel J. Elazar is President of the
Jerusalem Center for Public Affairs;
Senator N. M. Paterson Professor of
Intergovernmental Relations, Bar Ilan
University; and Director, Center for the
Study of Federalism, Temple University.